Oxwich to Om
American GI's in Sou

First published in 2020.

A CIP catalogue record for this book is available from
The British Library.

ISBN (paperback) on back cover.

www.llansadwrn.org.uk

Cover design by Karla Smith

OXWICH TO OMAHA
AMERICAN GI'S IN SOUTH WALES

CHRONOLOGICAL HISTORY OF US FORCES
D-DAY PREPARATIONS 07.06.43 - 06.06.44

Phil Howells

…. to all who served….

CONTENTS

PART 1 – OPERATION BOLERO

PART 2 – OPERATION OVERLORD and BOLERO (Continued)

PART 3 – OPERATION NEPTUNE and OVERLORD/BOLERO (Cont.)

APPENDICIES

LIST OF ILLUSTRATIONS

PHOTOGRAPHS AND SCANS.

US ARMY PLANS OF CAMPS, AERIAL PHOTOGRAPHS, APPENDICIES

*****

Acknowledgements

I find it hard to know where to begin with thanking those that have made this chronological narrative possible. Clearly without the men who took part and those whose task it was collate their unit's experiences, there wouldn't be a story to tell. Correction – there <u>would</u> be a story to tell, but it would have been almost impossible without the primary documentary evidence on which to construct the story of a year to D-Day in South Wales.

The aerial photographs taken during and just after the Second World War by the soon to be disbanded RAF Reconnaissance Squadrons for the Ordnance Survey has provided many a lasting image of the temporary camps of not just South Wales, but the whole of the UK. Whilst English Heritage is the custodian of their images, it is the Aerial Photographic Unit of the Welsh Assembly Government that safeguards our views from the sky. It's been some time since I was able to gain access to view the photo's held in Cardiff, but without the help of Derek Bailey and his staff, I probably wouldn't have been able to start putting together enough detail for a book. Discovering locations from scrutiny using 3D magnifiers of aerial photographs was stimulating to say the least and so rewarding.

Thanks are extended 'over the pond' to staff at NARA for their patience and help, especially David A Giordano and Gibson Bell Smith of the Textual Archives Services Division. Also to staff at the Donovan Technical Library, US Army Infantry Centre, Fort Benning; Carolyn A. Wright, US Army Transportation Museum, Fort Eustis; Bernard F. Cavalcante, Head, Operation Archives Branch, Department of the Navy, Washington Navy Yard.

More recent research since the advent of internet access to the huge file records held at Fold 3 has been immeasurable and I am especially grateful for the licence granted by them to reproduce those digital plans of Marshalling Camps where aerial photographs were unclear. The Corps of Engineers were responsible for preparing the detailed layouts in April 1944 as part of the Invasion planning schedule that covered the South Wales area.

'Over here' sincere thanks are extended to Stephen Brooks, D-Day Museum Portsmouth, Adrian and Neil Turley, staff at Cardiff, Swansea and Haverfordwest Libraries plus many smaller branches, and similarly staff at Glamorgan, West Glamorgan, and Pembrokeshire Archives. The Swansea Archives hold the original GWR Register of Arrivals and Departures for the Docks, a record painstakingly revealing shipping movements during the period in detail. Coupled with the memoirs of the Officer Commanding Movement Control Swansea Lt. Colonel Bevan RE, held in Swansea Central Library has provided so much definitive history especially as the Port carried the greatest troop burden for both Wales incomers from August '43 onwards and D-Day out-loading. This particular information was reproduced within the privately published volumes of *'Strands of World War II'* by local historian T.E. Stradling and fortunately Swansea Library recognised the importance of the submission by having the documents reproduced and professionally bound. The detail provided laid the foundation of how the Bristol Channel Ports operated under dual control of British and American command. What happened at Swansea and the adjoining sub-port of Port Talbot was replicated at Llanelli, Barry, Penarth, Cardiff, and Newport, plus Avonmouth and the minor sub-ports of Portishead and Sharpness.

Fortunately I have been able to exchange and share information with many individuals and agencies who had interest in other aspects of the Second World War in South Wales. Ken Murphy and Alice Piper, Dyfed Archaeological Trust were great sharers of information and I think I helped them in the preparation of their desk based research. Similarly, Ivor Jones preparing for his three volume *'Airfields and Landing Grounds of Wales'* was a good correspondent. Glenn Booker and his research into the 'G.I. Brides' revealed so much more as well, especially detail regarding the Liberty ship *Artemus Ward*, thanks to his 'letters from America'.

On the maritime side, the wealth of detail available on the web pages of two specific sites is quiet amazing. The late Arnold Hague and his successors have put together so much information in the *'Convoy Database'* that any interested party researching the Second World War could not do so without logging on at some time. Similarly the *'War Sailors.com'* database expands and correlates information so well. Backing up all this is the detail of *'The Chronology of the War at Sea 1939-1945'* by Rohwer and Hummelchen which linking with the official Administrative and combat histories of both the Royal, US and Allied Navy's makes for definitive summaries.

I am grateful as well to a number of friends whose advice has been so welcoming. The publishing journey was far more difficult that I could have ever imagined and I am so grateful to local author Karla Smith for her counsel and experiences, shared so readily. Nothing was too much trouble and without her this book could have remained just a manuscript waiting to happen. I may well have bored the socks of others too, when conversations turned to the war years and South Wales. Their inputs and suggestions have contributed in more ways than they possibly realise and I have tried to take note. John Lloyd and Kenneth Evans – both retired teachers – have provided valuable margin notes during the proof reading stages. Both had personal memories of the 12 months covered in this history; Swansea and Gowerton for Ken whilst Abergavenny born John had the unique experience at his childhood farmhouse home of sitting on the knee of a certain Rudolph Hess during one of those escorted walking trips the Nazi Deputy Fuhrer was allowed to make whilst at Maindiff Hospital.

I sincerely thank Dame Shân Legge-Bourke for providing her personal and evocative *Foreword* to this history and finally to the one person who has always been there in support, my wife Ros - a big thank you for putting up with me.

*****

Foreword

As time goes by and memories fade, it is so important to remember past history, and in particular through this very well researched book by Philip Howells, the build up of the D-Day preparations by the American Armed Forces who took over so many places including some of the historic and beautiful houses throughout Wales. One of which was my family home of Glanusk Park.

My earliest memory in 1950 aged 7 was an empty ransacked House, Stables, Courtyard and with numerous concrete bases where the Nissen huts had been in the Park, and doing PT and riding bikes in the Drawing Room with children from the estate, which was great fun.

At the beginning of the war my father 3rd Baron Lord Glanusk agreed with the War Office to hand it over for Military Training rather than use it as a Hospital or R & R home. This proved to be a costly mistake. October 1939 came and the first unit to occupy the house was the Herefordshire Regiment, who apparently looked after and cherished it. However as the years went by, the many units stationed here did not. The wonderful Library with a superb collection of books were burnt to keep the soldiers warm; they also broke into the steel doors of the cellars where my father had put the Meissen China and Waterford Glass collections for safe keeping. By the time the GI's arrived in 1943 there wasn't a lot left to damage or ransack!

My father died in 1948 having been offered a tiny amount by the Government in compensation for the damage, so my mother as a young widow with a 5 year old daughter was left with double death duties (my father died exactly 20 years after my Grandfather), and a complete shell of a 40 roomed house with the water pouring in, as the lead of the roof had been stripped to sell on the black-market! In 1953 my mother took the decision to demolish the House, but left the balustrade round the boundaries of the garden, which is still very much intact.

Looking back, sacrifices knew no borders in those days of war and eventual peace, but now, thankfully, the Park is farmed and many events take place.

The Hon. Dame Shân Legge-Bourke DCVO
Crickhowell 2020

Introduction

"Dad! Dad! What's that noise? What's that noise?" Around the street corner, turning into the dead end of Station Terrace roared the source. Still in its olive drab colouring, a GMC 'deuce and a half' six wheeled truck screeched to an abrupt stop at the entrance to J.L. Eve Construction Yard in Caerphilly. Where the liberation white star would have been painted on the door was the stencilled company name and even now I can remember it as clear as day. I couldn't have been more than five years old and had no knowledge of Americans being in my home town only a few years before and certainly didn't know anything about their huge vehicles. This truck had three rails running around and above the bed which some will instantly recognise as being of the Corps of Engineers style. To a little lad it was the size of the tyres (bigger than me) and the noise I remember so well.

During the course of researching this chronology it has been a revelation to discover so much about the war time history of the town I grew up in, through reading a number of excellent books and pamphlets published over recent years by local authors. In particular, the 'friendly invasion' of American soldiers (and their equipment!) dove-tailed so well into my own mission of detailing what had happened in South Wales during the twelve months leading up to D-Day 6 June 1944. It seemed to me that everyone knew through the hundreds, if not thousands of books that have been published over the past seventy-five years, about what had happened on the south coast of England, but there was hardly ever a mention of South Wales and the contribution to the overall effort of US servicemen and women based here. One book I read with the sub-title of 'The American Occupation of Britain 1942-1945' did not contain one single reference to any US serviceman stationed anywhere in Wales.

Great emphasis had been placed on the fact that the western part of Britain had been ear marked for US Army troops and the East for British, Canadian and other Allied formations, a geo-physical decision quite obviously which led to the western beaches of Normandy being American. Yet it seemed there was very little printed and published material about, for example, some of the most important exercises, actions and decisions that had taken place in South Wales and would subsequently affect what happened on the south coast of England. Many people in the UK would have little knowledge regarding the US Assault Training Centre at Woolacombe, North Devon unless they lived near there. What chance, therefore, would people know about the US Amphibious Training Centre at Scurlage or the US Transportation Corps Training School at Mumbles on the Gower peninsula? 'Gizmo's on the Preseli's? What's a 'gizmo'?

My curiosity was aroused when I started my own amateur researches around the time of the 50th Anniversary of the D-Day Landings in 1994. Obviously reading centred on published source's mainly of British origin, but gravitated more and more towards trans-Atlantic authors as I was discovering a distinct shortage of much information to do with the six shires of South Wales known to have played host to the US forces, Monmouth, Glamorgan, Brecknock, Carmarthen, Cardigan and Pembroke. That fascinating town of Hay-on-Wye and its bookshops proved a treasure trove for volumes including the 'Green Book Series' – the official history of the US Army in the ETO in WWII. I discovered in those lengthy but so well detailed tomes pictures merely annotated '…... somewhere in Wales'. 'Wait a minute', I thought studying them, 'I know where that is! Why didn't they say so? Well, perhaps they didn't know!' Strange when there appeared to be so much other detail. Many years back I was more than a little surprised to find an omission on the opening page of Chapter VIII in Gordon A. Harrison's definitive volume covering D-Day, *Cross Channel Attack* published in 1950. He wrote the following:

> *'Force U (seaborne units of the VII Corps) was marshalled in the Tor Bay area and east of Plymouth; Force O (1ˢᵗ Division), in the area of Dorchester; Force B (29ᵗʰ Division), near Plymouth and Falmouth; and the early build-up divisions, the 9ᵗʰ Infantry and 2ⁿᵈ Armored Divisions, near Southampton.*

Harrison went on to describe the locations of the 82ⁿᵈ and 101ˢᵗ Airborne and whilst being clearly factually correct, I can image more than a few comments from the veterans of the 90ᵗʰ and 2ⁿᵈ Infantry Divisions of which there was no mention and who had been ignored in favour of the later arrivals from Southampton!

However it was another more recent 'bible' that really spurred me on to put 'pen to paper'. Stanton's *'World War 11 Order of Battle'*, an amazing compendium of facts and figures which traces 'who, what, where and when' for all US Army troops from Battalion level and above, in all theatres of the war. Yet there is irrefutable fault in a few items of detail. For example, Chapter 39 Engineer Brigades, page 515 states:

> ### Provisional Engineer Special Brigade Group.
> *17 Feb 44 established at Pennlargaer England to control the 5ᵗʰ and 6ᵗʰ Engineer Special Brigades to be utilised in the Omaha Beach Assault on Normandy France; dissolved on Omaha Beach France 26 June 44 and assets used to form the Headquarters, Omaha Beach Command there.*
> ### Campaigns: *Normandy.*

Since when was Penllergaer [correct spelling] in England? No wonder South Wales has been ignored! It maybe a small parochial point to many, but perhaps it's a possible reason as to why there is so little knowledge in the wider world regarding one of the most important formations created during the Second World War. The men who were proud to have a 'castle' emblem as their Corps badge and who masterminded the OMAHA beach support operations deserve more praise. Were it not for the likes of Brigadier General William (Bill) Hoge, Corps of

Engineers, US Army, the OMAHA beach assault may never have 'stuck', but thanks to the sacrifices of his deputies such as Lt. Col. Lionel Smith, Commanding Officer, 37th Engineer Combat Battalion who died freeing Europe that fateful June morning, they made it. Forty percent of the men who became casualties on that one beach on that morning were from the Corps of Engineers.

Heroes all, with 'castles' on their collars, their unique corps insignia.

There is a lot more to tell now, devoid of the secrecy that surrounded so much information for so many years. Fifty years had to pass before the tales of Bletchley Park and 'enigma' were to surface. Likewise, the details of Operation FORTITUDE were closed to view for fifty years. Certainly it's taken those of us with an interest awhile to correlate information, as more accurate facts have surfaced from behind the plethora of regurgitated literature plus the inevitable publishing houses 'coffee table' books that have concentrated on glossy maps and photo's. I trust that doesn't sound arrogant and I apologise in advance to any of those well established and certainly famous authors who have related the same story under different covers year after year. D-Day and the preceding D-1 involved the south Coast of England itself and the north coast of France, but there was so much more to the overall story, including without doubt what had happened here in South Wales, that deserves to be told and which has been ignored. Bombarding forces and Corn Cob fleets voyaged from near and far as we know, but ships also sailed from the Bristol Channel, so where's the story behind that armada?

I understand and am told that facts can only be taken as 'fact' if verification comes from more than one source to confirm the detail (essential to a journalist, I believe) and it's only through cross examination and correlation of facts that one gets nearer to the truth. Going back to original sources has been necessary and 'surfing' the internet in order to build up a picture of events is quick, but confirmation is essential but painstakingly slow.

The vast majority of servicemen and women who crossed the Atlantic came by ship, embarked for Normandy by ship and if they were lucky, returned home more often than not, by ship, so consequently much of the story of the US Army (and Navy) in South Wales is interspersed with nautical information. The origins of the troop convoy structure, the safeguards that had to be put in place and the overall strategy of delivering so many US troops to Great Britain generally and the Bristol Channel ports specifically as part of the overall plan is a epic tale in itself. Likewise the story of US Army cargo that had to be delivered and stored and the measures that were undertaken to enable the support elements of the assault forces to carry out their prime function again covers volumes in itself. Operation BOLERO and the subsequent Operation OVERLORD, the overall strategic plan that spawned the tactical NEPTUNE, is again a massive tale of equal proportions. This chronology of the year leading up to D-Day deals with the elements of these massive operations, whether they may be on land or sea, but specifically focused on this part of Britain and how it affected 'visitors' and locals alike.

The discovery of so much further information relating to the Bristol Channel Pre-Loaded Build-Up Force has also resulted in, I think, a better narrative, and one that also deserves telling. Every book relating to the 'Normandy Invasion', or the 'Normandy Landings' or 'D-Day' relates to those that went before. Nothing wrong with that of course, and as any veteran will tell you, the 4,572 soldiers of several Allied nations, mostly American with British, Canadian, French and Norwegian plus 12 Australians and 2 New Zealanders who died that day are the real heroes. But some of the Americans who lost their lives on that fateful June morning on the beaches of Normandy had trained and lived for nine months in South Wales. There is therefore a wider story, devoid of the 'blood and guts' of warfare and it tells of what went on behind the scenes that made those heroic efforts of the vanguard assault troops a success.

However no narrative regarding the preparations for the events of the 6th June 1944 would make sense unless at least one chapter (albeit short) covered some of the detail of the warfare that morning and what happened to those who had spent time in South Wales. Seven pages is merely an attempt to put things in context and should not be seen as an authoritative description of the assault on one half of OMAHA. Neither do I offer reasons as to why the landings were ultimately to be seen as a flawed victory. There are many, many expert authors who have and no doubt will continue to expound on those theories. What I have tried to do is to capture the confusion and bravery of men landing in those first hours and their determination to get off that beach! Similarly reference to the UTAH beach landings is purely and simply an attempt to put events into context.

Normally a writer, I think, lists and gives all due credit to those who have assisted in the research and preparation of any book and I naturally am pleased to be able to do just that on the appropriate page. However there are three individuals – all Normandy GOLD beach Veterans who during the past twenty five years ago gave me the support and encouragement to tell what I and they regarded as an important story. They were not American, but they knew most certainly how much we owed to our major ally.

Gordon Davies, Royal Signals. Landed D+1 with his two comrades in their wireless truck and attached to General Collins V Corps to provide the 'signals net' between that US Army formation and the neighbouring British Corps. Standing on the slipway at Arromanches in July 1996 where we visited whilst on a day trip away from taking part in the Commemorations of the 80th Anniversary of the Battle of the Somme, I remember his quietly spoken words, delivered with all his typical reverence.

'We've got to come back to remember properly and you've got to write your book!'

Come June 1997 our choir did return and took part in the 53rd Anniversary of the Normandy Landings, but sadly Gordon suddenly passed away in the intervening December and never made it.

Ken Harding, trooper of 47th Royal Marine Commando. Landed on D-Day approx 0700 hrs to attack Port-en-Bessin and expected to travel and sing at the 53rd

Anniversary and pay his respects at the Bayeux graveside of his troop commander Captain T.F. Cousins, tragically shot when moving forward to take the surrender of German troops showing a white flag. Much to his regret, illness prevented Ken from attending.

'Do it for me please, Phil? And get a picture for the book perhaps.'

I was honoured to do so and he had that photograph six days later. He's gone now as well.

Then there's Bill Evans '31', as proud a 'Borderer' and Welshman as you could find anywhere. 'B' Company, 2nd Battalion South Wales Borderers. Landed 1200 hrs D-Day. He would belt out our Welsh National Anthem at any opportunity! Lobbied some of the highest in the land to preserve his Regiment threatened with amalgamation with the Welch Regiment and would never trust a politician again as a result of the promises given to him but never delivered. Veterans yes, politicians no! He related so many tales of his mates on that fateful day when on the extreme right of the British line, the 'Fighting 24th' was struggling and losing men as they attempted to link up with the delayed Americans coming off OMAHA. Bill always said that I had to get the book into print.

*'We need everyone to know what we did and including what the Yanks did.' (*his words*). 'There was only one thing that they did wrong by us. That's apart from being over sexed, over paid etc. - they were bloody late!'*

Evans '31' (the last two numbers of his army service number) passed away in 2014. RIP one and all.

This then is the story of just some of those American Servicemen and women and the Units they were proud to serve in during their 365 days in South Wales 1943-1944. It's late as well, but that's not their fault and any mistakes here-on are mine and mine alone.

Philip Howells
Llansadwrn, Carmarthenshire.
7th June 2019

*****

Prime Minister Winston Churchill's Statement
HOUSE OF COMMONS
Palace of Westminster
3.40 pm. 4 June 1940.

.....I have myself, full confidence that if all do their duty, if nothing else is neglected and if the best arrangements are made, as they are being made, we shall prove ourselves once again able to defend our island home, to ride out the storm of war, and to outlive the menace of tyranny, if necessary for years, if necessary alone. At any rate that is what we are going to try to do.

That is the resolve of His Majesty's Government – every man of them. That is the will of Parliament and the nation. The British Empire and the French Republic, linked together in their cause and in their need, will defend to the death their native soil, aiding each other like good comrades to the utmost of their strength.

Even though large tracts of Europe and many old and famous States have fallen or may fall into the grip of the Gestapo and all the odious apparatus of Nazi rule, we shall not flag or fail.

We shall go on to the end, we shall fight in France, we will fight on the seas and oceans, we shall fight with growing confidence and growing strength in the air, we shall defend our island, whatever the cost may be, we shall fight on the beaches, we shall fight on the landing grounds, we shall fight in the fields and in the streets, we shall fight in the hills; we shall never surrender, and even if, which I do not for a moment believe, this island or a large part of it were subjugated and starving, then our Empire beyond the seas, armed and guarded by the British Fleet, would carry on the struggle until, in God's time good time, the New World, with all its power and might, steps forth to the rescue and the liberation of the old.

Extracted from Hansard 5th Series, Vol. 361 cc787. Closing Remarks up to 4.14pm.

*****

Prologue

Operation BOLERO had its origin back in 1942 when the United States Government agreed to the notion of 'Germany First' despite being first attacked by Japan at Pearl Harbour. Putting troops into what became known as the ETO – European Theatre of Operations - was always going to be a massive and unprecedented task, getting them there and keeping them supplied an even greater problem. It was a means to an end as BOLERO only came about as a result of the commitment to the strategic OPERATION OVERLORD – the return of Western Europe from Nazi domination and its tactical naval off-spring OPERATION NEPTUNE – the amphibious assault on Normandy.

January had seen the start of planning with Lt. General Frederick Morgan appointed to the position of Chief of Staff to the Supreme Allied Commander (Designate). Not yet appointed, it was thought that the SAC would be British, hence Morgan's appointment. C.O.S.S.A.C was ordered to prepare three sets of plans.

a) An elaborate camouflage and deception scheme to keep Nazi forces in the West, including an amphibious feint with the aim of promoting an air battle employing both RAF and USAAF.
b) A return to the continent in the event of German disintegration with little planning.
c) A full-scale assault against the Continent in 1944 A.S.A.P!

COSSAC's staff at the start consisted of an ADC, two batmen and a driver, but gradually with US involvement the planning team grew. He wrote:

"Essentially what we are here trying to do is make an impossible situation reasonably possible for practical purposes..... Never were so few asked to do so much in so short a time" Lt. General Frederick Morgan – COSSAC, letter to Brigadier Leslie Hollis, Secretary to the British Chiefs of Staff. August 1943.

'Omaha Beach'- Balkovski

There was any number of factors that had to be dealt with by the planners from the outset. Provision of shipping, troops and army stores, safety and security of shipments, organisation in a foreign land, accommodations, training facilities, the list would go on and on. Not least was the constantly changing fortunes of war and the huge changes of direction that were made to satisfy the various Allied Governments needs, the Russian demands for the opening of a Second Front in Western Europe being one such example. The massive Operation BARBAROSSA in 1941 had decimated the Soviet armed forces and would continue to do so unless Britain and the United States could start 'turning the tide'. The Middle East was seen as a key to prevent further Nazi domination through the area and the

15

horrifying thought of possible geographic linking of Axis forces, consequently Operation TORCH was mounted from both the US and British shores to complete Montgomery's 8th Army defeat of Rommel's Afrika Corps. Whilst TORCH may well have provided many useful lessons in conducting amphibious operations and of course resulted in North Africa being cleared of Germans and Italians and gave a springboard for further southern Europe invasions, it also had the effect of turning operation BOLERO on its head. So much equipment and so many men were diverted away from the proposed invasion of France across the English Channel, that there had to be a revision of dates and agreements. An escalation in the movement of US troops and especially pre-shipped supplies was going to be necessary to achieve any sort of new date being acceptable to the Allies.

Convoys from across the Atlantic were organised and protected primarily by the Royal and Royal Canadian Navy supplemented by the RAF nearer home prior to Pearl Harbour and the United States entry into the Second World War. Early lend-lease arrangements boosted surface escorts for the SC prefix convoys consisting of mainly older slower vessels with the slightly faster HX and HXF convoys bringing all manner of cargo to the UK. From the South Atlantic the SL series from Freetown brought more foodstuffs including that from Australasia to keep Britain going, with convoys from the Mediterranean joining out in the North Atlantic. The well-escorted TC series had brought Canadian troops since December 1939 which was then superseded by the early AT convoys intermixed with the NA series in early 1942 with US involvement getting the US Army to Iceland followed by Northern Ireland code named Operation MAGNET.

Shipping losses in the North Atlantic due to U-Boat activity had been pretty horrific especially in the slower independent cargo ships and convoys, the 'wolf packs' sending hundreds of ships to their proverbial watery graves along with their gallant crews more often than not. It was later calculated that the total war time losses of allied shipping amounted to 21.7 million tons. Incredibly emergency construction of 2,710 Liberty ships provided replacement of 19.4 million tons. American shipyards would build some 5,000 merchant vessels from October 1941 through to the end of the war, but in 1942 losses exceeded replacements despite the ever-increasing number of new ships sliding down the slipways. The first few months of 1943 saw the U-boat attacks reach their full fury with 768,000 tons lost in March alone, however the Kriegsmarine dominance started to drop away thanks to the combined efforts of the allied navies, air forces and the code-breaking successes of Bletchley Park with 'ENIGMA'. Pre-shipment of US army cargo was slowly increasing after April 1943 and soon US organised troop convoys of the UT series would be on the rise to complement the fast independent AT super-troopers such as the *Queens, Mauretania, Aquitania, Empress of Scotland, Pasteur, Andes,* and *Ile De France* with the Dutch *Niew Amsterdam,* American *West Point, Wakefield* and *Mount Vernon* joining later in 1944.

Ashore in the UK it was evident that certain changes needed to be made by the SOS – Services of Supply. Pre-shipped cargo coming ashore had to be correctly manifested, labelled and loaded, accepted by trained service troops and moved forward to depots. Troops had to have accommodations and facilities prepared and given adequate onshore means of transportation. In 1942 there were problems caused by the absence of these requirements. The Casablanca Conference in January '43 pointed out that the proposed shipments of up to 150 per month could only be handled if US dock labour and locomotives were available as there was insufficient British stock of either. There was also a shortage of depot space as manpower was limited and no more could be built. SOS Chief, General Lee had spelt it out;

> *"He asked for 30 port battalions, 30 engineer regiments, 15 quartermaster service battalions and about 30 depot companies of various categories. All would be necessary in order to discharge 120-150 ships per month, construct the needed depots, properly store and issue equipment and supplies, and carry out the airfield construction programme."*
>
> Logistical Support of the Armies Vol. 1. - Ruppenthal

Then suddenly all this was to no avail. General Marshall wired General Andrews ETO Commander to say the decision to resume BOLERO was not firm. Other priorities were taking preference – North Africa again – and there would be "nothing for the months of March and April". Operation HUSKY was looming and the Sicilian Invasion was the priority with troops coming from North Africa. Anyway much of the stated requirements of BOLERO were academic as shipping availability still remained a problem. It was seen as a setback but Andrews stressed it was important that American troops were still seen to be continuing to arrive in the UK. The Trident Conference in Washington ruled out misgivings with 3 decisions.

1. Enlarge the U.S. / British bomber offensive.
2. Exploit the projected Sicilian operation in a manner best to eliminate Italy from the war.
3. Establish forces and equipment in the United Kingdom for a cross-Channel operation with a target date of 1 May 1944.

BOLERO was therefore very much back on course with definite allocation of resources. Twenty-nine divisions were to be made available in the UK and no further diversion of troops to the Mediterranean. In actual fact, four US and three British Divisions were to be on readiness after 1 November for return to the British Isles. Planners scheduled a build up of 1,300,300 American soldiers by 1 May of 393,000 air force troops, and 907,100 ground and service troops. More were to be available by 1 June if required.

The next thing to get resolved was the unsatisfactory labelling of pre-shipped cargo with incorrect manifests in the United States. The Zone of the Interior (ZI) command, meaning everything on the US mainland, felt that it was fine to get the necessary cargo tonnage on board and on the way to Britain as it was only a small country and unloading, sorting and delivery over short distance by truck was easy. They had no real firsthand knowledge of how narrow and therefore not serviceable many roads were. Coupled with the domestic imports required to help Britain survive with an obvious manpower and equipment shortage, limited wharf space and overburdened railway system things had to improve if the US Army was to supply its forces 'over there'. Cargo manifests were to be detailed and spelt out and telexed to a designated port area under the revised 'UGLY' system (which was designated for anywhere in the UK) and comprised three zones:

> Zone   I. (code name SOXO) being ports north of the county line from
> London to the west through Banbury i.e. Clyde & Mersey ports.
> Zone II. (GLUE) for Southern England and Wales.
> Zone III (BANG) Northern Ireland.

Service designation QM for Quartermaster or O for Ordnance etc., plus classification number of type of stores, plus sequence number (Quartermaster Service used 0-99 for example) meant that the right cargo should arrive at the right ports area and sorted (if required) and despatched to the right requisitioning centre without any reverse haulage or resending in the UK. Cardiff had a problem in the past before securing the use of the large GWR mainline railway Sorting Depot sheds located just to the east of the city, which also benefitted Newport. There was a specific problem regarding 'boxed' and 'crated' vehicles for assembly one of which was the weight and size for the already overloaded railway system. Boxed vehicles were simply cases containing one vehicle (SUP) whose wheels had been removed, thereby occupying less space aboard ship and offering the convenience of stacking. However in the instance of the larger trucks their size plus that of their timber boxes made for a pretty hefty lift. The crated vehicles using the title TUP (the T signifying duplicate parts for more than one vehicle) raised other problems as each crate could contain for example two cab units, another crate several axles and another chassis's. Moreover parts to make up one vehicle might not just be on different ships but end up in different ports! The British vehicle building assembly plants operating under the TILEFER scheme had managed to put together thousands of vehicles but would be overstretched to provide what was going to be required. The Ordnance Department were to take on responsibility for the supply of vehicles, so special companies were created boasting new titles such as Motor Vehicle Assembly, Tire Repair or Delivery.

Operation BOLERO was now firmly in place and there was now 365 days, a whole year, to go before Operation OVERLORD would commence with Operation NEPTUNE and D-Day heralding the liberation of Europe.

*****

PART ONE
OPERATION BOLERO

Bolero

*Music for a dance of Spanish or Cuban origin,
composed for performing in a single continuous movement,
highlighted by ever increasing tempo and volume,
culminating in a tumultuous finale.*

Lento - slow

Andante – a little quicker

Moderato – at a moderate pace

Allegro – lively

Sostenuto – at a sustained pace

Accelerando – gradually quicker

Tenuto – maintain and hold to full value

Presto – quickly.

Chapter I

5 JUNE / AUGUST 1943 – BOLERO LENTO

US troops had been setting up in various locations throughout South Wales for several months, in preparation for the influx of Field Forces. Service of Supply Headquarters had moved from London to Cheltenham to be nearer the area of US occupation, western Britain designated for the 'friendly' invasion. The Bristol Channel Ports had originally been under Southern Base Section control, but on July 8 it was changed to Western Base Section, which made much more sense. Western ports were points of arrival simply because southern and eastern ports were too close to enemy occupied territory and frequent incursions by Goering's Luftwaffe bombers. Over half the total number of troops that arrived in Britain did so via the Clyde at Greenock and Gourock, the only place for the *Queens* to safely moor as Southampton was recognised as too dangerous. Cargo wise, 70% arrived at the Mersey or Bristol Channel ports, much nearer to the centre of activity of the US Army. The all important import of oil, both crude and finished products - petrol, diesel, bunkering fuel and the essential aviation spirit, all had to come into Ellesmere Port or Avonmouth for access into the Government Pipeline and Storage System (GPSS) – the national fuel grid. Apart from the 8th Air Force in East Anglia with its supply train, the accommodation, supply and training of all American troops meant S. Wales was going to be heavily involved, especially the BCP's and hinterland.

Bristol Channel Ports naturally had a British Command since the outbreak of the Second World War and there were experienced Commanders at each port;

BCP. HQ. The Barracks, Newport. C/O Colonel S. Naylor MC

Newport	Alexander Road School	Major L.J. Osborne RE.
Avonmouth	Kings Weston House, Shirehampton.	Major G. Lomer DSO.
Cardiff	27 Dowlais Buildings, W. Bute S.	Major H.S. Thomas RE.
Penarth	The Spinney, Sully	Captain N. Miller
Barry	The Docks.	Major B.J. Burrows RE.
Port Talbot	The Docks.	(with Swansea)
Swansea	Old Guildhall, Somerset Place.	Major L.G. Bevan RE.
Llanelli		AN Other.

American Command ran along similar lines to ensure good liaison and co-operation especially as there were several civilian organisations that the US Army Transportation Corps would have to rely on – chiefly the Great Western Railway Company as rail provider and as docks owners – the Dockers! Originally the Commanding Officer of the 3rd Major Port of Transportation, Colonel E.H. Lastayo with Headquarters near Avonmouth supervised the unloading of individual ships, whilst the British supervised the ports. The autumn brought change with the 3rd Port transferred to North Africa as part of Operation TORCH, now more experienced following their time in the UK. During the winter part of the 5th Major Port continued with operations until 11th Port took over in July '43 with Headquarters in Newport. Command changed several times with Colonels Russell G. Simpson, Harry B. Vaughan, and Grover G. Heldenfels, succeeding each other until Brig, Gen. Joseph L. Phillips commanded in the busiest of times, his failing health through overwork resulting in Colonel Whitcomb assuming command for the Invasion with 17th Port under Colonel Crowthers taking over Bristol Channel Ports. All this was yet to come, for the time being the docks continued working well, minor problems being overcome through good liaison, resulting in the five sub-ports receiving the largest amount of US Army cargo.

Port Administration - Lt. Colonel R.E. Kernodle
Chaplain (Maj.) H.D. Buchanan – Chaplain
Captain V.F. Phillips – HQ. Company

Major L.D. Blount	-	Adjutant General Section
Major P.O. Johnson	-	Aviation Section
Lieut. M.M. Myerson	-	Chemical Warfare Section.
Major V.S. Bennett	-	Engineer Section
Captain A.S Kinsman	-	Finance Section
Major W.J. Flynn	-	Judge Advocate Section
Major F.J. Koenig	-	Port Surgeon - Medical Section
Major P.H. Fulstow	-	Port Dentist
Captain A.B. Rogers	-	Veterinarian Officer
Captain F.R. Schoenborn	-	Military Intelligence Section

Port Operations - Lt. Colonel A.H. Hall.
Captain J.H. Austin Jr. - Admin Officer-

Lt. Col. C.F. Poe	-	Quartermaster Officer
Major F.W. Greenhut	-	Port Signals Officer
Captain J.D. Cowan	-	Motor Transportation Officer
Captain J.S. Mowbray	-	Rail Transportation Officer
Major R.W. Buzzard	-	Ordnance Officer

Individual ports were sub-ports with their own CO, and a Signals Officer:

811th Port Signal Service Company - Major P.J. Grady.

Newport	Lt. A.L. Jung Jr. USA
Avonmouth	Capt. C. Biehl USA
Cardiff	Captain. W.S. Murison USA
Barry	Capt. J.S. Robertson USA
Swansea	Capt. C.L. Downey USA

Ultimately as Operation OVERLORD and its associated amphibious Operation NEPTUNE was enlarged in January '44, the role of Milford Haven and the ports of Llanelli, Port Talbot and Penarth were going to be more significant, even little Sharpness important, but to a lesser degree. Exactly twelve months before the day that the convoys of what became known as the Bristol Channel Pre-loaded Build-up Force (BCPLBUF) sailed in support of the Normandy Invasion, HX240 arrived with the *Charles M Hall* and the *Cyrus H McCormick* docking in Cardiff on the 5 June 1943. The new 'Liberties' were increasing all the while. From HX241 *SS American Press* unloaded at Barry and only a small number of troops on the *HMT Esperance Bay* with 346 men and *HMT Moreton Bay* with another 200 both putting into Avonmouth on the eleventh. HX242 with the *Peter Cartwright* docked at Barry and the *John P Holland* at Cardiff together with the *SS Bayano*. The *HMT Highland Chieftain* carried on up to Avonmouth, all starting to unload on the sixteenth and two tankers *SS Axel B. Byles* and the *SS Paul H Harwood* put into Swansea. Another Halifax convoy came in during the month with a few more troops on the *SS Ville D'Anvers* (80 all told) docking in Swansea along with *Smith Thompson*, the rest of the Bristol Channel section of HX243 saw the *Calvin Coolidge* going into Barry and *Noah Webster* to Cardiff on the twenty-second. Finally the independent and new C2 'Reefer' *SS Blue Jacket* closed out the month making her way into Avonmouth on the 26 June.

Away from the ports troops were enjoying their time in Wales. On Whit Monday, Llanelli residents also had the chance to watch the first game of American softball in the town when the US Army took on the US Navy at Stebonheath. The Army won 8-7 and both teams enjoyed a reception at the Thomas Arms Hotel hosted by the Mayor Alderman W.H. Charles with Major Kit Conyers responding to the welcome received by the US troops in Llanelli. Moreover the *Llanelli Star* in its report on 19 June stated that £150 had been raised with entry proceeds for the Bigyn War Comfort Fund.

The only troops to arrive at the Bristol Channel ports in July 1943 were those aboard the *USAT Cefalu* in convoy HX244 carrying part of the 360th E (GS) R to Swansea. The *Asa Gray,* loaded with US Army stores, was the only other vessel for the Bristol Channel in this convoy, arriving at Cardiff on the 1 July. From HX245 *Hubert H Bancroft* and the *SS Metapan* docked at Swansea, *SS Curacao* unload cargo including tanks at Cardiff and *William B. Woods* carried on to Newport on the ninth. From HX247 *Elmer A. Sperry* and *President Buchanan* went into Swansea, *Moses Cleaveland* to Barry and *Lucius Q.C. Lamar* to Cardiff leaving the *SS Abangarez* to sail alone up to Avonmouth on the twenty-third. The last convoy to use the AT (Atlantic Transit) prefix arrived on 27 July when the six vessels of AT55A, 4 troopships, 1 tanker and the specialist carrier *Seatrain Texas* made landfall, the later carrying 40 locomotives amongst other cargo. This was one of those occasions when the number of escorts (9) including the cruiser USS Augusta exceeded the number in convoy.

Liverpool was the destination of the *USAT Edmund B Alexander*. Significantly troops aboard included the 95th Engineer (GS) Regiment which would carry out major construction work in South Wales over the coming months. From now on the AT prefix was used exclusively by the big fast 'independent' troopers.

Photo: USAT Cefalu. 5,228 tons former Honduran banana boat. (Nav. Source)

Last of all, HX248 with 89 ships arrived on 29 July with *James B Richardson* and *Joseph Warren* berthing in Swansea together with the *Axel B. Byles* tanker, all the others docking at their respective scheduled ports - *SS Montgomery City* at Barry, *James J Hill* at Cardiff, *Samuel F Miller* at Newport and the *Francis Lewis* into Avonmouth in company with the *Esso Concord* and *Paul H. Harwood* tankers.

August would prove to be a key month for the planning of what would ultimately be known as Operation Overlord. The Quadrant Conference in Quebec was where the Trident decision was endorsed and the COSSAC plan for a cross-channel invasion planned for May 1944 affirmed. The success of the anti-submarine warfare carried out by the Allied Navies in the North Atlantic and the reduction in shipping losses meant that the BOLERO commitment could be increased. There were now to be 1,446,000 troops available in the British Isles by the projected invasion date of 1 May 1944. The original target date was extended to make available an extra month's production.

More General Depots were required to handle the huge amount of imported cargo and equipment leave alone troop accommodations that were required and although G-25 at Ashchurch near Tewkesbury plus a number of others were already active, some were only just starting. In Barry the former SRD No 2. was already in joint service with British and US troops operating, but it was earmarked for sole US Army use and on 13 August a Headquarters with 3 Officers and 90 enlisted men of the 187th Ordnance Company took over the renamed G-40. Two other sections of the 187th were similarly assigned to open depots at G-16 Wem and G-18 Sudbury- Eggington. By the end of the year those depots would have their own Ordnance Battalions in residence and the entire 187th Company would be at Barry.

> 'The progressive firming up of strategic planning was reflected in the implementation of BOLERO. The flow of troops and materials into the United Kingdom, a trickle during the North African operation, began to increase steadily during the summer of 1943, reached the flood stage in the final six months before the cross-Channel assault, and continued for several months thereafter'.
>
> The Transportation Corps: Operations Overseas. - Bykofsky and Larson.
> Office of the Chief Military Historian.

Operation TORCH had indeed caused a fall-off in both cargo and troops especially into the Bristol Channel ports, but there were now signs of an increase, but that was beginning to cause problems. Movement Control in Swansea made a formal application for 350 - 400 US port troops as delays were beginning to become obvious on occasion. However Lt. Col. Bevan was very concerned that the situation should be handled with great delicacy as he didn't wish to see a repeat of the strikes that plagued operations in the earlier part of the year. Simultaneously Brigadier General Ross (Transportation Corps Chief in the ETO) had come to the same conclusion. He was successful in gaining permission from British authorities to use US Army labour when he showed that every port was short of an average of 850 civilian stevedores or 'longshoremen'. During August the general shortage became more acute and practically all vessels were delayed in discharging because of insufficient labour. Ross therefore requested the shipment of 9 more battalions ASAP to complete the 15 allotted to the BOLERO programme.

Delays may have become obvious at the ports, but equally so cargo that had arrived which required attention before issue, particularly cased vehicles needing assembly, was also beginning to stack up. There were two Ordnance company types of organization that were sorely needed in the UK being the Motor Vehicle Assembly Company and the associated MV Distribution Company. The British 435th General Transport Company was greatly assisting in the movement of received transport to vehicle parks but they were getting swamped with the demands of the highly automotive US Army. The principle US vehicle depot for assembly was at G-25 Ashchurch under the astute eye of Major William Francis, who having visited the Austin Vehicle Assembly line at Treforest near Pontypridd, set up his 622nd Base Automotive Battalion plus the 147th MVA Company to assemble the crated parts of jeeps and trucks in a highly proficient manner. So much so that the lessons learnt enable production to be undertaken at Taunton and Tidworth together with eight separate assembly lines elsewhere including the 144th

Ordnance Vehicle Assembly Company at Cardiff with a detachment assembling GMC / Thornton 'deuce and a half' trucks in the former Cardiff Railway Lifting Shop at the Caerphilly 'Sheds'. These vehicles would be taken out for road testing along Van Road, through town and up the steep Mountain Road, then back down

Photo: Jeep assembly line at G-25 Ashchurch depot 194. (Signal Corps)

the Watford Road prior to returning to their assembly point. 148th MVA Company did similar up at Bromborough (Merseyside) and huge storage sites sprang up all over the country with both imported complete equipment and UK assembled vehicles. Acres of stored trucks and jeeps, tanks and guns were increasing in number and were scattered all over the country with quiet lane verges covered with miles of storage lockers containing ammunition and shells. Alongside and in the depots themselves mountains of cased stores and equipment were growing ever larger. Sub-depots specialising in certain commodities were being created for the Quartermaster, Ordnance, Engineer and Signals Corps and placed at strategic railway and roadside locations – all in preparation for the Invasion of France.

The 95th Engineer (GS) Regiment began their first camp construction assignment on 9th August at Mynydd Lliw, just outside Swansea. An extensive 'double' camp to house ultimately part of the soon to be created 5th Engineer Special Brigade, it was built with great difficulty by the newly arrived troops and the camps were continually being extended. For an experienced construction regiment the 95th Engineers were no novices when it came to construction in difficult situations. They had been despatched to the European Theatre of Operations because of acquired skills and had already received high praise for their work 6,000 miles away on not just the other side of the Atlantic Ocean, but in the northern wastes of Canada and Alaska bordering the Pacific. This service received extensive press coverage when they got back to the US prior to leaving for the United Kingdom. The Regimental History was proud to relate:-

> *'The 95th Engineers, one of the Army's crack Engineer Regiments has arrived at Camp Claiborne after spending the last eleven months in Canada helping to build and operate the Alcan Highway. The record of achievement on this assignment has earned for it the praise of many as one of the best coloured regiments in the Army.'*

Difficulties encountered included a lack tools and equipment, lack of materials and abnormal delays, long trips to haul in supplies which had failed to be delivered, and an absence of plans plus a general misunderstanding of technical details in relation to US Engineer and British Royal Engineer instructions. The daily commute from their base at Clase Farm Hostel, Morriston didn't help either. Eventually as other camp building work was assigned, progress in all areas improved, including community involvement. By the end of the year men from the Regiment were entertaining children and adults at parties and concerts all over the area – Regimental Chaplain Captain the Reverend Edward G. Carroll making a big impact with spirited sermons accompanied by soldiers of the Regiment.*

The question of accommodations arose again at a meeting of Movement Control Swansea on the tenth, as Major Oglethorpe (O/C 56 Transit Camp) at Singleton believed the US Army was to erect a hutted camp on the site, which would leave no room for the Port Transit Camp. Questions would be asked and by 19 August authorization was granted for the provision of a Transit Camp for 250 personnel with ancillaries for 500 in all. A week later a Royal Engineer company arrived to begin construction.

Two days before on the other side of the Atlantic five ships left Norfolk, Virginia in a fast convoy that had the prefix UT. Three troopships and two tankers made for a small complement in size but significant in many ways as it paved the way for others. One of the troopers was the *USAT Cristobal*, a former liner of some 10,000 tons built in 1939 for the Panama Railroad Company. Converted from a cruise ship designed for 1,200 passengers, she was now fitted out for well

---

* Footnote: *The Reverend Edward G. Carroll was the only black officer in the 95th Regiment and had an illustrious career following his US Army Service. Becoming Pastor of various Methodist churches in New York and later Baltimore, he was active in fighting for the human rights of black Americans. His devotion to duty – he volunteered to serve in the US Army – was recognised after the War and he was credited with being instrumental in stopping official segregation of troops through his actions and ministrations during the building of the Alaska Highway. Reputedly he was a source of inspiration to Martin Luther King.*

over double that number and would be a regular visitor to the Bristol Chanel.

Photo: USAT Cristobal – modern troopship and former Panama Railroad liner. US Army Ships and Watercraft of World War II - Courtesy of Naval Institute Press.

Among the units aboard was one that would take an active part not just in Operation BOLERO but also in OVERLORD and NEPTUNE ten months on and would spend much of their time in South Wales. The 487th Port Battalion under the Command of Colonel M.C. Jackson boarded at Norfolk, Virginia, being delighted to get away from the Port of Embarkation camp at Fort Patrick Henry. Dismay soon took over when they discovered that another unit was already in occupation of their assigned bunks; it turned out that each man would only have occupation for 12 hours! It was approaching evening so the 'longshoremen' would sleep by day and worry by night. Fifteen days they spent on the crossing, as a mechanical defect on one of the ships caused a three day stopover in Newfoundland whilst repairs were made. Troopships were not the most hospitable places to be and it was often said that the men were ready to fight anybody just to be able to get off, so the enemy had better watch out! For the 3,300 aboard the *Cristobal* they couldn't get to Britain fast enough. Brian Morse, in his 'A Moment in History' related the memoir of Pfc. Bernard Blumenthal from 186th Port Company thus;

> *On September 4th after five days of storm, seven days of diarrhoea and nine days of sub scares we finally sighted the mountains of Ireland, they sure looked good to us. Not long after that we docked at Greenock, Scotland.*

Naturally it was raining and the battalion set off south by rail to begin their tour of duty in the UK which would see them operate in the ports of Plymouth and Bristol before being based at Newport. The various companies would work both Newport and Cardiff Docks, being based at Camp Malpas and Tredegar Park before assignment the following year to take part in the invasion.

This was the first of 11 specific troop convoys from the US to the UK in preparation for the invasion of Europe, beginning with UT1 on 21 August and ending with UT11 on 6 April 1944. There was a minimum speed requirement of 15 knots for inclusion and they sailed at irregular intervals. Crossings took around 11 days with 5 days in the UK before returning with the TU designation over another 11 days and then 17 days in New York making a 44 day cycle that required two escort groups. A limit of 25 ships was increased to 30 following early success and increased ETO troop requirements. Port of departure in the US was primarily New York with additional transports joining from Boston, the port of arrival in the UK being listed in orders and schedules as Liverpool. Practically transports arrived a little earlier in Northern Ireland and Scotland with the Bristol Channel Welsh and English ports obviously being a day later. Convoy speeds were adjusted by the Convoy Commodore to ensure ships arrived at their respective ports at the correct time and date, especially important with the high rise and fall of the tides at the Bristol Channel ports. Port wharfing space was at a premium and the independent fast 'super troopers' also had to arrive during the dark of the moon. Liverpool was especially significant as it provided docking space for all vessel sizes except the 'Queens' but including the regulars such as the *Aquitania* and *Mauretania*. The Mersey was important too as it was one of only two in the west of Britain that had sufficient wharf space to accommodate a number of tankers at the same time at Bromborough and Ellesmere Port, the other being Avonmouth. The dedicated CU series of convoys were principally for the transportation of petroleum products plus crude oil from Curacao via New York and had commenced on 12 March 1943 with arrival at Liverpool on 1 April. Averaging around 15 ships per convoy with 6 escorts, these newly built T2 10,500 tonners would split up from their convoy in the Irish Sea with a number going into the Clyde to the Bowling terminal, others occasionally berthing at the Heysham refinery, more on the way into the Mersey and an average of 9 sailing on to the Bristol Channel, 7 being for Avonmouth and 2 scheduled for Swansea, including feed stock for the N.O. refinery at Llandarcy.

Although the South Wales port was not connected to the GPSS, there was an underwater link via the highly secret Hais Pipeline to North Devon from the Queens Dock. Nicknamed PLUTO (pipeline under the ocean) it had come into operation on the 4 April when the pumps started in Swansea and the 30 mile long 2" Siemens pipe successfully delivered fuel to Watermouth Bay near Ilfracombe. Providing training for the British RASC and RE troops under the guidance of National Oil Refinery engineers, the under-water link would see continual service up to June 1944. In fact it exceeded all expectations and as pressures were increased over the weeks a figure of 56,000 gallons of petrol was recorded as having reached N. Devon in one day, exceeding the Petroleum Board requirement for the Devon and Cornwall customers. Consequently supply volumes were reduced to the required 25,000 gallons. Despite being only a test line it proved its worth and like the Mulberry Harbours became one of the engineering feats of

OPERATION OVERLORD. Numerous pipelines were laid and fed from pumping stations set up by the National Oil Llandarcy Refinery crews on the UK mainland to Normandy. The last system was laid from Dungeness to the Pas de Calais as the Allies fought their way towards Germany and proved the most reliable and successful, greatly contributing to the availability of fuel for the Rhine Crossing.

Photo: A typical view of a T2 tanker – one of 533 built during World War II.
Courtesy of Nav. Source.

The CU convoys slowly grew in size as fast modern refrigerated freighters were added. Ultimately by May the following year the convoys would also contain almost as many troopships as tankers and freighters and be combined with the UT's as TCU's. Troop arrivals at the Bristol Channel ports during the period were:

June	626	making UK cumulative total of	329,143
July	176	ditto	382,417
August	178	ditto	424,098

Not a great contribution to the overall total by any means, but illustrative of the tremendous changes that would take place over the next few months as the Bristol Channel ports took on the burden of receiving the escalating number of troops.

Cargo statistics though remained high throughout.

June	93,613 long tons of a month's total of	176,093.
July	138,027	ditto	292,701.
August	150,647	ditto	324,328

GWR dockers and US 'longshoremen' would offload, together with the Mersey men, the amazing total of 70% of all US Army cargo landed in the UK by D-Day.

*****

Chapter II

SEPTEMBER '43 – BOLERO ANDANTE

Movement Control in Swansea were preparing for new arrivals whilst clearing their desks regarding Operation JANTZEN which had taken up so much of their time during the previous months. Although a logistical exercise to supply an Allied Army ashore with supplies coming in by sea, it did not involve US troops, but lessons learnt were certainly passed on. Lt. Col Bevan, as Port Commander for Swansea, Port Talbot and Llanelli was heavily involved together with his staff in forwarding the coasters, tugs and petrol barges to be offloaded to the No 1 Beach Maintenance Area to the rear of Amroth and No 2 likewise at Saundersfoot. Plagued by inclement weather, the exercise proved one thing – the use of ferro-concrete barges to convey petrol and fuel was no good in planning for invasion support. Possibly ten were used and all leaked and several broke their backs.

More problems nearly arose on 6 September with the discovery of cameras and photographs in the hands of the ships staff of *HMHS Llandovery* that docked with casualties from the Mediterranean. However it was deemed by the Naval Base Censor that the content was not a problem and as personnel had already been entrained, no further action was required.

US Engineer Regiments and other Service of Supply units had been arriving in numbers, with schedules drawn up to provide accommodations and supplies for the incoming Field Forces. Some had been on foreign duties already, the 95th Engineer (General Service) Regiment having been one of four Engineer units tasked to build the Alaska Highway. Regimental Headquarters, HQ & Service Company's plus 'D' Company, had moved into Camp Manselton from their first station at Morriston whilst working on the Mynydd Lliw project in August with 'D' Company assigned the construction of a 1,500 man Winter Tented Camp with waterborne sewage. Company 'B' worked on Camp Singleton and with the many changes in orders, from October 1st all the battalion training would be cancelled as per WBS instructions. Normal unit training and drills had been carried out on a one day a week basis but now camp building was a priority. 'D' Company had almost completed their work by early December but with 5th ESB troops moving in, they were re-assigned with 'F' Company to further enlargement of Camp Mynydd Lliw for 600 additional troops spaces, plus improving the Quartermaster Branch Depot at the railhead in nearby Pontardulais and expanding the US RTO (road traffic operation) office at Swansea Docks. The Depot was created in an abandoned tin plate works and required some 4,000 man-hours by one platoon of 'D' Company with a squad taking on the RTO job near the old Guildhall and using 1,350 man-hours. In the meantime the services provided by the 95th (now with the 55 trucks of a fully equipped 413th Dump Truck Company attached) meant they were stretched from Carmarthen, Llanelli and Port Talbot right up to Barry in the south-east Wales on various projects.

31

They were early arrivals in the summer, as was 372nd E (GS) R, with whom they shared so much work, getting off to an early start. Sailing alone from New York on 14th August on the fast former French liner *Pasteur* the 372nd Engineer (General Service) Regiment docked at Liverpool 6 days later, boarding trains for their journey to Bridgend. The two battalions of the Regiment marched to camp prepared by their advance party and began planning for their WBS mission of providing accommodations for the incoming forces. But to begin with, as this was for most men the first time that they had experienced being anywhere except the United States, there were things to see!

> *At the first opportunity, everyone walked to the nearby town of Bridgend and got first impressions of Britain and its hospitality. The neat hedged fields, narrow winding cobblestone streets, the economy with which every productive square yard of land was used for gardens, the frugal food ration which the British shared with these men, the British 'Bobby', fish and chips, all combined to form a pattern that became a part of everyday living in the days that were to come. The "Yank" was made welcome.*
>
> History of the 372nd EGSR.

The regiment began camp construction on 6 September, ranging from Pembroke and Picton Castle near Haverfordwest in the west, Kenfig Burrows, Ewenny Park, Heronston and St. Mary Hill near Bridgend, through to Barry, Wenvoe, St. Mellons and Llantarnum in the east, with Pontllanfraith 'up in the valleys' thrown in for good measure. Eleven major camps to house roughly 1,250 men each, most of which would also be used for marshalling the invasion follow-up force the following year, were built. Additionally a similar number of reassessments (alterations) and rehabilitations were carried out Tenby, Llangadock, Lamphey, Drefach Felindre, Llysnewydd, Burry Port, Fishguard, Llanelly, Kidwelly and the camps and accomodations at the big G-40 depot at Barry.

They were joined, initially in the WBS by the 333rd Engineer (Special Service) Regiment and the 342nd, 355th, 365th, 366th, 368th and 373rd Engineer (General Service) Regiments, all of two battalion strength – the latter who would again do so much construction work with the African-American 366th in South Wales during the coming months.

The first BCP's arrival of September from the US was the *Jim Bridger* from the 50 ship HX253 which docked at Newport on the fourth. The Liberty like so many at this stage of the war only brought US Army cargo, no troops. Much of that cargo consisted of cased vehicles in kit form, ready for assembly 'over here'. Despite additional timber to protect the vehicle parts, the 'boxes' reduced volume thereby enabling more to be shipped and made for easier loading, handling, transporting and storing. Efficient, providing contents were correctly labelled! Jeeps were the smallest and came packed in one case measuring roughly 10'6"x 5'x 2'9" weighing 1 ton 7cwt. Ambulances, Weapons carriers and other ½ ton vehicles were also single boxed, but larger and heavier. Chevrolet 1½ tonners required four boxes each containing two sets of chassis, cabs, axles and bodies. The 2½ ton 6 x 6 trucks were similarly packed although naturally heavier and in the case of the chassis considerably longer at almost 22 feet. Probably the biggest and most certainly the heaviest would be the three cases containing a Diamond T 4 ton 6 x 6 Wrecker with a crane, weighing over 10 tons. Oddly one of these cases contained 2 cabs which meant for a number of spares being available. Other large boxed cargo included gliders and some aircraft, although many were deck cargo aboard specially converted tankers. Tanks, tracked artillery and guns crossed the Atlantic sometimes as hold cargo or other times on deck, with locomotives always the latter.

The 756th Railway Shop Battalion debarked at Liverpool also on the fourth of the month with 'B' Company being detached for service at the Ebbw Junction (TC-203) engine sheds in Newport, the main part of the battalion being based at the Hainault Depot near Ilford, Essex, under their commander Lt. Col. Howard U. Bates. The battalion would be responsible for the reassembly of 'knocked down' freight cars, 7,106 being manufactured by D-Day with a proportion put together at the Sudbury-Eggington and Moreton-on-Lugg Depots. In South Wales a small company headquarters was set up at Tredegar House with accommodations for Major Edwin C. Hanly, 3 Officers and 174 men provided for at the former civilian hostel on Pontygwindy Road, Caerphilly. The term 'hostel' was a bit of a misnomer as this was a purpose built camp, albeit for bombed out civilians from Cardiff, rather than the more basic troop accommodations. They arrived by train on the seventh, marching down through the town. A number of residents were not too impressed as they were used to seeing and hearing smart British troops. 'Slouching' was more descriptive than marching and they carried briefcases, musical instruments and other personal items. A little unfair perhaps as they were about to set up home, and rifles and training were yet to come. They didn't march much anyway as they were mostly transported by jeep and truck to Newport. US Army Railway Battalions were sponsored by American railroad companies in the same way that US Army Hospitals were by civilian organizations, meaning men had often worked together before under the same management. In the case of the 756th it was the Pennsylvania Railroad Company – however now it was very much the case of '..*this is the Army, Mr Jones*'! Their duty was to maintain and service steam and ultimately diesel-electric locomotives of the Transportation Service that were continually being brought across the Atlantic with two roles.

The first was to assist the British Railway Companies who had lost equipment during the Blitz's earlier in the war and to strengthen the available rolling stock – something the US Army would have great need of in the coming months with the vast amount of cargo and personnel that would be arriving. Secondly a great number of locomotives would be needed on the continent once the invasion was successful. Operation POINTBLANK would result in large numbers of French steam engines being destroyed by aerial attack as the Allies attempted to paralyse the railway network to prevent German Army reinforcements getting to invasion sites.

Part of the 1942 lend-lease agreement set up between the American and British governments was for freight locomotives to be built in the US, but suitable for the European gauge railways. There would be a total of 1,893 produced plus another 192 of the 2-8-2 configuration for use in the Far East theatre in India, Burma and the Philippines.

Photo: No. 1604 arrives at Paddington 11December for formal hand-over. (IWM)

The first and only S -160 loco to gain real fame was No. 1604 which had arrived at Cardiff aboard the *SS Pacific Enterprise* together with No's 1602, 1607 and 1609 sailing into port on the 27 November 1942. No. 1609 was apparently the first to be offloaded onto UK shores but it was No. 1604 that was selected for a starring role. A big Public Relations exercise began with the loco' duly cleaned, polished and bedecked with the 'Union Jack' and the 'Stars and Stripes' pulling into Paddington Station on December 11th to a rousing welcome. Lord Lethers, Minister of War for Transport formerly received the engine from Col. N.A. Ryan, Acting Chief of the Transportation Corps with senior US Army Officers present and Directors of all four railway companies which would benefit from the use, on loan, of the first 400 loco's to arrive.

Lend-lease allocations varied slightly, but basically the Great Western had 174, London and North-east 170, London, Midland & Scottish 50 and Southern just 6 - south coast ports traffic not being busy due to enemy activity. There would have been more than 60 in the UK by the end of March '43, but a U-Boat and apparently an iceberg had accounted for the 10 aboard the *SS Southern Princess* and *SS Svend Foyn*, 2 of the 11 vessels sunk from the 29 ships in HX 229 - now both lay on the bottom of the North Atlantic. Sadly another 4 on the *SS Pacific Grove* including No's 2087, 2909 and 2991 joined them in April thanks to the attention of U-563. The 'Austerity' style locomotives were ordered by the Transportation Corps for service in Western Europe and were built to a design by Major J.W. Marsh CE by the Baldwin Locomotive Works at Philadelphia, the Lima Works in Ohio and the American Locomotive Works at Schenectady, New York. Many were still in service in Eastern Europe well after the war ended.

Photo: Cardiff Docks with Queen Alexandra Dock in the foreground leading to Roath Dock served also by Roath Basin. West and East Bute Docks (coal hoists evident) and Bailey Dry Docks to the left of the Pier Head approach. Smoke at upper centre from East Moors steel works. (Associated British Ports).

There were also smaller 0-6-0T 'shunters' brought into the UK and all would be maintained at Newport, 112 in total, plus diesel electric loco's the following year, the like of which had never been seen before in South Wales. These 0-4-4-0 DE's manufactured by the Whitcomb Locomotive Company at Rochelle would arrive later, something like 65 in total, with 6 stored down at the Llanelly Engine Sheds, none actually being used on mainline duties, but which proved extremely successful on the continent. Large numbers of bogie-wheeled tankers would also be brought across the Atlantic ready for use in France and the 756th RSB and their successors of the 757th would be responsible for maintaining these in both the Newport and Hainault depots.

One group who were both troops and troupers were the men of the 15th Special Service Company. Their and other Special Service Companies role in the great scheme of things was to keep up morale among US servicemen and women by performing shows, organising rest camps, cinemas and sporting events – in fact anything in the entertainment field rather similar to the British ENSA troupes. Sailing from New York the 15 September they were attached to the ETO and following a short period in Birmingham were stationed on Pontygwindy Road in Caerphilly, together with detachments elsewhere. Company HQ with the 1st and 2nd Platoons arrived by train in the middle of the night, tramping up the stairs through the booking hall and out on to the street before marching down Cardiff Road, Castle Street and away to the camp. Their first impressions of the town weren't that special, but after a sleep and a sunny dawn they changed their minds, finding themselves in a pretty valley and in proper accommodation. Joe Serpico got his musicians together forming the 15 piece 'Swing Band', rehearsing every afternoon until they were ready to perform. There were dances on 3 nights a week at the Plymouth Hall and their popularity soon had the band travelling all over South Wales to different camps. Doing likewise were the 3rd Platoon in Morriston and the 4th Platoon at Govilon, near Abergavenny.

The American registered *SS Hollywood* docked in Swansea and on the eleventh, Lt. Col. Bevan O/C Movement Control and Major Conyers, his US colleague, were delighted to be invited to lunch on board by her Captain, a much appreciated privilege. Major Conyers was having a busy time arranging for various locations to be used for both port companies to assist civilian stevedores and for accommodations for incoming troops. Newton Village Hall and Summerland Camp could be made available subject to inspection and he was hopeful that the former hostel at Clase Farm (similar to Caerphilly) would be suitable for US Port Staff and half or even the full complement of a Port Battalion, around a thousand men. He could provide the men if Swansea could provide the accommodation.

The following week four Liberty's from the 81 ship HX254 sailed in on the thirteenth with the *Artemus Ward* (to get unwelcome fame in March the following year) unloading at Swansea, the *James B. Weaver* at Cardiff and both the *Roger Williams* and the *Francis Asbury* at Avonmouth. However only one ship from HX255 sailed into the Bristol Channel with the *SS Pennsylvania* putting into Barry on the 16th . Troop Convoy UT2 brought the 101st Airborne Division and the 3rd Armored Division, making landfall on the 14th and was indicative of what was to follow over subsequent months as OPERATION BOLERO got into full flow. The earlier UT1 had consisted of only three American troopships, the *USAT Cristobal* bound for the Clyde with the *Argentina* and *Santa Paula* heading for Liverpool plus two tankers, with a large escort.

Convoy UT2 was a much bigger operation requiring an escort of Task Force 67 lead by the battleship *USS Nevada* with an impressive array of modern newly built destroyers – *Nelson, Murphy, Glennon, Butler, Gherhardi, Herndon, Cowie, Earle, Quick, Fitch, Capps* and the Destroyer-Escort *Weber*. Not surprisingly there were no fewer than seven US Navy fleet oilers included in the convoy to ensure a ready supply of fuel for the hardworking sub-hunting guardians. Former passenger liners, both American and this time British as well, graced the main part of the fleet. The Atlantic, Gulf & West Indies liners, now officially USAT's, the *Borinquen* and *Shawnee* and the Eastern Lines *Evangeline* plus the *John Ericcson* (formerly the Swedish *Kungsland*) were joined by the *USAT George S. Simonds*. From Britain there were two Cunarders, *Samaria* and *Scythia*, P & O's *Strathnaver*, Canadian Pacific's' *Empress of Russia*, the Orient lines *Orion* and the biggest of all the 27,000 ton RMMV *Capetown Castle*. Finally the *SS Mexico* completed the convoy line up bringing the unique 99th Infantry Battalion (Separate) which would spend the early part of 1944 in Wales.

Photo: USAT George S Simonds. Army Ships of WWII. - David Grover (Courtesy of Naval Institute Press)

Leaving New York for destinations unknown was often an exciting if not thought provoking experience for young soldiers who possibly had never ever been to sea before. Thronging guard rails and waving to people on passing ferries or gazing in amazement at the Statue of Liberty – symbol of freedom and gifted by France at the end of another war only 20 years earlier – left many a memory in most men's minds, some of whom would never see the shores of their homeland again. Then out in the rolling North Atlantic, other things were to occupy these 'citizen soldiers'.

Aboard *HMT Samaria*, designed to hold 1,000 passengers in peacetime, were 5,000 parachute and glider troopers of the 'Screaming Eagles'. George Rosie of the 506th Parachute Regiment recalled:

> *'Troopships are the pits. You're jammed in like sardines, sleeping in triple bunks with your clothes on, getting only two meals a day, if you could call them meals! We were allowed fresh water twice daily between 7.15 and 8am, and from 6-45 to7.30pm, which we used for shaving. Showers were salt water – better than nothing, but not much! On clear days we'd walk around the deck checking out the convoy, which was very interesting. To the right and back of us was a battleship that gave you a feeling of security. There were small cruisers scooting around between the ships checking for German U-Boats.'*
> 'Tonight We Die as Men' – Gardner & Hay. Osprey Publishing.

When approaching the relevant safety of the North Channel, the convoy split into various sections making for the ports of the Clyde or Belfast and Londonderry, Liverpool or the Bristol Channel with the escorts doing likewise. For so many of the nearly 50,000 troops aboard ship, this was the first time they had ever clapped eyes on Great Britain. The novelty of leaving ship after the best part of two weeks and getting aboard the trains with their individual external doors to small compartments remained in many minds for years to come. The *USAT Borinquen* landed 1,400 troops at Swansea with Movement Control providing a Welcoming Party on board, the *USAT Evangeline* unloaded 1,950 at Newport and *USAT Shawnee* 2,000 at Avonmouth. The arrival of the *Borinquen* at Swansea had highlighted the fact that there needed to be clarification in future of whether the incoming troops should be cared for British or American elements of movement control. This was, after all, the first occasion that US troop arrivals had the benefit of their own SOS troops being ashore to assist. Previously, as in the case of the *SS Uruguay* back in 1942, welcome and off loading had been handled by the Air Ministry, RAF and Movement Control. Some 6,000 servicemen aboard were moved on by train into England, with their barrack bags following as hold stowage could only be released when 50 US Port Company troops could assist. Despatch by train for the *Borinquen* troops was split between firstly from the LMS Victoria Station in Rutland Street to where the men marched ready for boarding for Stranraer with others entraining on the dockside from the special platforms that had been erected and which would see heavy use soon.

There was going to be an increase very shortly in the numbers arriving and it was vitally important that accommodations albeit temporary should be available. Colonel Conyers could secure more US port labour if camps could be found and he inspected Summerlands and Newton facilities plus the extensive Clase Farm and adjoining Ministry of Health hostel site on Morriston Hill. By the following month, these would indeed be needed as camps were not quite ready for all the three Engineer Combat Battalions that were scheduled for the area of Swansea. A storage area for offloaded 'boxed' vehicles was becoming an issue too. The site at Bryn Lliw Colliery was getting full and it was thought that Neath Fairground site could provide additional space prior to onward movement to USA depots.

Over at Cardiff two refrigeration fast C2 cargo vessels docked on 20 September, *SS Golden Eagle* and *SS Blue Jacket*. These were to be regular visitors to the Bristol Channel ports and the associated dockside refrigeration stores.

Photo: The newly launched C2-S-B1 reefer 'Golden Eagle' still to receive her armament, one of only six built at the Moore Dry Dock in Oakland California. Blue Jacket, Trade Wind, Bald Eagle and Great Republic were BCP regulars.
(Courtesy of Nav. Source)

Away from the Bristol Channel, much planning and discussion was taking place by various committees regarding the design and construction of two ports of a somewhat different nature, one British and one American. Protected areas for shipping off the shores of northern France had been deemed necessary for some time and the Artificial Harbours Committee had been set up to plan for the temporary 'Mulberry' harbours. There were various sub-committees such as the Caisson Design Committee and the Production (Contractors) Committee that would come up with the Anglo-American design for the re-enforced concrete caissons that would be constructed. No fewer than 147 of various sizes were required, contractors being household names by today such as Balfour Beatty, McAlpine, Bovis, Laing, Nuttall, Costain, Taylor Woodrow, Parkinson, Mowlem, Gee Walker Slater to name just a few. When it was decided that the harbours should have a longer lifespan than just the few months immediately following D-Day, more were constructed including some built by US Engineer troops from

South Wales. They were then towed out to Normandy just like their predecessors as part of a 'winterisation' programme to add to those there.

The thought of sailing to distant locations hadn't entered many minds, but for the men of one Ordnance unit reality dawned when they departed Camp Shanks by rail on Sunday 19 September, taking the ferry across the Hudson River to the New York Port of Embarkation. There at the Pier was their ship and not just any ship but NT353 the *Queen Mary*! One of two of the biggest ships afloat, the other naturally being the *Queen Elizabeth*, many Americans seeing them for the first time couldn't believe that they were boarding British ships – surely only the United States of America could have troopships this big! US authorities did plan to have big troopships, requisition of the 68,000 ton French liner *SS Normandie* was effected, but during conversion the previous November she caught fire and although extinguished, she capsized and sank at Pier 88. Soon though there would be the Navy operated *Wakefield*, *Mount Vernon* and the former *SS United States* now renamed for the duration *West Point*.

Sailing at noon the following day it was a rapid five day unescorted Atlantic crossing for the 82,000 ton *Queen Mary* with the time aboard spent on calisthenics and boat drills. Some 15,000 service personnel were aboard so personal space was limited, a far cry from the sumptuous surroundings enjoyed by travellers before the war*. Another night was spent aboard at Greenock before transferring by tender to a camp ashore in the afternoon. Supper for the C/O Captain Irving P. Nelson and all 210 Officers and men was followed by a rattling overnight train journey south, arriving at Cadoxton Station at about 10 am, marching to the nearby Hayes Farm Camp. The huts were to be home for the 863rd Ordnance Heavy Automotive Maintenance Company for the best part of a year.

The last transatlantic vessel of the month to the BCP's was the *USS Albermarle* (AV), a seaplane tender docking at Swansea on the twenty-eighth. She was bringing aeronautical cargo and passengers to support the newly inaugurated anti-submarine operations in the British Isles down on Milford Haven. An important vessel, she had two escorts for the lone crossing and coming in on the same tide were the hardworking escorts, the three stack veteran destroyers *USS Bulmer* and *Barker*, the crews no doubt looking forward to the delights ashore for the next few days.

A total of 5,400 troops had landed in the Bristol Channel ports during the month and it had been at least a year since anywhere near that number had arrived. The UK had now received over half a million US troops onshore, the figure standing at 505,214. US Army cargo stood at 126,854 long tons for the month as part of the 302,914 tons shipped into the whole of the UK.

*****

Footnote: Apparently Adolph Hitler recognised how important the use of the Cunard 'monster' was to the execution of the war and reputedly placed a bounty of one million Reichsmarks for any U-boat commander who successfully sank her.

Chapter III

OCTOBER '43 – BOLERO MODERATO

Ever since the first troopships berthed in the UK, it had been rumoured that there were Hollywood film stars aboard them. Thousands of USAAC crewmen, ground crews and support units of the 8th Air Force had landed and passed through the Bristol Channel ports in addition to those who had come in via Liverpool or The Clyde. South Walians had little chance to spot their celluloid heroes, so reading about them was a must.

> *MEDAL FOR CLARK GABLE. Captain Clark Gable has been awarded the Air Medal "for exceptional meritorious achievement while participating in five separate bomber combat missions over enemy occupied continental Europe" announced the USA 8th Air Force Headquarters.*
> 'Western Mail' 3 October 1943

The Public Relations Departments of the Army were gradually convincing the authorities that blanket press censorship would not help realising good relations between the friendly invaders and those they had come to support. Co-operation was the name of the game – all must be involved.

Meanwhile down on Gower a decision had practically been made by the military authorities to evacuate the south of the peninsula. Without warning the King Arthur Hotel in Reynoldston was requisitioned to be used as Headquarters and the occupiers Mr. and Mrs. Kneath, together with boarders, were given about a week to leave the premises. They left on 9 October and when the hotel had been evacuated, telephones were installed in each room and certain internal alterations were made. Appeals were made to the authorities by those involved and by other influential persons, not to carry out such a drastic overall scheme. These proved successful and the tenants of the hotel were allowed to return around the end of the month. The *'Herald of Wales'* reported:

> *'that Gower's gain was another's loss when it was decided to evacuate an area across the channel'.*

More developments were to follow though.

Over at Newport (Mon) the GWR Railwaymen at Ebbw Junction Engine Sheds were not happy with all of S-160 Class locomotives. West Mendalgief sidings had 42 of the imported US Army Transportation Corps 2-8-0's ready for checking out by the 756th Railway Shop Battalion. The GWR men had lost the use of the eastern lifting/fitting out shops to their military counterparts and were struggling for siding space as well. New storage sites were ear-marked and the first one was on the Barry Railway 'up-line' at Tonteg receiving its first 'Austerity' or

'Bolero' No.2616 on 11 October. Coming to a halt just outside the south end of Treforest Tunnel (the north end opening out to the old Pontypridd Graig Station) she would remain there the longest, in fact until 7 September 1944. A total of 118 identical locomotives were in storage in one long line calculated and quoted by E.R.Mountford in his excellent history of *The USA 756th RSB at Newport (Ebbw Junction)* at '1 mile 660½ yards plus a few extra for the roads and bridges that were left clear!' An incredible sight that would remain in people's memories for years to come. A popular rumour was that one locomotive not recorded was actually stored in the tunnel. The war ended, the line fell into disuse, the tunnel was blocked off and the loco remains there to this day!

Photo: Tonteg storage, looking south. Upper Boat Power Station visible at top of picture. (Courtesy of Oakdale Press)

An Engineer Regiment that would be one of those that would be responsible for a number of new and many reassessed camps in East Wales and the borders arrived at Chepstow Racecourse on 10 October. The black American 366th Engineer (General Service) Regiment was to be based here until March the following year carrying out the construction of 2 new camps, Glanusk Park and Monmouth, with 10 camp expansions including their own base at The Racecourse and at Sedbury, Bulwark, Llangattock, Hay-on-Wye, New Inn and Pontypool, Vauxhall at Monmouth, Crickhowell and Dan-Y-Parc. More work would be assigned following their move to Monmouth in March in the coming year.

The following day another US Army unit that would spend time in South Wales was beginning its journey to war, 3,000 miles away at Fort Dix. The 771st

Tank Destroyer Battalion had already covered much of their homeland during training in and travelling over 20 states and had the nick-name of the 'Gypsies' as they never stayed in one place long! On a dull Sunday morning 11 October a column of trucks arrived, loaded men and barrack bags and they were off. Several Officers had already disappeared a couple of weeks before which caused the men to wonder where they were off to next as it was clearly obvious that an 'Advanced Section' had left. Now in Quartermaster trucks, not their own, they had guessed right. Several hours later they were at the embarkation Camp Shanks, NY. Preparations for Overseas Movement (POM's) involved inspections, physicals, inoculations, briefings (which were very brief to say the least), film shows and finally that last evening 'pass' to New York. Hundreds of thousands of soldiers would do likewise during the course of the war. Then

> *'a never to be forgotten trip. The long walk to the train under heavy packs, the black-out train ride with much forced hilarity, the trek from the train to the ferry boat, a short ride down the Hudson and then the pier with the Union Castle Liner "Capetown Castle", looming up against the light of New York will always be vivid memories.'*
>
> History of the 771st TD Battalion.

Meanwhile on the other side of the North Atlantic at the Bristol Channel ports, October had got off to a quiet start with just the Liberty *Ephraim Brevard* from the 41 ships making up HX259 docking in Swansea on the fourteenth. Things started to move four days later as troopships in the biggest troop convoy of the war so far arrived in the UK from Boston and New York. Twenty three vessels carrying 87,000 troops had set out with a big escort on the seventh and although the USAT *George W. Goethals* had to turn back with engine trouble, the rest got in safely by the eighteenth. Convoy UT3 principally carried two entire US Infantry Divisions that will feature prominently in the months to come, the 2nd 'Indianhead' regulars bound for Northern Ireland and the 28th 'Keystone' National Guard unit from Pennsylvania set to be stationed in South Wales. The *SS Santa Rosa* with 3,460 men aboard docked in Swansea, her sister-ship *SS Santa Paula,* similarly loaded, debarked men in Cardiff, together with the new refrigerated *SS Bald Eagle,* whilst the former Panama Lines *USAT Cristobal* unloaded over 4,000 in Newport and the *USAT Henry Gibbons* transporting 1,900 soldiers landing them and cargo across the Bristol Channel in Avonmouth. Two special transports that were already a familiar sight in Welsh ports often bringing locomotives and tanks, the Seatrains *USAT Lakehurst* and the *USAT Seatrain Texas* did likewise.

Big convoys needed a large number of escorts – it was quite usual for a battleship to be the Command Post for the Task Force Commander, with a dozen destroyers and destroyer-escorts. Once through the North Channel the troop convoys would detach certain escorts with transports to Belfast or The Clyde, followed by Liverpool and the Mersey further south until the remainder entered the Bristol Channel splitting up again. On this occasion Swansea played host to the

Benson class destroyers *USS Parker*, *USS Laub*, and the *USS McLanahan* and the Buchanan class *USS Mackenzie*.

Photo: Santa Rosa arriving at her berth in Swansea.
(Courtesy of the South Wales Evening Post)

The 28th Infantry Division had been scheduled to occupy camps in the south west of England, but as they had been shipped slightly earlier than originally intended, they were stationed in South Wales as their planned accommodations were not ready. Headquarters under Major-General Lloyd Brown was set up in Tenby with units spread across the old counties of Pembroke, Carmarthen, Cardigan, and Glamorgan. Headquarters and two battalions of the 110th Regiment entrained at Newport travelling west over night to Pembroke Dock, causing alarm to many residents when 2,000 men tramped up the hill to Llanion Barracks in the early morning chill. Pfc Bob Pocklington recalled for a local journalist;-

> *'We heard afterwards that some of the local people thought we were 'German Parachutists. They hadn't seen US troops before and because our helmets were not unlike those worn by the Germans, they feared the worst.'*
> 'An Experience Shared'-Vernon Scott.

Over at Lamphey two companies marched from the railway halt the half mile to their camp up behind Lamphey Court and the old Bishops Palace, glad to be at the end of their journey at last. Disappointment soon became apparent as the sewerage system at the old RAF camp proved inadequate for the numbers now housed within the few huts and additional pyramid tents*. South Pembrokeshire would be a memory of the past when Companies 'I' and 'K' were transferred to North Pembrokeshire near Fishguard. Devoid of main equipment on arrival, the troops were able to take a little time to acclimatise themselves. Part of that 'acclimatisation' involved checking out the various hostelries in the proximity of camps. Difficult in some of the more rural locations, but certainly easier in the towns. Officers were despatched to seek out those premises that would welcome Americans and to decide whether those premises would be suitable for the regiment's 'innocents'! Major Bob Gaynor was ordered out on a foray by his 110th Regiment Executive Officer on a tour of Pembroke Dock pubs. He discovered at his first stop that the licensee, a former coal-miner, had been a resident of Scranton, PA – Bob's home town! The Major was able to report that at least one pub was clearly acceptable.

There were different problems elsewhere. Division Headquarters personnel were billeted throughout Tenby in hotels and private homes making their stay an extremely pleasant one for the 'Keystone' men. The problem here seemed to be the number of rich single ladies who were intent on the company of well paid smart soldiers. A favourite seaside location for amorous widows and spinsters, the genteel seaside resort must have appeared like heaven on earth to some! However most of the troops had much more mundane things to think about.

Harry Kemp of the 109th Infantry camped near St. Athens, Glam. recorded;

'The usual activities were ones established and mastered in a brief time. Requirements like where to sleep, the mess hall, the latrine, the command post, the motor pool, the supply point and the normal training area were easy. Military appearance and activities related to the overseas move had early priority such as sewing back the Keystone patch on uniforms, receiving the TAT equipment from the troop transports (some damage had occurred), and receiving and wearing the ETO service ribbon which all soldiers were now authorized. The aspects of arriving and living in a strange land during a war-time situation were not as simple. Fortunately the natives were very friendly.'

'The Regiment' – Harry Kemp.

Those friendships were yet to be made and some, sadly, were to be of short duration.

Overall the Americans in South Wales were welcomed by the locals where ever they were based and it was only occasionally that things got out of hand with the behaviour of just a few troops. There were so many men of differing services and nationalities especially in Pembroke Dock that just occasionally trouble flared.

---

* Footnote: Soldiers names carved on trees can still be seen in the lane fork where Lamphey Court Hotel drive turns off to the left where there was a guard post.

28th INFANTRY ('Keystone') DIVISION
Pennsylvania National Guard
Headquarters - Belgrave Hotel Tenby.
28th Divisional Artillery Headquarters.
Division Band, Signal Company, Quartermaster Company.
728th Ordnance Company – Saundersfoot.
28th Reconnaissance Troop (Mechanized) – St Clears

109th Infantry Regiment HQ. – Margam Castle
1/109th Kenfig Burrows. 2/109th Bridgend. 3/109th St. Donats.

Company A.	Company E.	Company I.
Company B.	Company F.	Company K.
Company C.	Company G.	Company L. - St Athens
Company D.	Company H.	Company M. - Miners Rest

Anti Tank Co., Cannon Co., Medical Detachment – Kenfig Burrows
Service Company – St Donats Castle

110th Infantry Regiment HQ. – Llanion Barracks, Pembroke Dock
1/110th Pembroke D.   2/110th Pembroke D. 3/110th Haverfordwest.

Company A.	Company E.	Company I. - Lamphey
Company B.	Company F.	Company K - Lamphey.
Company C.	Company G.	Company L.
Company D.	Company H.	Company M.

Anti Tank Company, Cannon Company – Cresseley House
Medical Detachment, Service Company – Llanion Barracks.

112th Infantry Regiment HQ. – Highmead, Llanybyther
1/112th Llanybyther.   2/112th Carmarthen.   3/112th Kidwelly

Company A.	Company E.	Company I - Pembrey
Company B.	Company F.	Company K - Burry Pt.
Company C.	Company G.	Company L. - Pembrey
Company D.	Company H	Company M. - Burry Pt.

Anti Tank Company – Trelog.
Cannon Company – Pembrey.
Medical Detachment – Llanybyther.
Service Company – St Donats.

103rd Engineer Combat Battalion – Llangadock (Abermarlais Park)
103rd Medical Battalion – Penally.
107th Field Artillery Battalion 105mm – Porthcawl
109th FA Battalion 105mm – Haverfordwest.
229th FA Battalion 105mm – Drefach Felindre
108th FA Battalion 155mm – Penclawdd.

The GI's got on well with the Australians in the flying-boat squadron, and generally with British troops, although it was inevitable that 'scraps' developed prompted by that old adage of resentment surrounding 'Yanks' being 'oversexed, overpaid and over here'. MP's were quick to quell problems between their own troops with judicious use of riot sticks, but sometimes it was the local constabulary which had to intervene. There was no love lost between a French-Canadian unit stationed near Pembroke and men of the 110th. Inspector R. J. Jones got wind of trouble brewing following the stabbing of a G.I. He arrived in the centre of Pembroke Dock with just his one Sergeant to find the opposite parties lined up on either side of the road hurling abuse and insults at each other. Stepping into the roadway between them, the young Inspector gave them 'a good dressing down.' He told them to stop behaving like overgrown children and to clear off back to their barracks. To his and Sgt. Bodman's relief, they did just that, dispersing rather sheepishly following a real telling off! The nearest thing Pembroke Dock got to a riot in World War II had been avoided.

Photo: Govilon Hospital. 4189 106G/UK392. 17 June '45. F/20//542 Sqdn. Courtesy of Welsh Assembly Government Aerial Photographic Unit.

As the 110th Infantry were settling into Llanion, across the Haven the 81st Naval Construction Battalion began building the US Naval Advanced Base and Hospital at Milford, providing Nissen huts for 900 men plus offices, chapel, shops, post office, galley, storage buildings, waterfront facilities and a 200-bed hospital. Simultaneously, the 'Seabees' set up the US Navy Advanced Amphibious Maintenance Sub-base at Penarth Docks. All facilities provided were the same as Milford, but on a smaller scale with accommodations for 561 Officers and men and a 50-bed hospital.

Whilst the US Navy construction crews were busy building their hospital in Milford and Carmarthen was seeing the rise from the mud of the Expeditionary Hospital, yet another US Army Hospital was already in operation. Further east the green fields of the Ty Mawr estate at Aberbaiden had disappeared beneath the wards, operating theatres and huts of the 279th Station Hospital with the 4th Platoon of the 15th Special Service Company also accommodated. The hospital would be enlarged with extra huts for the 703rd Medical Sanitation Company and later as D-Day approached, covered walkways and paths were laid plus extra accommodation for a Medical Battalion Ambulance Company. The local community would benefit in many ways from the hospital at Govilon.

Access from the camps south of the River Usk was fine, but north of the river the Cwrt-y-Gollen camp holding 3,000 men didn't enjoy the same benefit, so Army Engineers built a Bailey bridge at Glangwrney to make life and access easier and it is still in use to this day. It was good practice for the engineers after all. Certainly, there was to be no shortage of medical facilities for G.I's stationed in South Wales. With three Station Hospitals, it would only require one Field Hospital split into three 100 bed sections to provide that extra emergency cover required for the thousands of additional troops who would embark for the Invasion.

The G-40 Depot at Barry was getting busy when the 863rd Ordnance Heavy Automotive Maintenance Company began work, memories of sailing across the Atlantic on the *'Queen Mary'* still very fresh in their minds. There were around 350 men mainly from two depot companies engaged in Quartermaster activities at the depot, and they helped making the mechanics settle in. Two weeks were spent procuring vehicles and tools while awaiting modifications to their shop building located in a hangar. Getting to know what units might require their services – types of vehicles or armament – proved difficult with XXIX District Headquarters at Abergavenny and Western Base Section not much help. Just when they thought they had everything covered, then checks showed they hadn't. The idea was dropped and they just prepared for anything! On the 20 October the 863rd Ordnance Heavy Automotive Maintenance Company opened for business of third and fourth echelon maintenance. Seemingly to be the only heavy mechanical unit in South Wales, the Company became inundated with vehicle repair requests. Always happy to oblige, they had a huge parts supply problem as it appeared G-25 Depot (Ashchurch) never had enough and if they did, they kept them to themselves and others. Consequently salvage and repair became the name of the game. By the end of the month there were 80 or so vehicles requiring work and cannibalisation was the only way forward. A spate of accidents resulted in many jeeps and trucks becoming write-offs but a great supply source of spare parts. A steady production line was set up, but then parking became a problem as more and more damaged vehicles ended up in odd locations around the Depot.

THE EXPEDITIONARY HOSPITAL, CARMARTHEN

A peaceful cow pasture just outside Carmarthen had its bucolic tranquillity shattered early in the month with the arrival of an US Evacuation Hospital unit, closely followed on the fourteenth by the 'deuce and a half ' trucks bearing Company 'A' of the 1/95th Engineer (General Service) Regiment. Then followed by Company 'C' and a platoon of the 413th Engineer Dump Truck Co., another black American unit, they were all to assist in the creation of a totally new Medical Department venture.

The official History of The Medical Department: Medical Services in the European Theatre of Operations takes up the story.

'General Hawley's staff early took up the problem of housing general and station hospitals on the continent, where they had to assume that the battle would leave behind few ready usable buildings. In late 1943, after almost a year of work, the Hospitalization Division and the ETO Office of the Chief of Engineers completed draft plans for an expeditionary tented-hutted hospital. Designed to house a 1,000 bed general or 750-bed station hospital, this standardized installation was to consist initially of tents on concrete bases, on a site improved with paved roads and with water, sewer, and power lines. Each tent was to have space beside it for a parallel hut, which Engineers were to erect during hospital operations as circumstances permitted. Passing through several stages of development, from completely tented to completely hutted, an expeditionary hospital was supposed to be able to accommodate its full capacity of patients at each stage, even as construction and the transfer of facilities from under canvas to under roofs went on. In October 1943, to test the newly completed plan, SOS sent the 12th Evacuation Hospital to Carmarthen, Wales, to erect and operate an expeditionary hospital 750-bed station hospital serving troops in that area. The unit and an Engineer company arrived on the site, deliberately selected for unsuitability.'

Lt. Col O. Pickhart and his staff had a daunting task. They faced an empty field with poor drainage, with fewer personnel than Station Hospital units had for labour, inadequate equipment for a bare field site, and a rigid plan from Headquarters for the location of each tent and building. These conditions were worse than a Station Hospital would actually face in France, but in Wales, the 12th Evacuation Hospital was running a test and had strict criteria to meet. The roar of trucks bringing the men of the 95th Engineer Regiment Company was welcomed by some at least. Good access off the Carmarthen to Lampeter road with nearby housing at least meant that the men felt that they hadn't been condemned to spend the rest of the war only fighting the weather, as getting to know some of the neighbours and 'passes' into town were allowed early on. But they were in Carmarthen to work and that was the priority.

Photo: Early days of the 12th Evacuation Hospital at Carmarthen.
(Medical Department of the Army History ETO).

They started on the very same day that the first patients arrived on the 20th (as per test) and it took a day or so to sort out material requirements and detailed plans. Early on site difficulties were apparent immediately as the ground had become a quagmire during the setting up of the tents and the presence of continual rain – not unknown in Carmarthenshire. Days of hard, dirty, wet work were spent trying to get the hospital out of the mud before real progress on construction could be noted. The 95th E (GS) R History in retrospect stated that;

> *'the spirit with which the Officers, nurses and men of the 12th Evacuation Hospital carried on under adverse conditions, was an inspiration to our own men, and helped speed the work immensely'.*

Other phases of work were to continue in the coming months and they would be ready for the incoming Field Forces. Carmarthen Expeditionary Hospital provided the US Army Medical Department with all the information it needed, creating a learning curve that would have profound effect in the setting up of hospitals on the European mainland. At the same time it provided a station hospital servicing troops in West Wales.

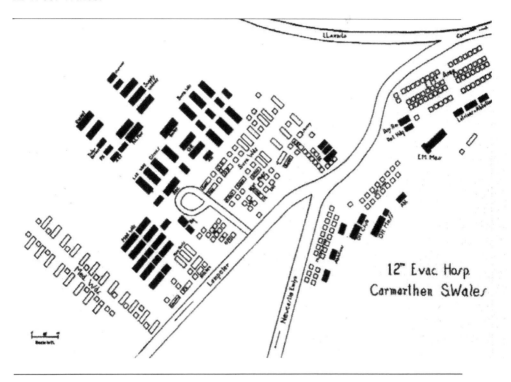

Plan: 12th Evacuation Hospital History. Courtesy; WWII Medical Research Centre (The main access to the turning circle outside the Hospital Headquarters building remains as the main entrance to Glangwili West Wales General Hospital.)

Not just the rain was causing despair. The ever increasing numbers of US servicemen and women was highlighting another problem, especially in the non-conformist heartlands of Wales. Historically the observance of 'The Sabbath' meant that there were no public entertainment or leisure facilities to be found open on a Sunday and certainly no pubs. As early as the first of the month the *'South Wales Evening Post'* ran a story headlined with the caption 'No Sunday Cinemas' for Haverfordwest'. Wherever anyone went in South Wales they could not help to see the large bill-boards outside cinemas advertising mostly Hollywood films – for example *'Immortal Sergeant'* starring Henry Fonda, Maureen O'Hara and Thomas Mitchell at the Milford 'Empire', or *'The Fleets In'* with Dorothy Lamour and William Holden at the Port Talbot 'Majestic'. Yet many servicemen were working

6 days a week and they could only get passes for recreation outside their camps on Sundays. Carmarthen Town Council placed the subject high on the Meeting Agenda at the end of the month as reported in the local paper.

> *'Councillor Treharne asked if there was anything the Council could do to provide entertainment for the members of American Forces on Sunday nights. They were unable to get to entertainment on week-nights, but there was nowhere for them to go on Sunday nights except the streets. The Mayor (Alderman P.W. Trefor Thomas) said they should do all they could to make the Americans feel at home, for it was the best way of fostering understanding between their two countries'.*
>
> 'Carmarthen Journal'.29 October 1943

Oddly the Council had adopted a section of the Public Health Act prohibiting music in local halls – management of 'The Lyric' who were showing James Cagney in *'Yankee Doodle Dandy'* and their competitor at the 'Capitol' where the appropriately titled *'Transatlantic Merry-Go-Round'* was showing were not keen to privately let out the use of their venues. There was no public hall in town at this time and it appeared that wholesome entertainment didn't include jitterbugging! Debate and outrage would continue the following month.

Troops of every denomination, who were church-goers of course, were very welcome at every place of worship. Invites were extended for US preachers to address congregations and Captain Edward G. Carroll, Chaplain of the 95th Engineer Regiment was delighted to open the 43'44 Session of the Calfaria Baptist Church Young Peoples Guild at Clydach the following month. His message - *'I Will Follow Jesus, but...'!* was accompanied by soloist Sergeant John T. Riley and they both proved a big hit.

Out in the North Atlantic troop convoy UT4 was ploughing its way to the UK with the 'Gypsies' of the 771st Tank Destroyer Battalion aboard. Original fears of submarines and seasickness proved unfounded, the monotony of ship-board life being interrupted by occasional drills and exercises. Much of the time the men lined the rails to bitch about the food, the double bunk loading, the lack of adequate toilet space causing many a helmet to become a 'total loss'!

A unit dedicated to the care of men rather than materials was the 12th Field Hospital which arrived at Gourock aboard the *'Queen Elizabeth'* on 20 October setting off south by train overnight to where they knew not! With black out curtains drawn and welcome arrival at Cardiff the following morning, they were trucked out to Rhydlafar, some five miles away which was to be their working home for the remainder of the year. The mission of the 12th Field Hospital with 20 Officers, 18 nurses and 188 enlisted men, was to prepare and open the newly built facility in advance of the arrival of the 348th Station Hospital. This was very much the role of Evacuation and Field Hospitals in much the same way that the Station Hospitals would ultimately be taken over by the larger General Hospitals as facilities and accommodations improved.

Unusually Swansea received three tankers all together on 24 October with

Photo: Rhydlafar Hospital. 4093CPE/UK1871. 4DEC46.F/20//MULTI(4). 58Sqdn.
WAG Aerial Photographic Unit.
The east-west A4119 Cardiff / Llantrisant road can be seen in the bottom left corner of the photo with the 'T' junction to St. Georges and Peterston-super-Ely. The Barry to Pontypridd Railway line runs up to the right of the picture.

the T2 *Seven Pines*, and slightly smaller T3's *Shabonee* and *Dartmouth* from the 17 strong fleet that made up CU5 which had left New York on the 13th. The next time three tankers would arrive together wouldn't be until the end of April 1944.

October was drawing to a close having seen a big increase in the number of troops arriving and remaining in South Wales with the 28th Infantry Division now in residence. All of the troopships of UT3 left their various ports in readiness for the predictable return in convoy TU3 across the North Atlantic, expecting the usual POW's or allied servicemen, especially aircrew, due for training in the United States. However on this occasion there was a major change as no fewer than fifteen* of the nineteen troopships and five other ships that had made up UT3 were diverted as part of Operation TIMBERWOLF.

This involved the transportation of the Canadian I Corps to the Mediterranean Theatre of Operations which, following continued pleading by the Canadian Army Headquarters and Government to be given a more active role in the war, began on the 27th of the month. They were to replace the British XXX Corps which was ear-marked to return to the UK in readiness for the invasion of Northern France. Included in the switch was the 5th Canadian Armoured Division which would utilize the tanks and equipment of the UK bound 7th Armoured Division, thereby making transportation a lot simpler. From their bases in Sussex and the southern Home Counties, over 33,000 troops crossed the country to Liverpool and the Clyde embarking on 26 vessels with 19 escorts that made up convoy KMF 25A. The ships wouldn't return to the UK until the end of November and only then following the off-loading of troops did TU3 return to the US following after TU4 and TU4A. (The Canadians got a bad deal. Equipment was worn out following North Africa and Sicily and not replaced until March '44).

The aftermath of increasing amounts of military traffic everywhere were beginning to appear in the press despite censorship restrictions. During the evening of Thursday 28 October a convoy of trucks preceded by Captain B.L Stein USA in a jeep was proceeding from Saundersfoot to Carmarthen along Begelly Common. At 8.35pm a truck driven by T.Sgt. Richard Kuhu struck Albert Probert. He died of a fractured skull, the *'West Wales Guardian'* reported on the 5/11/43. Unfortunately there would be more.

HX261 made landfall at the end of the month with just the Greek registered Liberty freighter *Hellas* going into Avonmouth. No fewer than 13,798 troops debarked in the Bristol Channel ports during the month of October, slightly less than planned with 2,000 men of the 28th Division remaining in the US following their ship breaking down. However the total for the UK of 610,000 remained accurate when they arrived at Gourock in the *Aquitania* on the 29th. Army cargo reached 163,681 tons with 395,359 nationwide.

*****

Anne Arundel, Argentina, Dorothea L Dix, Edmund Alexander, Hawiian Shipper, Henry Gibbons, James Parker, John Ericsson, Monterey, Santa Elena (sunk), Santa Paula, Santa Rosa, Sloterdijk, Thomas H Barry and XAP Thurston.

Chapter IV

NOVEMBER '43 – BOLERO ALLEGRO

The month got off to a busy start in Swansea Docks with the tail end of the latest US troop convoy UT4 making landfall, *USAT Borinquen* making a regular return to Swansea and *USAT Shawnee* this time unloading troops at Cardiff. *USAT Siboney* docked in Newport and the *SS Scythia* put into Avonmouth, four vessels unloading nearly 9,000 troops in all. In addition the *SS Santa Teresa* also landed her small troop contingent and cargo of stores in Newport. These ships brought Engineers and troops of the soon to be announced fledgling 5th Engineer Special Brigade who would play such an important role in SouthWales exercises and on the sands and bluffs of Calvados. The 5th ESB Headquarters, newly formed from the reorganised 1119th Engineer Combat Group on 12 November, moved from

Photo: USAT Borinquen, a former American Gulf and West Indies Line coastal liner on bare-boarded charter to the US Army.

Singleton to Penllergaer and during the next 3 months planned various operations mounted from Camp Corner House, Scurlage and carried out on Gower beaches.

The *USAT Borinquen* brought 1,450 troops for onward movement and as was now usual, some of the convoy escorts had a four day lay-over. This time they were Gleaves class destroyers, USS's *Butler, Gherardi,* and *Herndon* consecutively numbered DD636, 637 and 638. They were joined the next day by *USS Quick* which had returned having escorted the 19,000 ton former liner *HMT Scythia* up to Avonmouth to unload. Among the troopers arriving at a fog-bound Liverpool two days late, was the *'Capetown Castle'* carrying amongst its units totalling 6,194 soldiers one that would have its home for an appreciable time in South Wales. The 771st Tank Destroyer Battalion boarded train and travelled south through the Welsh Marches before turning west down to the far reaches of Wales. Off into the inky darkness of Haverfordwest Station, relieved by the Red Cross Clubmobile with hot coffee and donuts, then it was onto trucks and away up the rain soaked hill to Slebech, jumping down from the tailboards into ankle deep mud before gaining the sanctuary of their Nissen huts and tents at Camp Picton Castle. Getting their land legs back prior to re-assignment the following month was the order of the day together with learning that they were now assigned to the US First Army, V Corps, and the 28th Infantry Division.

On 1 November First Battalion Headquarters of the 95th Engineers moved to the Carmarthen project thereby putting the entire Battalion on the job. Gravelled pathways and roads were being laid, in one spot it needed fill of over 6 feet in depth. Concrete bases laid down for huts, gaps bull-dozed through hedgerows and water pipes laid, freeing up men from carrying buckets. The 12th Evacuation Hospital personnel found sanitation in mess halls improved with solid bases, food scraps no longer falling undiscovered into hay and attracting vermin. Living conditions started out rough but steadily improved. No baths or showers were available to begin with and laundry was difficult as uniforms got dirty. Local civilians allowed nurses to use their bath tubs and the men had a roster to use decontamination showers run by the local constabulary. Social divides were a little difficult to maintain as although separate messes and serving lines were maintained, there was only one kitchen. Carrying food to separate mess tents sometimes proved a problem. Most importantly and significantly their efforts meant they could carry out their principle duty - providing a station hospital for troops in the west of Wales.

Many of those troops were finding their way around the counties of the west whenever time permitted and were making friends with locals. These meetings were already leaving an everlasting impression on people of all ages. Carmarthen at this time attracted folk from all over as the County town boasted plenty of shops, markets, cinemas, pubs and, of course, chapels of every denomination with large, regular congregations. The war years had brought allied troops to camps in the area such as Starling Park and Ystrad Farm in Johnstown and to the Barracks by the Picton monument. Beyond and a little further out of town up at Job's Well Road lay the South Wales and Monmouthshire Training College, as fine a seat of teacher instruction as could be found anywhere in the country and students (possibly soon to be troops) in 1943 came from far and wide. Evacuations from 'blitzed' cities had swelled the numbers with relocation of schools and colleges for the duration. The site was shared with King Alfred's College, Winchester, not as a result of bombing, but simply due to relocation of seats of learning away from England. Premises were more often than not requisitioned for military use anyway. The College was also home to Wycliffe public school, the pupils safe in rural west Wales. The town became a real hub of activity, even more so with the arrival of the US Army. One young Pembrokeshire 'freshman', in company with a number of fellow trainees, well remembered meeting only the third US soldier he had ever spoken to, the other individuals being down in his home town. The late Lord Gordon Parry of Neyland recalled:

'Lammas Street was new to us. We were exploring the broad, main highway from Picton's Monument to Nott's Square and the shops that opened off its pavements, when we were hailed by an enormous "Yank". As big and strong as anybody that I'd ever seen, towering over the dylanesque, average height of the Welsh men and women around him, this senior warrant officer, in combat dress, held a tiny phrase-book in the palm of one hand. The forefinger of the other hand was pointed at a page and keeping the book open, "Prynhawn da, cockies!" he bawled, in a Welsh accent at least as good as mine. "Ma'en - braf iawn. Ydych ein siarad – Saes-neg?

Trinity '43-'44 A Legacy for Life - Gordon Parry

The boys revealed that, yes, they did indeed speak English and the soldier almost seemed more disappointed than pleased that he could now speak without his phrase-book. Now outside Conti's Café the warrant officer suggested "Say! Why don't we all grab a coffee? I want to ask you lots and lots about your great little city". The boys from Pembrokshire had much they wanted to ask him as well. The Top-Sergeant 1st Class turned out to be an academic himself and became a regular visitor to Trinity College, hailed as the first American to take his place at dinner one evening, standing for grace and

'towering between Principal Halliwell and Vice Principal Humphreys like a Californian Yoshemite Redwood planted in an apple orchard in Wales.'
'Trinity '43-'45. A Legacy for Life'- Gordon Parry.

Across in the boys home County the new camp building programme was well underway for the 372nd E (GS) R; work had started at Pembroke Dock and Picton Castle No.2 near Slebech. Llanion was extended with additional huts being erected to the east of the Barracks and Picton Castle had a mixture of Nissen huts and tents erected around the periphery of fields to the north of the main house. At the windswept Kenfig Burrows, a large double sized 'winter' camp was quickly erected and around Bridgend the Priory down at Ewenny Park was laid out by the Regiment to serve as their Headquarters. Nearby Heronston although a small camp overall, it would have an important role in May 1944. A somewhat windswept but well constructed camp at St. Mary's Hill a little further east sprang up during the month. Barry and Wenvoe Golf Courses were rapidly swallowed up with a camp on Port Road at Brynmill and along the road Wenvoe Castle Club similarly ended up under tin, concrete and canvas, with even more tents further extending the site later. Yet another golf course was taken over at St. Mellons, and the well sheltered fields at the Abbey at Llantarnum, just north of Newport was also laid out. Pontllanfraith completed the list of the 372nd new build assignments. Company 'E' would assist the 360th E (GS) R in a couple of month's time on their camp building programme in North Wales and Cheshire. Their Regimental History details just what was required to provide a 1,250 Summer Tented Camp: viz.

196 - Pyramidal tents	- 6'- 0" x 16'- 0" - Quarters, etc.	
41 - Tents	- 8'-10" x 9'- 2" - "	
7 - Tents	- 16'- 0" x 50'- 0"- Infirmary, vehicle repair.	
1 - Nissen Hut	- 16'- 0" x 72'- 6"- Officers Mess.	
1 - " "	- 24'- 0" x 42'- 6"- Enlisted Men's Mess.	
1 - " "	- 24'- 0" x 54'- 0"- " " "	
1 - " "	- 16'- 0" x 36'- 0"- Officers Bathhouse	
1 - " "	- 16'- 0" x 48'- 0"- Enlisted Men's Bathhouse	
1 - " "	- 16'- 0" x 36'- 0"- " " "	
1 - " "	- 16'- 0" x 48'- 0"- Enlisted Men's Dry Room	
1 - " "	- 16'- 0" x 36'- 0"- " " "	
1 - " "	- 16'- 0" x 36'- 0"- Headquarters Office	
1 – MOWF Hut	- 18'- 6" x 30'- 0"- Infirmary	
5 – Camp structure	- 11'- 6" x 30'- 0"- Enlisted Men's Ablution	
1 - " "	- 11'- 6" x 17'- 6"- Officers Latrine	
5 - " "	- 11'- 6" x 20'- 0"- Enlisted Men's Latrine	
3 - Vehicle Parks	- 17,500 sq. ft. - Laid with cinders/gravel.	

Water, sewer, electric lines plus roads and paths as required for access.

Early occupants of the Brynhill Golf Course camp at Barry included the 115th FA Battalion – a separate ETOUSA unit that had a training role in the Replacement System similar to the 771st Tank Destroyer Battalion that would eventually be up the road at Wenvoe, the 115th specialty being Field Artillery and they were with the 79th Replacement Battalion comprising the 458th, 459th and 460th Replacement Companies, looking after the 1st Field Force Casual Detachment No.4. Come April and the 79th Battalion would be moved out to Braunton, part of the large redistribution of units occupying the South Wales Marshalling Area.

Nearby at G-40 provision of service was high on the agenda for the 863rd Ordnance Company. Having satisfied the wishes of the Depot Commanding Officer by creating a much needed vehicle hard-standing on a much vaunted but unnecessary cabbage patch adjacent to their workshops, they were gaining a reputation for getting the job done. A detachment of 65 men under Lt.'s Jones and Spicer were placed on detached service to Llanelly on the third day of the month to supply maintenance to the newly arrived 28th Division. Breakdowns and especially accidents attributable to some men forgetting which side of the road they should drive on, was causing concern – in the five weeks they spent down west they completed one hundred and thirty major repair jobs and a further three hundred and eight modifications! Command of the Company reverted to their old training overseers when the 183rd Ordnance Battalion took station at G-40 and with a more senior ranking Officer in command supply problems eased.

Meanwhile transatlantic shipping was increasing all over British western ports with the Severn Estuary taking even more of its share. Convoy HX262 with 59 vessels included the *Benjamin Hawkins* sailing into Barry, *Henry M Rice*, and *John L Sullivan* docking in Cardiff on the fourth and the *SS Taranaki, SS Gallici*, and *SS Salacia* continuing up to Avonmouth. Swansea, as was so often the case, took her fair share unloading general cargo from the *Abel Parker Upshur*, and sugar from the *SS Empire Chivalry* together with alcohol. Finally the tanker *Paul H. Harwood* pumped ashore petrol in Queens Dock.

The previous month the 'Keystone' 28th Infantry Division from the Pennsylvania National Guard had arrived in South Wales as their proposed camps in the South West of England were not ready. The first of the Division regiments was due to start detailed instruction at the Assault Training Centre in North Devon shortly, so it was that a cadre from the 109th Regiment Headquarters at Margam Park travelled over on 8 November and joined up with the 115th RCT of the 29th Division who were scheduled to start school. The extensive site under command of Col. Paul Thompson (eventually to be placed in command of the 6th ESB) had been in use since March and had already trained troops, starting with the 'guinea pigs' of the 116th Infantry, the 175th RCT from the same division and the experienced 16th Infantry Regiment from Hubner's 'Big Red One' 1st Division plus numerous other units. Regiment Executive Officer Lt. Col. Carl L Peterson with 34 Officers and 70 enlisted men greatly benefitted from their time spent at Woolacombe and were able and eager on their return to camp in South Wales to prepare the rest of the Regiment. Sited in the wind-swept north-west corner of Devon with extensive open beaches at both Woolacombe and nearby Staunton, the Assault Training Centre Staff were responsible for creating the 31 man assault teams. Not universally popular with infantry commanders to begin with, but the merits of a change in platoon structures became obvious during training as each team was comprised of specialists as well as riflemen. Lt. Col. Lucius Chase, Chief of Training reported:-

This was approximately all the US Manual on Amphibious Operations had to say about the subject. 'FORTIFIED AREAS ARE AVOIDED IN THE INITIAL ASSAULT AND TAKEN FROM THE REAR'. Our feeling was – nice work if you can get it!

'Omaha Beach'- Joseph Balkovski.

They were going to have to attack beach fortifications from the front and were not able to go around them. The teams were made up of 1 Officer with an 8 man rifle section, 4 man Bangalore Torpedo section, 4 man B.A.R .section, 4 man light mortar section, 4 man bazooka section, 4 man explosives section and a 2 man flame thrower section. The infamous Higgins boats (LCVP's) and the British LCA's were the right size for these assault units. (Higgins, a New Orleans based boat builder lead the way in equal employment rights for all - same pay!)

Company 'A' 103rd ECB would be going from their camp at Abermarlais with the 109th, but in the meantime they were getting used to being in Wales.

Photo: Abermarlais Park*. 2384 106G UK 1471 4.5.46. Courtesy of WAGAPU.

The camp had originally been started by Canadian troops but Company 'C' of the First Battalion 372nd Engineer General Service Regiment began reassessment and enlargement work in September 1943 to accommodate 33 Officers and 772 men.

*Footnote: Abermarlais site had an amazing history. A previous incumbent had commanded the Welsh archers at Crecy, later home to Henry Tudors' supporter Rhys ap Thomas who reputedly slew Richard III at Bosworth making Henry king, and in the 1800's Admiral Foley had served with Nelson commanding HMS Elephant. The house in 1944 was the one he had built. Mrs Cambell-Davy aimed to buy the Neuadd Fawr estate in Cilycwm after the war and have another camp so she could enjoy the generosity of the Americans even more if there was another war! Soldiers had reputedly painted their names on the door lintels, but nothing now remains, the camp being dismantled in 1947and the House destroyed in 1978.

Similar works were going on all over Britain. Abermarlais had become home to the division 103rd Engineer Combat Battalion – one of the oldest formations in the US Army which could trace their Philadelphia origins back to American War of Independence. Happy times were spent in and around Llansadwrn, children being frequent visitors to the camp getting rides on their tracked 'Weasels' (similar to Bren Gun carriers) and being generally spoilt by the generous Americans. Come Christmas and a party and concert would be staged by the troops in the school on Boxing Day. The big changes would take place in April '44 when the 28th ID was replaced by the 2nd Division slated as the immediate D-Day follow-up force.

Typical of aerial photographs taken by the RAF just after World War II, the enlargement highlights the familiar 'halo' effect of concrete bases laid for tents of the 'winter' camps and the faded trampled grass of 'summer' camp tent bases. Abermarlais House can be seen at centre. The A40 runs top to bottom partially obscured by trees with the Marlais stream at right. The drive approach to the house and camp can be seen leading up from the foot of the picture where the existing entrance still lies complete with the so-called 'Bosworth' standing stone. It crosses an east to west footpath from the main road before widening out for truck parking before swinging to the west. A diligent local council roadman caused concern at one time when the sentry down near the road spotted him sweeping up following a convoy of trucks leaving a mess on his patch. Investigation showed it was just Leonard Bone doing his bit, although the surveyor had to come down from Llandovery to identify him! The southern corner of the walled garden can just be seen at the top with grassland of what is now the caravan park. The mansion housed the Headquarters and Officers Mess with Nissen huts erected to the west side for troop messes and canteens, stores, workshops etc. Tents provided accommodation for the men and the camp became a 'Bolero' camp to allow for training and accommodation for US troops in preparation for the Invasion.

Also at this time an extensive 2,500 man 'double' camp was constructed on Gower in November '43 as an Amphibious Training Camp for the 5th ESB during their formation and before their subsequent arrival in S Wales. They exercised and trained on Port Eynon and Oxwich beaches in preparation for the Invasion of Europe, developing engineering and transportation strategies that would assist the assaulting infantry Regimental Combat Teams. Camp Corner House was located around the junction of the Rhossili and the Scurlage to Port Eynon road, covering 8 level pastures exclusively to the west of the A4118 which provided direct access to the beach at Port Eynon. Many exercises would be carried out in the following months, but it wasn't all work and no play, as we shall see.

Bigger and faster convoys were arriving in UK waters from North America as Operation BOLERO escalated. The slow SC series continued bringing cargoes that had kept Britain going during the days before the US entry into the war. Likewise the faster HX series had continued and enlarged with newer Liberty ships in commission. The UT troop convoys were on the rise and the independent AT series headed by 'the Queens' continued to pour troops in. Keeping the fuel tanks stocked fell to the new 10,500 tons T2 tanker fleet which was also growing all the time. CU6 with the majority of 18 such vessels arrived on 12 November with 11 entering the Bristol Channel. Swansea took the *Conastoga, Murfreesboro* and *Samoset* and Barry the *Churubusco*. Congestion arose at Avonmouth. *Julesburg, Monacy, Pan-Pennsylvania* and *SS Seakay* all docked on that day, but *Crown Point* and *Shilloh* had to wait until the following day. *Powder River* didn't even get into port to unload her cargo until the 14th, spending 48 hours anchored in Barry Roads. On the 13th the C/O of the 108th FA Battalion was pleased to lead his baseball team out to play an exhibition game for the townsfolk of Gowerton on the local sports park down the road from their camp at Penclawdd. Meanwhile Gower residents and farmers worried about the influx of troops and talk of land acquisitions as witnessed at Scurlage were coming to a head and by the middle of the month there were signs of action taking place. It was decided that there should be open discussion, so that people could put their concerns to the powers that be and to stop any rumour mongering that would be harmful to all concerned. Newspapers were quick to respond. Reporting restrictions at the time were in place, so press coverage was somewhat delayed. An office was established at Cefn Bryn House, where all claims for damage would be met. The office was controlled by Captain Peate with a staff and members of the local War Agricultural Committee and everyone was happy. Gower farmers, realizing the importance of the training and with a sigh of relief that they were not to be evacuated, worked in total harmony with the troops. Many lasting friendships were made too.

'AMMENDED SCHEME'

Gower was abuzz with rumours when, on November 23, 1943, the farmers were asked to attend a public meeting in Reynoldston. Sir Gerald Bruce, the Regional Commissioner presided and on the platform were General Halstead, General Macaulay, Captain Peate, Mr D.R.Grenfell MP and Mr Hubert Alexander, representing Glamorgan War Agricultural Executive Committee. An amended scheme was fully explained at this meeting. It was pointed out that farmers would be disturbed as little as possible by the proposed influx of troops, that a considerable area of land at Scurlage was to be requisitioned to house amphibious craft and personnel and that a line west of Parkmill to Llanmorlais would be required for manoeuvres. The farmers were assured compensation would be paid for damage to crops or buildings and an appeal was made to them to co-operate with the authorities so that the work would not be hampered.

'Herald of Wales Saturday June 9th 1945'

Ironically the following day an item appeared in the Swansea *'South Wales Evening Post'* indicating things were not quite as harmonious as everyone would have liked. Printed on the same page as an article headed *'Taxi Cab Hold Up. Americans Sentenced to Five Years'* (a report of a Courts Martial at a castle 'somewhere in Wales'), the paper duly reported that *'Troops Walk the Streets -*

Swansea Sunday Cinemas Appeal Refused'. It appeared Councillors were divided in opinion, many stressing that they were mindful, as was the Chief Constable, that there should be something done to make the soldiers feel welcome but not at the expense of observing the Sabbath. There was talk of it being the 'thin edge of the wedge' and if allowed public houses would be next! However, unbelievably, the Watch Committee did agree to the opening of cinemas on Christmas Day subject to the Chief Constable's approval of the films! Letters to the Editor followed rapidly.

HX263 made shore by the eighth with the *SS Robin Sherwood* docking at Newport. Explosives from the *SS Jacob Luckenbach* and sugar from the *Charles Folger* were unloaded at Swansea, general cargo from the *SS Alcoa Cutter* at Barry and similar from the *SS Ameriki* in Cardiff, and the *SS Alabaman* and *John Catron* discharging at Avonmouth. Earlier on the fifth of the month the repaired *USAT George W. Goethals* with a small number of other vessels and troopships that made up UT4A left New York, arriving in the UK on the sixteenth including the *SS Ocean Mail* which unloaded at Newport. The 462nd AAA AW Battalion were part of the shipment aboard the *Goethals* that set out from Boston. No repeats of engine problems occurred on this trip and the 11 days voyage was pleasantly uneventful, disembarking at Greenock on 17 November. Coffee and doughnuts dished out by American Red Cross girls was a lovely surprise and then they were off, rattling along to Camp Crookston just down the track under 3 miles from Glasgow. For the next three weeks they would spend time here getting their land legs back, attending classes and receiving their new 'forty's, their automatic anti-aircraft guns, before departure south to Pembrokeshire.

The 6,726 tons *USAT Examiner* was also part of UT4A, in her case bound for Liverpool with the 111th Ordnance Medium Maintenance Company aboard. The report of the troops on the much larger 12,093 ton *Goethals* made no big deal regarding the weather but it was November and a pretty rough crossing with even the 11,420 ton escort carrier *HMS Khedive* with her cargo of 55 aircraft almost disappearing in the wave troughs. The Irish Sea was thankfully like a mill pond and the men were delighted to receive on disembarkation coffee and doughnuts, cigarettes and gum from the attentive Red Cross girls. Then it was on the train and away to Barry. Parked up at the station were trucks from the 115th FA Battalion who ferried the Ordnance men to their camp on Brynmill Golf Course, setting up their tents which would be their home for a couple of weeks. Then at the beginning of December they were transferred to the camp at G-40 on the other side of town. It looked like the mechanics of the 863rd Company were getting help at last.

The next convoy HX264 included the Liberty *David Starr Jordan* before she diverted to dock at Newport on the eighteenth, *Roger Williams*, *SS Hawaiian* and *SS Pan Maryland* off loading in Swansea, *SS Alcoa Trader* in Barry and 6 more cargoes earmarked for Cardiff and Avonmouth. Likewise HX265 released the *SS Bayano* into Avonmouth and two general cargoes into Newport on the twenty-first. By the last week in November, the troopships that had originally sailed for the Mediterranean following UT3 arrival in the UK were making their way back into British ports having left various locations with some of the chosen troops for the Invasion of Normandy, experienced men like those of the 82nd Airborne Division changing Theatres of War at Eisenhower's and Montgomery's request. The Augusta part of Convoy MKF25 with 21 ships and a similar number of escorts had a good passage, unlike their voyage out to the Med the previous month when they lost two of their number to bombing by the Luftwaffe – the Dutch *Marnix Van St Aldegonde* and the *SS Santa Elena* – the latter carrying 1,848 troops and 101 nurses, of whom only 4 perished. The *SS Santa Rosa* returned to Swansea with her sister ship, the *SS Santa Paula,* unloading in Cardiff with the *Lakehurst,* the *USAT Henry Gibbons* carrying further on up to Avonmouth. The *SS Carnarvon Castle* docked in Swansea carrying Italian POW's and it turned out arrangements were far from ideal with delays experienced by Movement Control in getting the dockside cleared. Eventually escort guards were provided and the POW's were marched off to entrain at High Street Station.

Two naval convoy escorts berthed at Swansea being the *USS Ordronaux* and the *USS Mackenzie.* Another twenty-seven troopships left Algiers in convoy for the UK with the *Largs Bay* and *Esperance Bay* docking in Cardiff and the *HMT Moreton Bay* and *HMT Tamaroa* in Avonmouth. Still more convoys from the Mediterranean including LST's would arrive over the coming months as Operation BOLERO escalated. The Liberty *William Sturges* docked in Swansea and *James B Weaver* from HX266 completed a busy month when she put into Barry.

Thanksgiving Day was always a big event for any American and all unit commanders ensured that their men enjoyed the traditional feast whether they were in camp or out on exercise, a special meal would be ready for them at some stage. Staff Sergeant Williams and his kitchen crew of the 109th Infantry Regiment Cannon Company at Margam Castle boasted, as did any mess sergeant worth his 'salt' their 'menu of the day';-

THANKSGIVING MENU
Roast Turkey - Snowdrift Potatoes - Giblet Gravy
Nut and Onion Dressing - Creamed Peas - Cranberry Sauce
Raisin Pie - Parker House Rolls
Sandwich Spread - Cookies
Butter – Sugar – Cream
Coffee – Candy - Cigars
'The Regiment' – Harry Kemp.

All in all 19,723 troops had arrived in the Bristol Channel ports in November alone, bringing the UK cumulative total to 784,631.

US Army cargo stood at 145,497 long tons, a decrease from the previous month with 322,757 as the total for all ports, also down.

*****

Chapter V

DECEMBER '43 – BOLERO SOSTENUTO (XMAS)

The U.S. Advanced Amphibious Base at Milford Haven received the first of its operating personnel from the Bureau of Yards and Docks on the first day of the month with the A2 Administrative Section of WOFA-29 under Comdr. W.L. McDonald making preparations. The unit comprised in addition to the A2 Section the C3-Radio Section, C8-Visual Station, C9-Radio Station (Harbour Defence), E9-Repair Small Amphibious Craft, E10-Standard Landing Craft Maintenance and G7- a 50 bed Dispensary. The composition of the unit indicated it would be primarily concerned with the training of landing craft personnel and minor repairs as and when required. Early on the G7 dispensary was transferred to the sub-base at Penarth when G4- a 200 bed Hospital and G9- a 10 bed Dispensary was assigned.

Set up in a field to the north west of the town the U.S. Navy property included the old Hubberston Fort which was remodelled to house the administration, operations and communications offices with 66 British built Nissen huts to which the 81st Construction Battalion had added another 69 standard concrete huts, two more Nissens and one Romney hut for housing, extra offices, galley area, hospital and recreation facilities. Separately there were two other areas under the jurisdiction of the base, namely Hakin Dock with 600feet of wharf with cranes plus workshops and warehouse, and Ward's Pier with a number of Nissen huts for a theatre and store and including one concrete hut for the Dispensary. The Hakin warehouse floor sloped to enable good washing down from the railway platform at the rear to the dockside.

Apart from training and repair facilities the USNAAB under Captain Glyns' command was to provide supplies and fiscal services for transient US shipping. Accordingly an additional 40' x 100' storage shed was erected at Ward's Pier. Refrigeration was inadequate so through the usual excellent co-operation of Royal Navy fresh meats and provisions would be brought direct from Haverfordwest as required by visiting shipping.

Further up the Bristol Channel at Penarth the USN Advanced Amphibious sub-Base was set up with a complement of 28 Officers and 425 men in hutted accommodation and a further 47 Officers and 514 men billeted in hotels, public buildings and private homes. Repair and training were the principal duties and would continue well into 1944. The 50 bed hospital was built by the 81st Construction Battalion up in Victoria Road (today it's part of Stanwell School field). The shore based seamen down in dockside buildings and huts had an interesting time of it when it came to getting up to Penarth for a beer as the near vertical face of the headland overlooking the wharf and dock below could be climbed by a wooden staircase built on to the rock face. Good exercise going up, but a bit dicey getting back down, although no falls were recorded!

LST 216 briefly called into Swansea on the third day of the month, sailing the same day, nothing especially notable except she was on her way to John Browns yard on the Clyde for fitting out and changing her role and title to *FDT 216*. One of only three manned by the Royal Navy but in RAF service as Fighter Direction Tenders, she would have a major role off OMAHA beach on D-Day. HX267 with 61 ships plus escorts made landfall on 4 December with the Liberty *Edward W Scripps* sailing direct to Cardiff, *Stephen B Elkins* and *George Durant* parting company with her to berth in Swansea, the New Zealander *SS Mataroa* easing over to starboard aiming for Avonmouth and 18 days repair.

Invasion training began in earnest for the 109th Infantry Regiment early in the month with all its support troops making it a proper RCT (Regimental Combat Team) – over 3,000 men similar to a British Army Brigade – leaving for the Assault Training Centre in North Devon. Their composition was straightforward and was mirrored by all Division RCT's:

109th Regimental Combat Team
109th Infantry Regiment Headquarters and 3 Battalions.
107th Field Artillery Battalion.
Company 'A' 103rd Engineer Combat Battalion.
Company 'A' 103rd Medical Battalion.
728th Ordnance Company (part).
28th Quartermaster Company (part).
28th Signal Company (part).

In addition a cadre of 190 Officers and men from the 110th Regiment at Pembroke was attached as observers to prepare their units to go through the same training later. The 1st and the 9th US Infantry Divisions also sent 30 Officers each to observe and learn from the 109th RCT beach assault training. On the first day the men witnessed a demonstration by the resident Training Centre troops demonstrated how to 'Assault a Fortified Position'. Individual learning techniques progressed to squad, platoon, company and then battalion level with an assault on the thirteenth in bad weather. The following day with better conditions another battalion exercised so that by the sixteenth all 3 had experienced the perils of assault from the sea, especially as one 105mm round from the 107th FA fell short injuring two 109th enlisted men and wounding another seven of another unit plus two fatalities. On the eighteenth a full live-fire RCT Assault supported by the 743rd Tank Battalion was launched in inclement weather resulting in 3 of the tankers craft overturning losing thirteen soldiers*. General Brown commended the RCT on accomplishing its training mission and after clean-up on the following day, units returned to Wales by rail and motor.

All the while unit training at company, battalion and regimental level was

---

Footnote. A monument dedicated to those who lost their lives on this exercise is extant on Woolacombe seafront in memory.

gathering pace in preparation for the ultimate Invasion, there remained the fact that replacements would be required to fill the ranks of the expected fallen. Basic training in the US – the boot camps - would turn the 'rookies' from citizens into soldiers in a matter of weeks, but further training would be required for the specialties of units which would receive the newcomers.. On 8 December the Headquarters First United States Army issued Movement Orders to various units instructing changes of location and assignment to the T & S Division of the Services of Supply for the purpose of training field force replacements. Three of the units notified, 745th Tank Battalion, 38th Cavalry Regiment (soon to be reorganised and broken down into Reconnaissance Squadrons) and 471st Quartermaster Regiment (Truck) were in Wiltshire and the West Country, but the 771st Tank Destroyer Battalion with its M10's were down in West Wales at Picton where they had been in camp since arriving a month before. MO V-253 specified that an advance party consisting of the CO, S-3, S-4, Operations Sergeant, Supply Sgt. and 1 Clerk Typist should report to Camp Wenvoe, with the battalion (less one company) to follow at the earliest opportunity. Thus it was that replacement training was centred in S.E. Wales for Field Artillery (115th FA) at Camp Barry and Tank Destroyers at Camp Wenvoe. The 771st TD Battalion which was assigned by the ETO as the specialised Tank Destroyer training Battalion for the Field Force Replacement system played an important role at the Assault Training Center as well with Company 'A' stationed at Braunton for a period.

By Christmas the 771st was madly planning courses, training instructors and assistants, building training aids, searching for firing ranges, and making up schedules and making as many friends as possible with the people of Barry and Cardiff. The battalion was all together for the festive period before Companies 'A' and 'B' moved to Camp St. Mellons. For the next few months there wouldn't be an idle moment with training classes in camp, range firing expeditions to the Black Mountain, firing at the Anti Aircraft Artillery site at Barry Island and exercises right across the county. Fraternization with the natives continued and there were sounds of wedding bells as well!

The saga regarding cinemas in one West Wales town had been continuing. Headlines in the oldest newspaper in Wales *'The Carmarthen Journal'* read "Sunday Opening For Cinemas" being somewhat misleading as the Carmarthen Town Council meeting on Friday 10 December voted 11- 4 against acceding to Military Authorities request! There had been an emotive discussion attended by Major R. Cottle representing Colonel MaCartney (Carmarthen Sub-Area Commander), Lt. Col. A.N. Holmes USA, Chaplain Robert E. Keiffer USA and representatives of local churches. Suggestions put forward for consideration included cinemas open only after divine services, admission to Forces personnel only plus one guest and only suitable films to be shown. It was all to no avail, Carmarthen Free Church being 'unequivocally opposed to the request as they felt it was something quite foreign to this country. It was noted that the 'Capitol' cinema was happy to open "like Swansea" but unfortunately for Carmarthen the 'Lyric' bosses said "No".

Repairs and maintenance had been going on at a pace in the Ebbw Junction sheds with the 2-8-0 loco's being taken often two or three at a time for storage on the line at Tonteg. By the 8th there was no more room, so the next site started receiving the US Transportation Corps engines. Routing from Ebbw Junction to Tonteg had been through the old Barry / Rhymney Railway exchange sidings at Penrhos where a total of 8 double-ended rail tracks lay either side of the 2 main through lines. All through the rest of December and the following first two months of 1944 a consistent flow of boarded up mothballed massive engines were hauled up via the Bassaleg Junction onto the old Brecon and Merthyr line through Machen before branching off to join the Rhymney Line at Caerphilly East Junction. Then through the impressive four-platform plus terminal bay Caerphilly Station and branching off for the Penrhos Junction, over the Watford level crossing by the Miners Hospital at the end of St. Martins Road and finally to the storage site – completing a 12.5 miles journey. The site had been well chosen. It was unused, lying in a natural break of the hillsides between the Rhymney and Taff valleys, surrounded by woodland in an area with little habitation and only approachable along country lanes. In fact many residents near the Hospital although knowing of an Officers Mess at Redlands House on St Martin's Road, were totally unaware of the 756th RSB armed guards that watched over 156 locomotives.

Photo: S-160's in store at Penrhos Sidings looking east. The incline of the old Barry line is visible to the extreme right of the picture. (Courtesy Signals Corps).

Some temporary messing facilities for the guard detachment were provided at the Community Hall at the end of Bryngwyn Terrace off Watford Road, but it really was too far away.

At Pentre in the Rhondda Fawr, an extraordinary meeting had been called by the Secretary to the Rhondda Urban District Council. There was nothing unusual about that, with the exception of the subject matter.

> *The Clerk reported that he had communication with the Welsh Board of Health relative to the billeting of American troops in the Council area and informed the Board of the accommodation available in hotels and other places; that the Board had replied that they were faced with the necessity of billeting large numbers of American troops in the near future and it was proposed to billet two thousand in the Rhondda, that the billets were required for lodging only, as feeding centres would be provided by the Military Authorities'* etc.etc.

Rhondda Borough Council Minutes.

What? Armed Forces of the United States coming to the Rhondda! Heated debate amid great excitement ensued in the chilly chamber as individual Councillors vied with one another (again not unusual) to offer suggestions to help cope with the arrival of troops. However, reticence and disquiet began creeping in as members brought to mind the events of 1910 when the then Home Secretary Winston Churchill sent troops in to quell the Tonypandy riots. Billeting in private homes? Not so sure. Council considered the matter and duly resolved:

> *1. That the Clerk be instructed to make further representations to the Board for billeting of troops in hotels and other suitable places and not in private houses.*
> *2. That on the arrival of the troops, the Chairman and the Clerk be authorised to make the necessary arrangements for extending to them a welcome on behalf of the Council and residents of the Rhondda.*

Next meeting would be on 12 January by which time a reply should have been received.

For some Councillors down in Swansea there was also great excitement but for another reason. For American and British sportsmen alike, in or out of uniform, the towns' home of rugby at St. Helens was to be the ground for staging the spectacle of 'The European Theatre of War Championship' on Saturday 11 December – American Football in Swansea! The US Officers Mess at Bryn Road provided a lunch for their British counterparts before the game and Lt. Col. Bevan among others was pleased to join with the newly promoted Colonel Kit Conyers USA and Captain Connel USA, eagerly anticipating an eventful afternoon. The home side 'Invaders' in a blue strip were taking on the visiting 'Screaming Eagles' in green and yellow helmets and it was going to be some occasion with the Band of the Royal Artillery and a US Forces Band providing music. Organised by the Swansea Garrison Royal Artillery Prisoner of War Appeal Committee it was attracting interest from near and far. Plenty of voluble support came from the Americans in the big crowd, but the 'tanner' bank filled with Welshmen was quite

Great AMERICAN
FOOTBALL MATCH
(In aid of the ROYAL ARTILLERY
PRISONERS OF WAR FUND)

Invaders
v.
Screaming
Eagles

AT

ST. HELENS GROUND
SWANSEA

Saturday, Dec. 11, 1943
KICK-OFF 2-45 p.m.

EUROPEAN
THEATRE OF WAR
CHAMPIONSHIP

OFFICIAL
PROGRAMME - 3d.
(Proceeds in aid of the above)

quiet, many studying the game that they were witnessing for the first time. The teams boasted many a top NFA professional or maybe college player now in the army, names and pedigrees all listed in the newspaper prior to the game and the match programme. The 'Invaders' team were all men of the 28th Infantry Division from Pennsylvania who had been in the area for only 6 weeks, their opposition being provided by the 101st Airborne Division who appropriately were flown from their Oxfordshire bases into Fairwood Common airfield. VIP's witnessing the game would include Lt. General Gerow US Army V Corps Commander and Brigadier-General William Hoge 5th Engineer Special Brigade Commander and himself a ball player of renown in his college days. From the British Army were the Brigadiers Rance and Hancock and honoured guests from Glamorgan County Council and Swansea Council. The result was a 6-6 draw, the only casualty being Lt. Edward Sauer who suffered a broken leg following a collision with a player. The sight of a US military ambulance being driven onto the turf to attend to the casualty did cause some misplaced mirth. Welsh rugby games didn't have ambulances on the pitch! Unfortunately the crew of the *K.J Luckenbach* were unable to get to the game as they only docked that afternoon having sailed in with a cargo of general cargo and small arms as part of HX 268.

Up in Scotland the 462nd Anti Aircraft troops after spending a memorable 'Thanksgiving' amid the warmth and generosity of the locals received orders to move and on the thirteenth boarded another train, dined on English meat pie and were off to the coastal area near Angle, South Wales. Now attached to the 'Keystone' Division, home for the next few months was to be at the East Blockhouse Fort, right on the tip of the Castlemartin peninsula on the south-east side of the 'heads' entrance to Milford Haven, with 'C' Battery housed at Camp Penally, near Tenby with the 28th Division Medical Battalion.

Photo: East Blockhouse, Angle, Pembrokeshire. 106guk16295120 8.7.46
An early morning photo of the most westerly windswept camp on the Castlemartin Peninsula, complete with Anti-Aircraft gun emplacements. (WAGAPU)

Under the command of Lt. Col. Charles E. Howard, the 462nd was attached to the 'Keystone' Division and had already undertaken some amphibious training at Camp Gordon Johnson in Florida following their initial 'proving' as a unit at the Mojave Desert Training Centre. At Camp Bradford (VA), more amphibious training culminated in a mock invasion with the 28th ID. off the Solomon Islands in Chesapeake Bay. Now, with the N. Atlantic behind them and the welcomes of the Scots, the seriousness of advanced training began in West Wales. All aspects of anti-aircraft warfare were covered at the Aberaeron School under the astute, highly experienced eyes of British Army instructors and the 'Dome' trainer proving very popular and beneficial, shooting down images of German aircraft projected by pretty ATS girls manning the equipment also being appreciated! All military training had begun in earnest, mostly based at their new home up to Christmas though much fun and enjoyment was found in the neighbouring towns of Pembroke and Tenby. The only trouble was there were loads of G.I's doing the same thing!

CU8 arrived on the 14 December, the *USAT Exceller* off-loading 550 men at Swansea, the *SS Mormacmoon* 1,750 at Barry and the cargo loaded *SS Sea Serpent* in Cardiff, plus the *SS Shooting Star* in Avonmouth.

Convoy UT5 consisting of 22 troopships, 2 specialist carriers and 3 tankers arrived in the North Channel on the sixteenth and although not many vessels were scheduled for the Bristol Channel ports, there were over 60,000 troops on some famous ships taking part. The British *Athlone Castle* was bound for the Clyde with Liverpool due to receive the *Britannic*, *Capetown Castle*, *Stirling Castle* and P/O's *Strathnavar* The former French liners *Athos II* and *Colombie* plus the British *Durban Castle* were slated for Belfast together with the American *Bienville*, *Excelsior* and *Shawnee* all bearing elements of the 8th 'Golden Arrow' Infantry Division.. All others were USAT's or US Navy transports, *Borinquen*, *Cristobal*, *Explorer*, *Florence Nightingale*, *General George W Goethals*, *J W McAndrew* and *Susan B Anthony* heading into the Clyde. The *SS Mexico* brought 1,200 troops to Swansea, the escorts USS's *Cowie* and *Knight* coming in with her. *USAT Lakehurst* with 228 men plus locos docked in Cardiff, the *USAT Sibony* with 1,212 on board and *USAT Seatrain Texas* 118 men and more locomotives both docking at Newport. Finally the British *SS Highland Chieftain* set down 1,900 men in Avonmouth.

The 43 ships of HX 269 closely followed UT5 and included the Liberty *John G Whittier* going to Newport, *Samuel Nelson* docking in Swansea and the *HMT Akaroa* from S. Africa via New York into Avonmouth on 17 December.

Also on the same date the slow SC148 convoy spread its 40 plus ships to all ports with the merchantman *SS Pan Gulf* and the fleet escort oiler *SS Gulf of Mexico* berthing in Swansea. US *LST 264* on its maiden active service voyage, made the crossing with 146 passengers (the designed limit) making landfall as usual in Milford Haven to offload the fuel oil ballast. By the nineteenth, unloading would be complete for the American transports of UT5 and they departed with the escorts for the Clyde to make the return TU5 convoy on 20 December. Christmas would be spent at sea but they would be back in New York for New Years Eve. During the time these ships were in port one of the big convoys from the Mediterranean arrived in the UK. MKS 32 with 6 escorts looking after 67 ships including 12 US Navy LST's (Landing Ship Tanks or more often referred to by their crews as Large Slow Targets!). All were provisioned in Milford Haven and they sailed for various UK destinations the following day with the crews having been paid as well. The USNAAB facility was already starting to function well.

None of these arrivals and departures were reported at the time, of course, but back down west the '*Carmarthen Journal*' was continuing to report on the cinema saga. With headlines such as *"The Sunday Cinema's Controversy"* on 13

December describing protests to the Council and *"Carmarthen and the Troops"* on the 24th with calls for public meetings supporting home visits. By the month's end the headlines screamed *"Irregular Proceedings!"* There were suggestions that the conditions regarding Sunday opening imposed by the Council were wrong as they had no power to impose restrictions. Therefore they would be open to the public! By the twenty-first of December the ETO had the definitive number of troops in the UK standing at 761,309 of which 34,283 were in South Wales.

Monmouthshire	5,525	Carmarthenshire	5,007
Glamorgan	15,919	Cardiganshire	1,351
Brecknock	Nil	Pembrokeshire	6,491

The detachment of 863rd mechanics and fitters were back in G-40 on the 14th, their work done for the time being, having carried out 130 major repair jobs and modifications to 308 other vehicles of all types. The 28th Infantry Division would have another Ordnance unit assigned to look after their vehicle casualties. Work continued back in Barry on a wide range of repairs including some that they had no experience of – British impressed cars for example. The unit was also having its services in demand with output increasing all the while sending out repair and inspection teams hither and thither. In their workshops at G-40 on Christmas Eve, Lieutenants Jones and Smith with a number of technicians were emptying cartons of Ordnance material taken from a foundering ship. Another team carried on during Christmas Day before salt water damaged contents beyond use.

Seasonal expectation was growing for the 5th ESB troops around Swansea.

The holiday spirit seems to have hit the fellows at last. Many are planning to spend them with British friends which they have acquired within the last few weeks. This is the second Christmas we have all been together in the Army and we hope that we shall be back in the States by the time the next one arrives. On Christmas morning there was a very inspiring Catholic Service was held in St Joseph's Church, Swansea. It commenced with a parade through the streets of Swansea leading to the Church. The parade consisted of about 1,500 people and the Swansea Home Guard Band. Many persons lined the streets and cheered as the parade passed. It was a very impressive sight. Solemn High Mass was celebrated at the Church and an inspiring sermon was given by Father John: The Dunvant Players, a group of Swansea dramatists, produced the Nativity Play for all men at Camp Manselton at 0950 hours Christmas morning. The Recreation Hall was filled to overflowing and from the many comments the men obviously appreciated and enjoyed the production. After the events of the morning an excellent dinner was served to all.

The 348th Engineer Combat Battalion History

For the 109th Regiment it was back to training although the First Battalion were pleased to be housed in new barracks at Penclawdd. Christmas meant a day off and it was the same for all troops. Parties were being arranged for local children and the cooks were having their own field days making preparations for the traditional turkey dinner – not chicken or anything else – but TURKEY! Sergeants were ensuring mess halls were decorated appropriately and invitations to share festivities extended to new found friends from near and far. On Christmas Eve the 1st Battalion 112th Infantry put on a party for 200 underprivileged children in Llanybyther, fifty sergeants acting as 'daddies'. The Masonic Hall in Port Talbot had a special licence to enable American troops to entertain local children. The 110th Regiment organised parties in Pembroke and Haverfordwest for 2,000 children in all, other Regiments doing likewise with gifts of candy for every child. The Church School Room and Wesley Schoolroom had parties put on and there were 150 in the Drill Hall, Haverfordwest. The *Western Telegraph* reported on the twenty-third that 800 children were to be entertained at the USNAANB in Milford with a party and a carton of US candy and a card for the children of HM Forces with the very best wishes of the 'Seabees' USN. Brynhyfred Baptist Chapel in Swansea had a Xmas party with soldiers gifting a silver coin to every child.

Even the school room in the little village of Llansadwrn near Llandovery had a concert given by men of the 103rd Engineer Combat Battalion based at Abermarlais Park. The Grand Pavilion at Porthcawl had a special Programme of Events with a Dance on Christmas Eve and a Boxing Night Concert to which troops were invited at 2/- each. At each and every US Army camp and location an inspiring Christmas Message from the War Department Chief of Staff Gen. George C. Marshall was read. Little did many of the troops know that the lavish meal was the last such Christmas Dinner they would enjoy in Europe.

The holiday was short lived for the 112th Infantry – a splendid Christmas turkey dinner was bracketed by a 15 mile road march in the rain and a five day field problem, again in the rain. Men were remembering what an army major had said to them when they docked in Cardiff.

"Welcome to Wales. If the sun is shining it's going to rain; if the sun's not shining, it's raining."

No holiday either for the 110th RCT on Boxing Day as they loaded up for their turn at the Assault Training Centre in North Devon. By train and road they had a lengthy trip via Gloucester which would take not just the day but part of the night as well. Training got under way before the New Year and the 110th got a new Commanding Officer as well, with Colonel May re-assigned as C/O of the 112th Infantry and Colonel Theodore A. Sealy taking over. It was under his command that the 110th received its baptism of fire in Normandy.

Down on the water another primarily fast tanker/cargo convoy CU9 arrived on the 27 December, the SS *Santa Teresa* to Newport and SS *Surprise* to Avonmouth. The Cardiff-bound refrigerator *Blue Jacket* had a bit of an adventuresome passage having been involved in a friendly-fire incident in the North Atlantic. Detached from the convoy on the sixteenth and making nearly 16 knots in overcast, misty weather, windy with a moderate swell running, 500 miles east of the Azores and watching out for U-Boats, one of the ships' Armed Guard spotted a red flashing light. Running a zigzag pattern at 0315 hrs several reports were received on the bridge reporting the sightings of red flashing lights and the

Officer of the Watch was unable to determine distance. Then the *Blue Jacket* found herself engaged by three warships of the RN Escort Group 3 comprising *HMS*'s *Berry, Cooke* and *Duckworth*. Damage was inflicted by both sides, before the almost two hour long battle ceased. The RN Commanders were all heavily criticised or reprimanded and the duty officer Western Approaches HQ was also found to be at fault. Two members of *Blue Jacket*'s Armed Guard detachment were commended by the USN for having acquitting themselves well by returning fire from their forward mounted 3" gun. More importantly they got to Cardiff.

Most units were arriving in South Wales at this festive time, but one was leaving after providing anti-submarine protection over St. Georges Channel and beyond. The Catalina Seaplanes of VP.63 had been stationed at Pembroke Dock since July under Coastal Command 19 Group but were now off to pastures new. Christened the 'MADCATS' after their submarine Magnetic Anomaly Detection device, the squadron had been popular with many PD residents due to their unfailing friendliness and generosity. Another Sunderland Squadron would ultimately take their place making the Pembrokeshire seaplane base the biggest in Britain. VP.63 had been the first and only US Naval Air Squadron to be attached to the RAF and during their time in Pembroke and had flown 338 missions, each one an average duration of 11.8 hours. They had suffered the loss of only one aircraft over the Bay of Biscay, but seven crewmen had perished, two remaining airmen being rescued after 24 hours adrift by *HMS Bideford*. The rest of the squadron were hardened by the loss and they resolved not to forget their fallen 'buddies'. Their morale remained high for the duration of their time in West Wales.

Season's Greetings were flowing combined with morale lifting messages of support. Col. Blanton found time for a New Year missive to his 'Maremen', the old First World War nickname for the 109th Infantry;

> *"1. The Commanding General has informed the Regimental Commander that all reports of the activities of the regiment, while on the recent specialized training were excellent and he is very gratified with our record. 2. As Regimental Commander, I desire to commend the various units and particularly the personnel, men and officers, for their enthusiasm, hard work, and ability to take and absorb the difficult training under adverse conditions.*
>
> *William L. Blanton*
> *Colonel Infantry*
> *Commanding*

Appropriately local civilian leaders also found time to thank the Regiment for its service and friendship. The Mayor of Port Talbot Horace H. Macey, J.P. wrote to Colonel Blanton the following letter of thanks.

> *"On behalf of the Borough Council, the Education Committee and Welfare Officer and myself, I would like to sincerely thank you and all the members of your staff for the excellent and generous way in which you entertained*

the school children on Sunday last. I feel confident these pleasant memories will remain indelibly impressed upon the minds of us all, and the significance of the gesture is such that it should tend to further cement the understanding and good relationship that already exists between the United States and ourselves.
Best wishes to you, your officers and men, for 1944."

The Regiment' – Harry Kemp

By the end of the month both HX271 and SC149 would be in the safety of UK ports ready for the New Year, the regular *Ephraim Brevard* being back in the Bristol Channel, this time at Newport. New Years Eve was celebrated in the usual way, troops and nurses far from home wondering what 1944 would bring them.

Not all got to celebrate the end of the year for the 31 December saw the start of the first of six Exercises down on the South coast of England at Slapton Sands with DUCK 1. An RCT based around the 175th Regiment from the 29th Division down in Cornwall was to take part – 5,000 troops and 1,000 vehicles - would be embarked in a variety of assault ships, primarily LST's and would include not just an assault landing but also offloading of stores ships. Another 3,000 troops from the 1st Engineer Special Brigade and Corps troops would also be involved. Four coasters were loaded at Avonmouth as part of the exercise and a large number of mistakes were duly observed by the umpires – so much so that the number of exercises were increased to the point that as soon as one finished it seemed another started. The conference at the conclusion of the two day exercise for the contributing units and others scheduled to take part in similar exercises made everyone well aware of the exposed deficiencies. Marshalling and loading was deemed a success and laid the foundations for NEPTUNE. However all communications, off loading, waterproofing, congestion and organising the beaches was poor - the ESB roles being well highlighted. The ATC Commander Colonel Paul Thompson, soon to be given charge of the 6th ESB and William Hoge of the 5th ESB would certainly take note, as we shall witness.

The rate at which troops were arriving dropped by the end of the month with all UK ports recording figures of 7,263 making it ashore in the Bristol Channel Ports. Nonetheless there were now 918,347 US troops recorded as landing in Britain, including Northern Ireland. But almost to compensate, Army cargo offloaded had risen at the BCP's to 187,238 long tons as part of the 378,078 recorded nationwide.

*****

END OF PART ONE.

PART TWO
OPERATION OVERLORD
(AND BOLERO CONTINUED)

Chapter VI

JANUARY '44 – BOLERO ACCELERANDO

Christmas was over for another year and as the New Year dawned the sound of Bing Crosby and his *'I'll be Home for Christmas'* had reached the top of the hit parade with the result that those far away passed frequent comment that Bing hadn't sung <u>which</u> year! The sub-title had added *'If only in my dreams'*, indicating that the lyricist and record company recognised that if they wanted popularity for the song, then they had better choose the words carefully!

There would be greater irony twelve months ahead when the most popular recording of all time, *'I'm Dreaming of a White Christmas'* from the film of the same name put Bing at the top again, just when tens of thousands of freezing GI's were up to the necks in snow fighting for their lives in the Ardennes against the German onslaught (the Battle of the Bulge) during one of the coldest winters on record. For those fortunate not to be in the front line, then there would be the frequent United Service Organisation (USO) shows organised by the Special Service Companies for troops recuperating, with the likes of Bing, Bob Hope, Frank Sinatra, and the ever popular forces sweethearts like the Andrews Sisters or film stars such as Lauren Bacall and Dorothy Lamour entertaining the men.

But for now there were no Allied troops on the continent except, of course, for those in POW camps; soldiers, sailors and airmen of all nations who had only the possible treat of a Red Cross parcel to enjoy. Men captured 3 years ago, leading up to and including the Dunkirk evacuation had been joined by those captured in North Africa and early survivors of Dieppe, not to mention the RAF and United States Army Air Corps crews who had managed to escape shot down and burning aircraft only to be incarcerated in camps all over Nazi held Europe.

Many new films doing the rounds in the UK included a number that were almost propaganda, designed to harden the resolve of soldiers and citizens alike. Hollywood produced films such as *Watch on the Rhine* with Bette Davis and Paul Lukas – an anti-isolationist piece highlighting the evils of Fascist theories with an anti-Nazi German engineer hero working in the US. Another film in a similar vein was the Ernest Hemingway classic *For Whom the Bell Tolls* set in Spain during the civil war starring Gary Cooper, Akin Tamiroff and Ingrid Bergman. Hemingway

was to land on Omaha as a war correspondent. Another actress set for stardom featured in *Jane Eyre* - a very young Elizabeth Taylor appeared with Joan Fontaine and Orson Welles. *Madame Curie* saw the usual pairing of Greer Garson with Walter Pigeon. For pure escapism Jane Russell (pictured) set hearts beating in *The Outlaw*, no doubt inspiring some nose-artists in USAAC bomber crews to decorate aircraft.

The Assault Training Centre in North Devon was proving to be of great benefit in the preparation of Infantry Regimental Combat Teams for the Invasion. Similarly, the Amphibious Training School for the Engineer Special Brigades at Scurlage and down on the beaches of Oxwich and Port Eynon was showing the way forward. Now yet another training school, this one run by the Transportation Corps, opened in the New Year.

The training of Port Battalions was largely in the hands of the Maritime Training Branch. This Branch was responsible for improving the efficiency of field units by initiating and supervising training programmes. In order to secure efficiency in the work of Port Battalions during the initial phases of the invasion, a Training School at Mumbles in Wales was opened on January 1st 1944, under the command of Lt. Colonel Hugh Allison. At Mumbles on terrain much like the coast of France, battalions were trained to unload ships under actual battle conditions. The training was conducted in conjunction with other units of the Army, such as the Assault Engineer and Infantry Teams and the Navy, with whom the Transportation Corps would work when the invasion started. Hitherto, Port Battalions had become adept in port operation which involved the unloading and discharge of cargoes and goods under the more or less normal conditions of protected harbours in Britain. The School stressed the reverse process which consisted of getting the cargo ashore by DUKW's from coasters lying offshore. The discharging would have to be undertaken under enemy fire at beaches where none of the normal facilities of a port were available. Therefore, the chief object of the School was to train battalions equipped with a limited amount of gear to discharge cargo in difficult seas onto a bare beach head.

Physical features of Caswell Bay at Mumbles so closely resembled an actual beach head that only the absence of casualties and the enemy differentiated it from an actual combat area. The natural features of the terrain had been churned up beyond recognition by the heavy equipment of the units stationed in the area. These other units were ground force units with whom the Port Battalions would have to work if they were present during the early operational phases. Because of this possibility it was deemed of primary importance that the battalion was able to defend themselves under enemy action. Thus the Transportation School constantly stressed basic military training so that the Battalions would not constitute a burden which would have to be defended by others. Also experience had proved that organisations of specialists who were also well trained in military conflict worked better under fire than similar specialists who had not been so trained.

In view of this, the Training School set up the following curriculum by which two Port Companies could be trained every three weeks.

a) Military. – Military courtesy, customs of the service, close and extended order drill, interior guard duty, road marches, overnight bivouacs and command post exercises along the line of beach operations.

b) Technical – The deck force was trained in signalling, winch operation, rigging and splicing. The hold force was trained in the proper handling of stowage of cargo, the various types of lifts and the use of dunnage. Checkers were taught cargo identification, storage plans, manifests and hatch lists with cargo in its proper priority receiving considerable attention. Service Sections were trained in maintenance of ships gear and deck or pier apparatus, to include coopering, blacksmithing, electrical welding, rigging and operating forklifts and tractors.

Approximately 1,000 measurement tons of cargo were loaded and documented on two coasters weekly entirely by training personnel. The coasters were then sailed approximately 1 mile off shore where the cargo was discharged on to the shore with the use of DUKW's. This constant training greatly increased the ability of the Port Battalions to work under unusual conditions.

Around the first of January it was also becoming increasingly evident that as part of the preparations for staging an assault on 'fortress Europe' the Ordnance Department would have to ensure that all vehicles and equipment was in tip top condition. Moreover 'waterproofing' measures were being developed and instructions prepared for issue to all troops to ensure the right actions were taken before and after the sea crossing, and landing. The 72nd Ordnance Battalion set up a Training School at Bideford (Devon) where cadres of Ordnance men could learn the correct procedures and return to their units to pass on their new-found knowledge. The material used was a mix of asbestos and bostick which when coated over any potential water ingress points, set hard. Once ashore it had to be removed otherwise engines would rapidly overheat for example, and would result in huge numbers of wrecked and totally unusable transport.

Additional measures including the raising of air inlets and exhaust outlets were also part of the training schools itinerary. Lieutenants Jones and Specter, Staff Sergeant Ed Bydynkowaki and Tech 4 H Holcomb from the 863rd Ordnance HAM Company spent ten days during the middle of the month at the school, returning to G-40 at Barry where they instructed the rest of their company. Soon teams were out and about instructing units of the First and Third US Armies in the vicinity and carrying out wading trials at Barry Island. The Lieutenants were becoming acknowledged experts too in the use of waterproofing, as well.

The New Year had dawned and it was business as usual for the 110th RCT in Braunton. Assault training was ongoing in exactly the same manner as their brothers in the 109th RCT experienced. They readily took on board the required changes in the Tables of Organization required by the ATC teachers, companies being broken down into assault squads of 1 Officer and 30 men including teams of riflemen, of Bangalore torpedo wire cutters, demolition men as well as Bazooka, automatic weapons and mortar teams. All designed to fit into the US LCVP's or British LCAs assault craft. There were congratulations given to one battalion for their performance and the manner in which they carried out a particular assault in the dunes. Lt. - Col. Messee, G-2 at the ATC, wrote to the 28th ID Chief of Staff:-

"I have been informed by Lt. - Col. Learnard in charge of the battalion 'hedgehog' problem that the 1st Battalion 110th Infantry was the thirteenth such unit to run through the problem, and from an infantry standpoint was the best of the thirteen."

Ironically, at the very time part of the 28th 'Keystoners' were receiving high praise, a cadre from the engineers of the division that would replace them had been earmarked for training. Lt. Snetzer and 21 officers of the 2nd ECB were arriving at the ATC having been sent to N.Devon from their camp on the Drumbanager Estate in Northern Ireland. The 112th Infantry cadre was equally well impressed, returning to Highmead keen to show that they could do as well if not better when the whole Regiment took their turn the following month. Various training activities had been involving the far flung elements. The Anti Tank Company out in the woods at Trelog above the River Cothi were getting in some good practice on the small Cilweni Range above the camp and were building up their fitness with road marches down the valley to Abergorlech and back. A visit to chapel on Sunday was often undertaken and individual groups of soldiers were often seen doing a forced march on other days – usually to the 'Black Lion' pub! Improving relationships between British and American Forces was high on the agenda of both ETOUSA and The War Office – too often the powers that be kept hearing of fighting taking place on the highways and byways not to mention the pubs and dancehalls of the UK. The 28th Infantry Division was earmarked to carry out exchange visits with the 15th Scottish Division and each unit was aligned with a sister unit of the opposite one. Consequently the following links were established, many of which continued after the war but started in January 1944.

28th Infantry Div.   **15th (Scottish) Division**
109 Infantry   - 44 Lowland Bde: 8/Royal Scots, 6/R. Scots Fusiliers, 6/KOSB's
110 Infantry   - 227 High'd Bde: 10/HLI, 2/Gordons, 2/Argyll/Sutherland High's.
112 Infantry   - 56 High'd Bde: 9/Cameronians, 2/Glasgow High's, 7 /Seaforth.
107 FA Battalion - 181 Field Regiment Royal Artillery
109 FA Battalion - 190 Field Regiment Royal Artillery
229 FA Battalion - 131 Field Regiment Royal Artillery
108 FA Battalion -   no corresponding unit
103 EC Battalion - 624 Field Park Company RE; 278, 279, 20 Field Co's RE.
103 Medical Bn.   - 133, 93,194 Field Amb.; 22, 23 Field Dress' Station RAMC
28 QM Company   - 62, 399, 283 Infantry Bde Co. 284 Div. Troops Co. RASC
28 Signals Co.   - 15 (Scottish) Divisional Signal Co.
28 Cav.Recc. Tp. - 15 (Scottish) Reconnaissance Regiment.
728 Ordnance Co. - 44, 56, 227 Infantry Brigade Workshops.

Fraternity was building elsewhere as well. The 'Keystone' Division was happy to accept a shooting match challenge to take place on the Penally Range from the 1st Pembrokeshire Home Guard Battalion. The 112th Regiment was designated to provide a team of eight marksmen as the other regiments were away from their home stations busy training. The Home Guard team won all 4 sections – slow, rapid, quick fire and 'falling plate' by a narrow margin. CSM Williams of 'F'

Company won the individual best shot much to the delight of his fellow Saundersfoot 'squaddies' and was presented with the Champions Cup by General Perry USA 28th Division Artillery Commander and his C/O Lt. Col. Peter Howells. The 28th Infantry Division football team was also reformed, accepting a challenge from the 29th 'Blue and Gray' Division for a game on neutral ground in Bristol much to the delight of First Army Headquarters personnel who hadn't been able to get to the game in St. Helens before Christmas. The 'Invaders' lost this game of 'armoured rugby' 28-7.

The 7th Armored Group Headquarters arrived at the beginning of 1944 at Camp Llangattock Park, Monmouthshire with 41st Ordnance Battalion also taking up camp accommodation as it was completed. Armoured training for US Forces on the Castlemartin Tank Range began on the fourth with the 759th Tank Battalion being transported from Camp Dan-Y-Parc near Crickhowell all the way down to Pembrokeshire. The entire battalion from the First US Army spent three weeks of live-firing practice before travelling back, not to its original home, but further on to Orchardleigh. Their place in Castlemartin was taken by the 743rd Tank Battalion Company 'A' with their M4 Sherman's and 'D' with their light Stuarts, the other two companies training elsewhere and being equipped with Duplex Drive (DD) Sherman 'swimming' tanks.

The first incoming Bristol Channel ships of the New Year turned up and *HMT Highland Princess* with 1900 troops returning from the Mediterranean docked at Avonmouth on 4 January. The crews of the sixteen ships including 14 tankers in CU10, having been on the North Atlantic over the New Year, were more than pleased to reach the relative shelter and safety of the Irish Sea by January 5. Nearly all T2 tankers, with 6 destined for Avonmouth, just the *SS Robin Locksley* voyaged with them to offload general cargo and a few troops at Barry on the following day. These arrivals were closely followed by *HMT Tamaroa* and the *Samuel Parker* from the 72 ship HX272 berthing on the sixth to unload their men from the States. Shipping movements were increasing all the while and as the weather improved over the coming months both cargo tonnage and troop numbers would continue to rise.

Convoy UT6 had left New York on 30 December bringing the 4th Armored Division and 508th Parachute Regiment among others. Twenty-three troopships with the Escort Carrier *USS Santee CVE 29* split up with the *SS Santa Paula* disembarking 2,366 troops at Swansea together with the *SS Bantam. SS Exchange* carrying 1,920 unloaded at Cardiff, the *SS Santa Rosa* 2,500 men at Newport and the *USAT Thomas H Barry* 3,481at Avonmouth on the 8th. Swansea hosted the escorts *USS Champlin* and *USS Nields* and Movement Control in Swansea had got concerned that the arrival of the two ships was at 1800hrs on the sixth – a Saturday and wanted to bring forward the timings of the dispersal trains. However this wasn't possible due to technical difficulties in the Severn Tunnel as maintenance work was being carried out over the weekend. The GWR continued to request that incoming troops should be allowed ashore whilst awaiting trains, but the Army issued a definite 'no' to allowing any 'shore leave' for either troops or crew until after 'disembarkation'. BCP HQ in Newport was involved and enquired how many troops could be accommodated at the 56 Transit Camp – simple answer of "not enough" even with extra tents, only 650 could be accommodated. The ships duly arrived and the *Santa Paula* on board Transport Commander suggested that the troops should be allowed ashore for exercise under supervision of Officers. The request was forwarded the following morning but US HQ still refused. Following another night aboard Colonel MacCarthy O.B.E. Commander of Carmarthen Sub District had the delicate task of providing the Welcome Address via public address. Disembarkation commenced without incident!

The Clerk of Rhondda Urban District Council reported back to Councillors at their monthly meeting that had received a reply from the Welsh Board of Health regarding the billeting question and that the representations had been noted and pointing out;

> *'That the issue was one for the Military Authorities, who after investigating possibilities had decided that this particular contingent of troops should be accommodated in private dwelling houses.'*
>
> Minutes of the R.U.D.C. Meeting 12th January 1944.

By the middle of the month the 110th RCT had completed its ATC training and had returned to Pembrokeshire. A new location had been ear marked for Companies 'I' and 'K' formally at Lamphey which was proving unsatisfactory due to drainage problems as they now found themselves in the north of the county at Fishguard. Camp Cwmbrandy on Maesgwynne Road had been occupied by Royal Marines earlier in the war, unfortunately for three of them. Many of their comrades were away on a night exercise so on the night of September 23rd 1941 there was only a picket guard on duty. Fishguard and Goodwick were pretty quiet during the war, but on this night the peace was shattered. A lone German bomber picked out by searchlights dropped what turned out to be a parachute mine. The young marines seeing the parachute descending must have assumed it was a member of the crew bailing out over the camp and rushed to capture him, with tragic consequences. Marines Connolly, Brunt and Wyles were killed instantly and widespread damage caused to buildings all around. Many claims for compensation by locals were genuine, but it was noted by the Council Surveyor Mr Arthur Jones, that many buildings known to be in poor repair for years previously were included – naughty, naughty!

The hutted camp was in a reasonably good state when the Yanks moved in. However exercises kept them busy and a week later after spending time on improvements they rejoined the rest of the Regiment at Penrice Castle on Gower for training in 'the occupation and organization of a position after landing on a hostile shore' under the direction of Brigadier General Buchanan, Assistant Division Commander. Artillery practice on Gower was extremely limited and the adjoining small range at Kittle Top was not a live-firing range, so was limited to deployment and exercise.

Mid January also saw the arrival of the 99th Infantry Battalion (Separate) at Glanusk Park. This unique unit took station in January having arrived in the UK the previous autumn and been based at Perham Downs Camp in Wiltshire. All men were US citizens but of Norwegian origin and had been recruited to augment the First Special Service Force that was created in 1942 to undertake potential operations in Norway as part of Operation PLOUGH. Abandonment of that plan meant re-assignment for the battalion, although some 100 men who had trained as paratroopers, skiers and mountaineers volunteered for OSS clandestine duties. In Wales the 99th Infantry Battalion continued with mountain warfare training, less 52 men - all 6ft tall or more - who became the active and ceremonial guard to the US First Army Headquarters in Clifton, Bristol. Competitive exercises and target practice was encouraged by the Commanding Officer Colonel Turner with the local home guard which mightily impressed the Welshmen. The Norwegian-Americans had only recently taken part in an exhausting US Army / British War Office exercise on Dartmoor designed to evaluate fitness training of troops. Fit they most certainly were and scaling nearly all the nearby mountains followed by manoeuvres kept them so.

Camp construction and extension programmes were coming to an end for the 95th Engineers in South Wales. The General Service Regiment had been split into various camps as work was being completed and by the 20 January 'F' company was rejoining the Regiment which had relocated to Shropshire five days earlier. More summer camp building was under way and the Regiment took over from the 373rd Engineers who were assigned the major extension to G-40 Barry Depot, which had just been authorised. The Headquarters and HQ Service Company had moved to Port Talbot on the 15th for the duration of the Barry Project and the Regiment would not be together until the following month for specialised training.

Convoy CU11 separated in the North Channel into the usual sections with two ships sent on to the Bristol Channel on the 20th with the *SS Santa Cecelia* setting down troops and cargo at Barry and the overworked ex cargo liner *HMT Moreton Bay* taking on 22 days of repairs at Avonmouth, much to the delight of her crew. Five more heavily laden Liberty ships this time from the 62 ship HX275 docked on the thirtieth with *Henry W Grady* and *Clara Barton* into Swansea, *Charles W Peale* to Cardiff, and *Ezra Weston* and *Josiah N Cushing* going into Newport.

Developing the ESB's both in organisation and training had been high on the agenda of the First United States Army and the Brigades showed typical forethought even before the High Command issued directives. On 22 January the

84

5th ESB published a directive effectively dividing itself into three 'Battalion Beach Groups', at the centre of which was an Engineer Combat Battalion –No's 37, 336 and 348 – and around which were attached the service troops. Precisely the same grouping of troops took place not just in the 5th ESB but also in two of the 6th ESB Engineer Combat battalions. The 203rd ECB would be the reserve battalion and go to Normandy as part of the Bristol Channel Pre-loaded Build Up Force. Part of that training involved fitness and ability to cover some distance on foot. Accordingly most of the units' road marched one way or the other, a distance of some 23 miles. Each of the 5th ESB Beach Groups would spend 3 weeks or so training on Gower starting with the 37th BBG in January, 336th BBG in February and the 348th BBG in March. Gradually as their individual roles developed, the Engineer Combat battalions would concentrate on those specific aspects which had been highlighted in the overall plan.

The History of the 5th Engineer Special Brigade highlighted the significance of facilities afforded by this special location.

> *The terrain and beach conditions on the Gower coast, especially at Oxwich Bay, closely resembled those to be encountered later by the troops of the Brigade, upon landing in Normandy, France. Every effort was further made to promote realism in conducting landings and operation on the beaches selected. Thus, prior to each exercise, beach obstacles were set up and the dunes planted with mines and activated booby traps. Pillboxes and concrete blocks were also constructed and attacked with rifle grenades and rocket launchers during assault landings. Casualties were assessed by umpires and men were furnished to act as Medical casualties, being tagged to indicate the nature and extent of their "wounds"; the evacuations of "casualties" to naval landing craft was also practised in connection with handling the wounded. "Prisoners of War" were received into custody at a stockade and processed. Simulated air attacks were staged by a nearby squadron of the Royal Air Force*.*

The beach at Oxwich changed considerably during the period US troops were preparing for the Normandy Landings, with sand dunes levelled in places to provide training sites. Access down from the main A4118 road near Nicholston was improved by Engineers cutting a military treadway road down through the sloping scrubland and woods and laying perforated metal planking or paling enabling trucks to take a short cut down to the beach from the east end, rather than the more lengthy route via Oxwich Marsh. This roadway was in addition to that created as a bypass to Port Eynon where there were constant transport issues with DUKW's gaining access to the beach having come from Camp Corner House at Scurlage.

---

* Footnote: Both RAF Stormy Down near Bridgend and Fairwood Common both provided aircraft when required.

336th Battalion Beach Group - Camp Mynydd Lliw.

336th Engineer Combat Battalion
4142nd Quartermaster Service Company
Company B, 61st Provisional Medical Battalion
2nd Platoon, 30th Chemical Decontamination Company
2nd Platoon, 210th Military Police Company.
3rd Section, Shop Platoon, 3466th Ordnance MAM Company
Company 'A', 6th Naval Beach Battalion
1 Platoon; Company 'A', 203rd Quartermaster Gas Supply Company
Sections, 616th Ordnance Ammunition Company
1 Platoon, 294th Joint Assault Signal Company
458th Amphibious Truck Company.

Elements of a new division ordered to the ETO for the Normandy Invasion arrived in South Wales, although this time they were literally passing through. The 'Ivy Leaves' of the 4th Infantry Division, so named in the usual manner after their divisional badge, were bound for Devon and Cornwall. Unlike the early UT6 a couple of weeks before, UT7 arrived 12 hours late on the morning tide of the twenty-ninth with Swansea taking the *USAT Cristobal* and 2,201 troops plus the *SS Robin Sherwood's'* 600 men. Colonel Phillips from 11th Major Port provided the welcome address to both ships personnel via the Tannoy extension as both ships had docked on the same tide. A hot meal was provided aboard with the men then disembarking direct to their trains on the dockside. A schedule allowed for up to 12 trains a day making port clearance of troops a straight-forward affair.

The *SS Bienville's* 1,709 troops and the 168 from the *USAT Seatrain Texas* went ashore at *Cardiff;* the *AP 72 Susan B. Anthony* landed 2,583 men at Newport together with the 228 from *USAT Lakehurst*. Avonmouth received the *USAT Frederick Lykes* with 2,817 troops aboard, with the *SS Ocean Mail* going into Barry sending ashore 1,850 men by the last day of the month. With CU12 also arriving on the same day, the *SS Exceller* brought 550 men to Barry with the *SS Jamaica Producer* and *SS Warrior* docking at Cardiff and Newport for cargo unloading respectively. HX 275 despatched the *Henry Grady* and the *Clara Barton* to Swansea on the 31st. The port hadn't received any oil shipments for a couple of months but a T2 tanker did arrive from CU12 with the *MV Washista* docking during the last night of January.

Bristol Channel ports had received 23,120 troops in January alone, as if to make-up for the drop off in the preceding month – the highest monthly total to date. UK figure now stood at 1,084.752 servicemen and women and cargo at 109,692 long tons and UK total at 281,588.

*****

Chapter VII

FEBRUARY '44 - BOLERO TENUTO

By February the men of the 111th Ordnance Medium Maintenance Company were well into their assignment of providing mechanical support to the 28th Infantry Division. Stationed at what was termed Albro Castle, the building was in fact built as a workhouse in St. Dogmaels, near Cardigan, their stay was as good as it could get. Friendly locals, sandy beach within a mile and the nearest other US troops 30 miles away, so not much competition for the attention of the girls. The unit was kept very busy though, with the Division they were serving spread right across South Wales even if breakdowns often occurred almost on their doorstep. The main coast road ran through Cardigan to the frequently visited range between there and Newquay at Aberporth. A British Army creation earlier in the war, the Light Anti Aircraft Training School had been receiving US Army units during 1943 and increased in 1944 as more and more battalions arrived, rotating on weekly training missions – aircraft identification, radar familiarity, live firing etc through the highly technical site referred to by the Americans as the 'University'.

February 1 and the 110th Infantry Regiment returned to Pembrokeshire where immediately all NCO's were promoted one grade and many privates became PFC's, recognising the success of weeks of training. Around the middle of the month the Regiment ran a series of exercises on the Preseli Mountains to the north-east of Haverfordwest with the two companies based in Fishguard providing defensive positions in the north facing the attackers from the south! Valuable experience was gained as the Regiment had just received some rookie replacements from the field force replacement centre. Extensive manoeuvres had been taking place for the 109th Regiment as well, individual battalions rotating over two days on the Black Mountain Manoeuvre Area enabling live firing of rifle, machine guns and mortars. During this time elements of the 771st TD Battalion were also attached for coordinated training with the rifle squads, platoons and companies.

Some people were not happy down in Barry though. The paper reported:-

'A Sully Road Complaint'. Complaints by a senior member of the nursing staff about the Sully Hospital road condition "Why can't we have some concessions as afforded to others in this vicinity."
The following evening, on 3 February, the South Wales Echo ran another report:-
'Sully Road Swamp – Public Services Suspended'. An alternative route was not available due to security reasons. Complaints were justified and it was odd, especially when mechanical appliances were available.'

The equipment being referred to belonged to the 373rd E (GS) R which actually started extending the G-40 Depot on the first day of February. The Second Battalion had been on site since the middle of January but had been unable to start construction having been delayed due to the failure of promised material and equipment arriving. Locals would not be aware of what work had been planned and the Engineers had a pretty big operation to get under way as detailed from the WBS Project Assignment dated 13 January 1944.

> *"1. The following construction work is assigned to your unit for construction: Project No. 588-D-90, expansion of Engineer Section, Depot G-40, approved 1 December 1943. Approximately 1,000,000 sq. ft. of open storage, five miles of railroad, and five miles of road, together with a 250 man winter tented camp.*
> *2. The above construction is urgently required, and Supply Division, OCE (Office Chief Engineer) will require partial activation of the depot prior to final completion, in accordance with the following schedule...."*

This was no small order; the British had set up a schedule of between six to nine months for the work. The 373rd agreed to accomplish it with one battalion in 90 days. The men worked through sleet, rain, cold, mud and more mud (hence the complaints to the papers), on ground so swampy that it could only be opened as roads were worked on, and would have been completed in 85 days had the unit not been taken off the job to train for the invasion. The project was organised in three distinct sections with 'Dog' Company responsible for drainage, bridges, culverts and modifications to the existing Haynes Lane camps; 'Easy' Company the 250 man 'winter' tented camp and concrete roads on rock and cinder base, with 'Fox' Company all railroad construction. Road haulage of material was the responsibility of the attached 420th Engineer Dump Truck Company whose 55 tippers were augmented by another 100 dump trucks driven by men of 373rd as tonnage was increased to 2,500 tons a day from no less than eight different quarries. No wonder the public highways were getting into a mess as over 150,000 cubic yards of rock and cinders were used for road bases, crane ways and railroads. Gradually public road conditions improved as it was in everyone's interest to have it that way.

A 'repple-depple' trooper, John Mackenzie in a replacement artillery battery, was trucked in following arrival at Liverpool on 10 February to extend the nearby Camp Wenvoe, planned as a future Marshalling camp.

> *"A few miles inland from Barry was a low, swampy meadow in a vale just below a beautiful manor house. Someone said it was a golf course, which it may well have been in a peacetime summer, but that February it was a cold swamp. We were given a hundred 8 man tents and ordered to build a camp there. Water squished under foot when we walked and any hole dug instantly filled with more water!"*
>
> 'On Time, On Target' – John Mackenzie.

Using a primitive transit, a compass, some string and a 100 foot tape, three officers and the rookie laid out a tent city for 800 soldiers. The methods used were similar to those used by the Roman Army 2,000 years earlier!

From the Mediterranean MKF28 arrived at this time with *HMT Highland Brigade* landing 1,927 troops at Avonmouth. The Bristol Channel section of the 69 strong HX277 came in on the 13th with *James B Weaver* unloading at Swansea, the *SS Reinholt* at Cardiff and the *David Starr Jordan* at Avonmouth. Simultaneously CU13 arrived again on the 13th with the T2 tanker *Powder River* berthing at Queens Dock, Swansea, the mixed freighter *SS Mormacmoon* unloading at Barry and the reefer *SS Sea Serpent* at a busy Avonmouth also taking 8 more tankers to feed into the GPSS via the Berwick Wood and Hallen Fuel Storage Depots.

Trucks with the 366th E (GS) R rolled into Dan-y-Parc Camp on the other side of the river from Crickhowell on 12 February to carry out re-assessment and camp enlargement, moving on a month later. The following day the 225th AAA Searchlight Battalion turned up expecting to find a finished camp, but had to set about improvements as well. They were in Wales for just two weeks whilst in transit from Blandford Forum to their new assignment of air defence at Newcastle on Tyne. Other arrivals included the 407th AAA Gun, the 792nd AAA AW and the 759th Tank Battalions before all were 'cleared out' in readiness for the creation of one of the Sub Area 'U' Marshalling Camps in late April '44.

There were continuing problems elsewhere including complaints to the *South Wales Evening Post* regarding speeds of military trucks. Accidents were commonplace, but possibly none as tragic as that which occurred in Swansea to a serviceman who had come across 'the pond' to serve his country and allies. On Friday 11 February at 10.55pm Pvt. Thomas Baggerley had been run down and killed, not by a speeding truck, but by the Mumbles Train at the town end of the Promenade. Almost on cue and possibly conscious that people really ought to be looking out for these 'boys far from home', the paper reported on 16 February that the Swansea Railwaymen proposed a plebiscite on the Sunday Cinema question. This subject had been the topic of so much argument and discussion in the Council Chambers, chapels, churches and pubs - not on Sundays, of course - and covered in the columns of many newspapers ever since it had been raised back in October '43. Five days earlier, the Carmarthen Journal (11.02.44) carried the headline *No Sunday Cinemas Carmarthen Decision Reversed*. A meeting back on 8 February noted that Hereford had allowed Sunday cinema during the First World War and had been open ever since. Swansea was not opening as reported previously on 8 January. The council had debated the subject before a full public gallery and there were now claims of intimidation. The previous debate and decision by the Council had been taken before Independents had had the chance to speak. A Councillor quoted from a letter he had received stating *"your place is to represent the electorate and not to cater for a fleeting population of Americans who will only be here for a few weeks anyway."*

This 'fleeting population' now included the 2nd Embarkation Hospital in Cardiff which was billeted all over Whitchurch with tent facilities on the Common. Having arrived aboard the *Queen Mary* in '42, they had been providing the Cowglen Station Hospital for any sick troops that had come ashore from the Clyde troopships, but now were now preparing for early Normandy duty.

In Swansea the 5th ESB received their Operation Memorandum #5 from First US Army HQ on 13 February. ESB tasks were very clearly defined:-

a)   Mark hazards to navigation on beach and determine landing points (Navy).
b)   Effect emergency boat repairs (Navy).
c)   Establish medical facilities to collect, clear and evacuate casualties to ship.
d)   Control boat traffic in the vicinity of the beach (Navy).
e)   Direct landing, retraction, & salvage (emergency repair) of boats. (Navy)
f)   Maintain naval communications with Task Groups and vessels (Navy).
g)   Mark landing beach limits regarding a), (Engineer)
h)   Construct and maintain beach roadways and exit routes. (Engineer).
i)   Establish and mark debarkation points. (Engineer)
j)   Unload supplies from ships and craft. (Quartermaster Service Company, DUKW Company, Port Company and Engineer).
k)   Assist in removal of underwater obstacles.
l)   Clear beaches of mines and obstacles.
m)   Erect enclosure for, guard & evacuate prisoners of war. (MP & Engineer).
n)   Establish Army communication with brigade and adjacent units. (Signal).
o)   Construct landing aids where required. (Engineer).
p)   Maintain liaison with senior commanders ashore and afloat.
q)   Maintain order and direct traffic in beach maintenance area (MP platoon.)
r)   Provide bivouac, troop assembly, vehicle parking and storage area for units crossing the beach. (Engineer and Ordnance).
s)   Regulate and facilitate movement of unit personnel and equipment across beach and ensure rapid movement of supplies into dumps. (Engineer, MP, Quartermaster Service Company, Amphibious Truck Company)
t)   Select, organise and operate beach dumps for initial reception and issue of supplies. (Battalion Beach Group).
u)   Select, organise and operate until relieved beach maintenance area. (ESB).
v)   Maintain records of organisations, materials & supplies landed (Service)
w)   Provide for decontamination of gassed areas in BMA. (Chemical)
x)   Maintain information center for units landing. (Combat Bn & ESB HQ.)
y)   Operate emergency motor maintenance service to assist vehicles and equipment damaged or stranded in landing and requiring de-waterproofing assistance. (Ordnance).
z)   Provide local security for beach maintenance area (Engineer)
Finally coordinate offshore unloading activities (Brigade Headquarters and Navy).

The 5th ESB Commander William Hoge together with the soon to be re-appointed Colonel William D Bridges was able to devote time to study the lengthy directive with its tables of organisation, missions and tasks, gradually coming to the conclusion that the scale of the OMAHA landings was going to require a larger organisation than that previously envisaged.

More increases in US troops, this time in Caerphilly, took place in the middle of the month with the arrival of the 'Bubble Boys'. American soldiers loved nicknames – 'Snow Whites' were nurses, 'Snowdrops' were the white helmeted Military Police, 'Grease-Monkeys' were mechanics, 'Polly Dollies' were Petrol, Oil and Lubricant Quartermaster supply men, 'Dough Bashers' had to be bakers, so naturally the 634th Quartermaster (Laundry) Company could only be 'Bubble Boys'. They had arrived at Liverpool in January aboard the Navy Assault Transport '*Anne Arundel*', part of the UT convoy and had spent the past 6 weeks at Camp Merevale near Atherstone, minus equipment, and carrying out all the usual fitness and basic training under their C/O Captain Harold "Andy" Devine.

Arriving by truck, the 634th spent the first two nights at the Pontygwindy Road Camp sharing with the Railway Shop Battalion which really meant serious overcrowding resulted. Officers with the assistance of the local constabulary set about billeting the 260 men all over town. Messing facilities were provided in Nissen Huts on Mill Road near Piccadilly Square with the Mobile Laundry Trailers set up on the old fairground site behind the Workmen's Hall, between the Tannery and Social Club. Getting all the new trailers from depots took some time; motor pool men had to get up to Blackpool on one occasion but finally all sixteen units were in operation by mid March. The unit was not too popular on one short lived occasion – to get 'up and running' they needed water and it was taking far too long to get the authorities to make the connection to the mains supply, so they did it themselves. Overnight after the last bus passed, they dug, located the pipe, tapped in, refilled the trench, patched the road and swept up. A job done the American way! Unfortunately as soon as they drew water they lowered the water pressure all over the town causing uproar! The unit quickly sorted things out by securing two 5,000 gallon tanks which they slowly filled overnight, so everyone was satisfied.

Their time spent in Caerphilly was indeed happy for the 'Bubble Boys', the Quartermaster Company was going to get very busy soon so they made the most of their peaceful situation. A number of men married local girls whom they had met at the Plymouth Hall for example, the dance hall above Woolworths. They had the upper floor of the splendid black and white 'Clive Arms Hotel' overlooking the Castle as a recreation centre and the town was well blessed with pubs, Railway Inn, Kings Head, Wheatsheaf, The Bell, Boars Head, Castle and Piccadilly Arms plus two cinemas. Cardiff and Newport were also nearby; so there was plenty to do when time allowed*.

Meeting on 17th February Cardiff City Council Transport Committee Engineer Section reported on traffic accidents involving US Army vehicles. The Chief Engineer submitted a schedule showing details of collisions involving the Department's passenger carrying vehicles and those of the United States Army for the 4 months ending 31st January 1944. It was resolved that the issue be referred to

---

* *Footnote: Another popular nickname was that applied to not troops but to ladies of the night in London, who were referred to as 'Piccadilly Commandos'. Perhaps in Caerphilly as well?!*

the Watch Committee recommending that the US Authorities use diversion routes.

No diversion for CU13 with the largest tanker convoy so far containing 19 ships in all, with just the one T2 *Powder River* scheduled for Swansea, another four – *Harpers Ferry, Hartford, Pan Pennsylvania* and *Seakay* carrying on up to Avonmouth. The other ten had earlier split into various ports, 1 for Belfast, 5 to the Clyde and 4 to Liverpool and Stanlow. The modern refrigerator vessel also in the convoy saw *SS Blue Jacket* berthed at Glasgow, and *SS Shooting Star* docked at Swansea and *SS Sea Serpent* at Avonmouth. Finally a small number of troops aboard the *SS Mormacmoon* together with cargo docked at Barry. The even bigger but slower HX278 with 51 merchantmen made landfall with the *Florence Crittenton* arriving at Swansea, the *James I McKay* at Barry and *HMT Mataroa* landing 500 men at Avonmouth on the twentieth.

The 320th Anti-Aircraft Barrage Balloon Battalion was a new arrival to Pontypool on 21 February, not by sea of course, but by truck as they had been in a camp at Chepstow temporarily after leaving their Checkendon, Oxfordshire camp where they had been since their arrival on board the *Aquitania* back in November. They had a rough crossing deep in the bowels of the ship as per usual for black Units, delight being apparent when they viewed the rolling hills of Scotland rather than hearing the rolling waves of the North Atlantic crashing against the hull of the over laden former liner. It had been planned for the unit to relieve a Royal Air Force squadron of their assignment providing Low Altitude Balloon Defence at Cardiff, but as was so often the case, their equipment didn't keep up with them as it was shipped separately. British and US kit was totally different so the 320th AABB (VLA) Battalion had to bide their time. Ten and fifteen mile route marches in the rain seemed to be their main occupation in Oxfordshire, but eventually they were on their way to Pontypool. Very soon three dozen Very Low Altitude Barrage Balloons could be seen rising and falling over the Polo Fields at New Inn as the men trained in readiness for the Invasion. Enjoying the pleasures of home in the domestic billets of Abersychan and Pontypool was something the men never forgot – the only problem being that it didn't go on long enough. Exercises interrupted their stay, trucking down to Slapton Sands in Devon in preparation for D-Day.

On the twenty-second UT8 passed through the North Channel, sections turning away in the usual manner to the Clyde (9 ships) or Belfast (4 ships) with the rest ploughing on down the Irish Sea before the Liverpool contingent of 9 broke away and the remainder steamed through St. George's Channel turning to port and up the Bristol Channel. The troop convoys were getting bigger and bigger, this one consisting of 31 vessels plus escorts including seven troopers of over 20,000 tons each. Aboard were three entire divisions, the 30th Infantry Division plus the 5th and the 6th Armored Divisions. The *USAT Thomas H. Barry* off-loaded 3,481 men at Swansea, with the *SS Flying Eagle* landing her cargo of US Army stores and escorts USS's *Liddle* and *Newman* a welcome three day sojourn. The *XAP76 Anne Arundel* unloaded 1,894 men in Barry, the *SS Santa Paula* 2,366 including the 749th Tank Battalion, together with stores from the *SS White Squall* at Cardiff. The *SS Exchange* put 1,216 men ashore at Newport which also included the 553rd

Engineer Heavy Pontoon Battalion bound for Foxley Camp, near Hereford with the 'tankers'. Finally the *USAT James Parker, APA13 Joseph T. Dickman* and *APA11 Barnett* put ashore a total of 4,500 men at Avonmouth. This was the first time that the US Navy APA's brought troops to the Bristol Channel Ports area. From now on they would remain in UK waters carrying out various exercises right up until their role in Operation NEPTUNE. Two CU14 ships came in on the 23rd with the *SS Marina* unloading at Barry and the 'reefer' *SS Golden Eagle* at Avonmouth.

February would prove to be very important down on Gower. The 37th ECB had been training through the previous month, now it was the turn of the 336th Battalion. Three exercises kept the 336th men busy with Operation CRANE on Port Eynon Beach between 13th and 15th. ROOK was staged on Oxwich Beach between 20th and 22nd and SNIPE took place between 25th and 28th February, a

combined loading and engineer exercise at Port Eynon. Exercise CHEVROLET started on 25 February lasting through to 1 March. A 'Mounting' exercise designed to train troops and supply staffs in the loading out of supplies from the UK for a continental operation, to train Chemical Warfare Service troops in screening a harbour and beach area using chemical and generator smoke and to test the feasibility of extended operations in a completely smoked area. When the 336th completed training the 348th would take their place at Camp Scurlage.

Creation of the Provisional Special Engineer Brigade Group was to be one of the most important and big decisions taken in preparation for the assault on Omaha Beach. Aerial reconnaissance of northern France was continually highlighting the ever increasing number and range of obstacles that Germans were planting as part of the creation of Fortress Europe and it would be down to the Corps of Engineers to gather sufficient forces to deal with them both during and immediately following the assault. So it was as these exercises were ongoing, an important document was published, being the First Plan of 'Operation NEPTUNE'. Part of that plan saw the creation of a totally unique

Footnote: Hoge (pictured) was one of those senior Officers who would receive high praise for his war service. A clever Engineer who directed the construction of the 1,519 mile Alcan Highway in 1942, he was a great commander of men. Later he showed his tremendous versatility when ordered to the Command of Combat Group 'B' of the 5th Armored Division and successfully secured the Ludendorff Bridge over the Rhine at Remagen.

organisation and one that would have a major role in the months to come.

On the 26th February 1944 First United States Army (FUSA) officially sanctioned the creation of the Provisional Engineer Special Brigade Group which would have under command the 5th and 6th ESB's and the 11th Major Port of Transportation – it's duty to plan and control all the support elements of Gerow's V Corps in their D-Day assault and follow-up of 'OMAHA' beach. Newly-promoted Brigadier General William G. Hoge CE (pictured previously) would be in command – in fact as the organisation was his idea, he had already brought together a group of specially selected Engineer Officers to a meeting at Penllergaer House a few days earlier to begin the massive task, despatching two Officers to liaise with the 6th ESB command in Torquay the following day.

Photo: Penllergaer. 4091.106G 1419 15APR 46 F.20"//541SQDN. (WAGAPU)

The former commander of the 5th ESB was only too well aware that the size and complexity of the invasion planned on just OMAHA would need a Command Headquarters to ensure success, eventually being in command of a HQ with an approved T/O of 1,462 men. Ever mindful of his men, he stipulated to

Footnote: The house and gardens fell into decay after the war and was subject to theft and vandalism – lead stripping and timber thieving creating a danger. A weekend explosive exercise for 146th Royal Engineer Company resulted in total destruction. Even now many people do not know of Penllergaer's importance. New Lliw Valley Council Offices were built on the site and even that organization has disappeared into the Unitary Authority. The grounds are now a Park and Ride facility for Swansea with the woods a nature conservation site.

his deputies that every PESBG soldier had to know his precise role in the invasion.

PROVISIONAL ENGINEER SPECIAL BRIGADE GROUP
HQ & HQ Company – 270 men
14th Finance Disbursing Section – 17
Detachment A, 246th Signal Operations Company – 51
Detachment A, 255th Signal Operations Company – 57
Det. D7G1, 6901, European Civil Affairs Division -8
Team No 402 Military Intelligence Interpreters. - 6
Detachment No. 31 (Provisional) Counter Intelligence Corps. - 6
Co. 'C'. 783rd Military Police Battalion. – 175
302nd Military Police Escort Guard Company – 138
Second Battalion 358th Engineer General Service Regiment – 601
440th Engineer Depot Company (-3 Platoons) - 119
Det. 4 Fourth Platoon Company 'C', 602nd Engineer Camouflage Bn. – 14

Brigade strengths of 6,500 each, plus 3,000 attachments followed by the 8,600 men from 11th Major Port, gave Hoge's PESBG some 29,000 troops.

Camp Penllergaer therefore was possibly the most important location for the US Army in the 29th District, if not in Western Britain. Sir John Llewellyn's grand home and gardens, requisitioned some two years earlier by the British Army (following a period when it was part of the Bible College of Wales), provided accommodation for 39 Officers and 177 other ranks in both the house and huts & tents. Not the most extensive of camps with only a few Nissen huts and tent bases visible from the air but it was well situated for road communications with the other 5th ESB camps especially opening on to the A48, the main S. Wales east-west highway. During training the 5th ESB troops would rotate through Camp Scurlage (Corner House) often on only a weekly basis from their stations at Singleton Park, Manselton, Clase Farm, Mynydd Lliw and Penllergaer. It was quite common for units to road march to or from the camps covering 18 miles as part of fitness training. The camps were now well and truly occupied to capacity and Company 'D' 95th Engineers were completing the enlargement of Mynydd Lliw No 2. Change of station was imminent for the 1/95th E (GS) R as their sister battalion needed help with the work load in South-east Shropshire.

The under strength 2/95th Engineers had been charged back in mid January with the construction of nine 'summer' tented camps each for 1,250 men with two each at Davenport House, Kinlet and Sturt Common and one each at Chyknel, Gatacre Hall and Coton Hall*. Their original job on the extension of the G-40 Depot at Barry had been turned over to the 373rd E (GS) R whom they

*Footnote: Coton Hall was actually the ancestral home of General Robert E Lee, the overall commander of the Confederate Army during the American Civil War.

relieved in Shropshire. In similar fashion the First Battalion passed over their work on the Expeditionary Hospital at Carmarthen to the 372nd E (GS) R and headed north. The black engineer regiments were well used to being moved from job to job as they suffered from an even greater lack of equipment than the white counterparts at the best of times. Segregation in the US Army would continue for a considerable time and to add insult to injury the number of decorations received by black troops was infinitesimal despite proven valour.

Perhaps the 'powers that be' had more than just a twinge of regret in the way that they were treating some of their assigned units, as the Commanding Officer of the Western Base Section wrote a letter of thanks to the outgoing Commanding Officer of the 95th Engineer General Service Regiment Lt. Col. Frank F. Bell. He wrote following with a conclusion regarding the Hospital project;

> *"1. In the Western Base Section we are faced with an Engineer construction mission of considerable magnitude. Your regiment has performed its missions in a creditable manner, and will be, in all probability, called upon in the future to carry a heavy construction load.*
>
> *3. I want you and your officers and men to know that I fully appreciate the work that is being done, and the importance of the missions that you are carrying out."*

History of the 95th Engineers.

It is worth noting that during the period 1st February to 8th March in Shropshire 'the greatest difficulty encountered on this construction was the procurement of materials and in order to meet the deadline the men worked ten hours a day, seven days a week . Equipment over T/E employed on the job were 4 Motor Graders, 3 Power Shovels, 2 Portable Rock Crushers, 1 D-8 tractor, 1 D-7 tractor, 3 ditching machines, 8 concrete mixers and 50 dump trucks.' A great achievement was the task of laying 3.5 miles of asbestos-cement water main between Sturt Common and Kinlet camps.

Back down south and the month had seen a constant flow of railway engines travelling from west from Ebbw Junction to the old exchange Barry Railway sidings near Caerphilly. By the last day of the month the last siding space for the storing of the Transportation Corps 2-8-0 locos was taken at Penrhos, 152 'Bolero's in the care of 'B' Company 756th RSB. Now with Tonteg storage track full as well, where next could they be stored as the shipments continued?

Incoming troop totals for the month stood at 14,937 through the Bristol Channel Ports with 1,221,436 now having been landed in the UK. The month saw US army cargo on the rise again, figures now standing at 115,703 long tons as part of the overall UK total of 233,722.

*****

Chapter VIII

MARCH '44 - BOLERO PRESTO

The 348th Engineer Combat Battalion trucked to Camp Scurlage on 2 March from Manselton and for the next week held their first training exercise at Port Eynon with the various attached units, as a fully fledged Battalion Beach Group. Operation GOAT was in the form of individual demonstrations set up by one section of troops to be reviewed by others, a method of instruction and familiarization successfully pioneered by the 37th Engineer Combat Battalion.

Photo: US 7PH GP LOC 202 6-3-44 F24" SECRET. Courtesy WAG. APU.
Port Eynon with DUKW's heading towards the shore during an exercise. Clearly visible to the left is the additional roadway Engineers cut through fields to provide a one-way system bypassing the village.

This was followed by a two day exercise, Operation RAM on March 15th at Oxwich. By mid afternoon 327 tons of supplies had been off-loaded from the usual coaster off shore, continuing overnight until 1400hours the following day when the troops returned to Scurlage.

During this training the 37th Engineer Beach Group had entrained at Pontardulais to travel to Dorchester to take part in the much bigger Operation FOX where they would support the 16th RCT from the 1st Infantry Division. In the same exercise the 149th Engineer Beach Group from the 6th ESB would support the 116th RCT attached from the 29th Division – just as they would do in 3 months time. Taking place on Slapton Sands, many lessons had been learnt after Exercise DUCK earlier, but there were still concerns regarding communications. The 37th returned to Singleton, Swansea on the 15th to continue with 5th ESB training. Whilst the combat engineers of the brigade were busy, things were changing elsewhere in South Wales.

Cadoxton Sidings turned out to be the next storage location with the 2-8-0's taken there in twos and threes by a GWR engine from Ebbw Junction sheds down the Relief line to Cardiff, then Penarth Curve South Junction on the Taff Vale line to Cogan Junction, then the Barry Railway line to Cadoxton and finally the storage site. In all eighty-four locomotives would be stored here.

Total harmony was not being witnessed everywhere. The *Tenby Observer* ran a report of proceedings at St. Clears Police Court on Friday 4 March headlined by "Wanted to Pick Fight with Americans". A Whitland man was fined £5 for using obscene language at a dance in the Gwalia Hall, St Clears. PC Enoch stated it was the worst he had heard in ten years and when asked what were the reactions of the US soldiers, he informed the Court that they behaved like 'perfect gentlemen', which he thought was a pity because in his opinion "some people could do with a bloody good lesson", causing some amusement throughout the court. (The troops probably were from Pen Y Coed House on the outskirts of town, home to the Reconnaissance Troop of the 28th Division.)

The Liberty *James Caldwell* from the 59 complement of HX279 docked in Swansea on St. David's Day and just one vessel carrying troops came into the Bristol Channel from CU15 being the C2 *Santa Barbara* which offloaded troops again at Swansea on the sixth of the month. The T2 tanker *Fort Fetterman* from the same convoy also came in but on the following morning tide. Probably a good job as port and debarkation space was going to be at a premium.

The day before WBS HQ published OVERLORD "C", the master plan for the XXIX District detailing the mission statement for the marshalling of troops in the Bristol Channel area. The amount of detail was impressive, even though at this stage it only called for the utilization of two marshalling and embarkation camps to serve just Avonmouth and Newport which would each despatch 6 MTV (motor transport vessels) over a 24 hour period carrying a total of 2,800 troops and 720 vehicles. There were no plans for dispatching troopships from the Bristol Channel Ports at this stage of the planning, although the scale of the proposed landings had already increased from three beach heads to five. Both Eisenhower and Montgomery as the land commander had made it clear in January that for OVERLORD / NEPTUNE to be a success, additional assault forces would be required. SWORD and UTAH would be added as 'single' Brigade fronts in addition to the three 'double' Brigade fronts of JUNO, GOLD and OMAHA. At this time it was envisaged that the rolling programme of a 'back-up' to the assaulting divisions would be sufficient. Within three weeks the powers that be determined there had to be an immediate back-up force, pre-loaded as well.

However, for the time being, under great secrecy, preparations were made and the 58 pages in 22 sections were issued dated 8th March 1944. Instructions had been forthcoming as a result of a meeting at the War Office in London back on 12th January when the Services of Supply delegated responsibility to the WBS XXIX District for the Mounting of Cross Channel Operations. The contents table detailed:

Tab	1	General Plan – Command channels
	2	Port Allocation
	3	Capacities – Marshalling Camps
	4	Present Occupants – Marshalling Camps
	5	Personnel Requirements
	6	Transportation Corps – Flow Chart of Movement Instructions
	7	Ordnance
	8	Quartermaster
	9	Engineer
	10	Signal. Circuit Diagram – Signal Communications
	11	Medical
	12	Chemical Warfare Service
	13	Provost Marshal
	14	Finance
	15	Security
	16	Army Exchange
	17	Adjutant General and Postal
	18	Chaplain
	19	Special Services
	20	Joint Administrative Plan. British – Civil – Military
	21	Miscellaneous
	22	Maps, showing Marshalling Camps, Road Net and Supply

The camps selected were Muller's Orphanage for Avonmouth and Llanmartin for Newport, with only the latter being used, together with many more, in May. Although superseded by OVERLORD "D" and its subsequent revision, the 8th March plan had covered much of what was required to facilitate the successful concentration, marshalling and embarkation of the Bristol Channel build-up force. (Even this relatively straight forward document with its typically precise text made for a fairly 'chunky' missive. There were no fewer than 76 individuals who had to be in receipt of copies including other Commands and Base Sections, so it had to be duplicated for distribution far and wide, with no fewer than 150 copies!)

UT9 sailed in, despatching twelve vessels down the Irish Sea with the *USAT Cristobal* landing 2,201 troops, *AKA 1 Arcturus* 400 and the *AKA 2 Procyon* another 400 at Swansea. Two strangers to Swansea also docked for the usual escort respite with the destroyer-escort *USS Blessman* plus the *USS Gates*. The *SS*

Bantam unloaded stores and about 100 troops onto Barry wharfs. The US Navy *AP 70 Florence Nightingale* brought in 2,085 troops to Cardiff with the *USAT Seatrain Texas* bringing locomotives and 168 troops, together with the *AKA 14 Oberon's* 400 servicemen. Another USN assault transport, the *AP 69 Elizabeth C. Stanton* debarked 2,159 troops in Newport together with the *USAT Lakehurst's* 228 and the *AKA 66 Andromeda* with a compliment of 400 servicemen. To finish off the *HMT Highland Princess* landed 1,900 men in Avonmouth with yet another USN transport, the *AP 71 Lyon* putting ashore 2,032 men by 11th March.

This date was significant for Company 'F' 366th E (GS) R as they were the last to arrive at their new station of Monmouth having completed their construction schedule. A detachment would be absent whilst building a two hut plus seven tent Ration Distribution Point for the Quartermaster Corps at Abergavenny whilst the Regiment entered a nine week intensive training programme. Main subjects covered included Bailey and timber bridge building, and road construction. Other topics included the laying and removal of mines and booby traps plus full weapons training with rifles, carbines, sub-machine guns, 30 and 50 calibre machine guns, bazookas and hand grenades. Identification of aircraft and tanks both friend and foe, was interspersed with physical conditioning and road marches. The weapons training was carried out on the 600 yard Home Guard range and at the artillery range at Cwm De near Crickhowell.

To the west another company of port battalion troops were beginning their additional training at the Transportation School at Mumbles near Swansea. The 226th Company, part of the 490th Battalion would spend the next four weeks working with an amphibious truck company and their DUKW's practising the loading and discharge of cargo from a coaster into these seaborne trucks and running into Caswell Bay, before then departing on completion to undertake duties at Penarth Docks.

Further down into the West Wales countryside, Cresselly House had a bit more room for the men of the 110th Infantry Regiment Cannon Company when their comrades of the Anti-Tank company left them on the twelfth. The trucks towing their 37mm 'pieces' left to journey up the A40 through Carmarthen and Llandovery to take in the delights of the high, desolate moorland of Mynydd Eppynt and the Sennybridge Firing Range for nine days of 'problem firing'. Simultaneously the 108th FA Battalion from the Division arrived on site to conduct their own target practice. Specifically set up for the Royal Artillery in 1939, the range would enable live-fire practice and also provide for the 'zeroing-in' of new guns as they were received by the US Army Field Artillery Battalions. Sometimes the visiting units would be able to spend their sleeping hours in the relative comfort of the hutted camp down in Sennybridge village, but mostly the men bivouacked in pup tents, and in all weather, with their guns. They missed Lt. Col. Sealys' Regimental Parade witnessed by the visiting Officers of the 15th (Scottish) Division but it turned out they were back for the Division Inspection by the Deputy Commander of the US First Army Lt. General Hodges at the end of the month.

Even further west and the 462nd AAA AW Battalion were off for more training, this time trucking all the way across South Wales and down to Camp Blandford in Dorset. Day and night convoy tactics and manoeuvres were carried out under the critical eye of General E.W.Timberlake overall Artillery Commander for the First Army. By the end of the month they were as polished as they could be and returned to Angle.

Twenty-seven ships of CU16 made landfall on the twelfth with just the T2 tanker *Sweetwater* and the cargo carrier *SS Rosemount* coming into Swansea. *SS Moremacswan* docked in Cardiff and *HMT Arawa* unloaded her 1,900 troops at Avonmouth the following day, no doubt delayed by the 8 tankers needing to get into the docks. A couple of days later another tanker *Great Meadows* from the same convoy berthed in Swansea, re-routed from docking at the refinery at Heysham. On the same day the *James Fenimore Cooper* from HX281 and the *SS Michigan* from the slower SC158 also berthed in the King's Dock to unload.

On the following tide the *US LST 389* docked for the last time at what had almost become a second home for the past month or so. Ever since leaving the Mediterranean in convoy MK30 and arriving at Liverpool at the end of the previous November, the well seasoned and battle weary crew under Lt. George C Carpenter had been based at Milford Haven following repairs and 'R and R'. Invasion experience had been gained during Operations 'HUSKY' and 'AVALANCHE' in Sicily and Italy and that was to be put to good use through involvement and further training with 5th ESB troops off Gower beaches. A further period of repair would now be possible before transfer to Northern Ireland for fitting out with new replacement anti-aircraft weaponry in readiness for the Invasion. *LST 389* would be part of Force 'B' loaded with elements of the 175th Infantry RCT from the 29th Infantry Division. Other LST's including *72, 314, 317,* and *369* would be regular visitors during the next month on similar activities, together with others which would require minor repairs and alterations in readiness for June. The month was turning out to be busy on the fraternisation side, according to the papers which were carrying a variety of reports about the 'friendly invaders'. Whilst there was still opposition to the Sunday cinemas question, there was naturally a big welcome for any US serviceman who wanted to become part of any church or chapel congregation. The *South Wales Evening Post* reported on the twentieth that the Walter Road Congregational Chapel in Swansea held an American Friendship Service and Concert with Chaplain McEldowney of the 336th ECB co-hosting assisted by the singing of Corporal Hooberry. Encouraging friendships of a different nature was headlined in the *South Wales Echo* on the seventeenth. "*Missed last Train*" led the story of a Newport woman who lodged a soldier and a girl in Charles Street, pleading guilty to accommodating an American soldier and a girl with a night's lodging without keeping a signed statement of particulars. She was fined £5 and reminded that the maximum penalty for Evasion of the Aliens Order was £100 or 6 months in prison. Wartime special orders regarding secrecy were highlighted, again in the *Echo,* under the headline *"Troops Movements – First Newspaper Prosecution"*. Connell & Bailey, proprietors of the *Stockport Express* were summoned under the General Defence Regulations 1939 with unlawfully publishing information in respect of the disposition of certain of His Majesty's Forces: Fined £20.

Other units were on the move again. The 95th E (GS) R were 95% complete on the nine 1,250 man camps they were building in Shropshire when they received orders to undertake a period of extensive training in preparation for the invasion. Moving back down south with their assigned 413th Dump Truck Company they set up camp at Llanelwydd, over the river from Builth Wells. For the next four weeks it was basic training designed to improve fitness. Their engineering capabilities had been proved, and with assignments to road and bridges construction and repair they were fine. Their Regimental History relates:-

> 'The regiment was quite proficient in Engineer specialties but badly needed combat and weapons training; and mine and booby traps training. The rugged, semi wild nature of the Welsh countryside and the liberal allotment of training ammunition and explosives greatly increased the effectiveness of this phase of the training'

By mid March it was time for the next construction phase to start at the Expeditionary Hospital at Carmarthen, but some nearby residents were beginning to find problems with the ever increasing construction work. The site had already extended across to the other side of the Bronwydd Road with accommodations for nurses, officers and enlisted men; between Dolgwili Road and Abergwyli Road and the public footpath had been closed, much to the locals' dismay. The Carmarthen Borough Council Minutes of Meeting of the Reconstruction Committee on the 13th showed that US Engineers in occupation of land agreed that the footpath along pond side would be re-opened; the 'No Thoroughfare' sign to be removed.

THE EXPEDITIONARY HOSPITAL – (Phase 2)

The 12th Evacuation Hospital unit was successfully operating the facility and had been ever since the first tent had been pitched back in October. But as per plan it was time to move on. The 1/372nd Engineer (GS) Regiment began work on the 14 March whilst the hospital carried on providing care for patients who must have wondered what exactly was going on with excavation and concrete being poured on all sides for the new 24 x 96 feet hut bases. About 11,000 cubic yards was batched off site with dump trucks delivering the ready-mix for 96 hut slabs. Intense competition arose among the Nissen hut erection crews, one of which set a record of 190 man hours to complete a hut. In other words a ten man team could construct a fully finished hut including plumbing and electrics in two days under ideal conditions. The mud was a thing of the past with concrete walks and covered passageways inter-connecting the surgical-clinical buildings. Complete utilities were provided, even a high pressure steam boiler to give central heating to the surgery and clinical buildings. Furniture and other woodwork was prefabricated at a civilian operated army requisitioned saw-mill and put together on site – so successful that the same type of furniture was used throughout the US hospitals in France. The day of the flat pack had arrived!

Exactly a month passed from start to finish and during that time the hospital staff changed as well. The 12th Evacuation Hospital had welcomed the advance party of their successors earlier in the year and now it was time to move on, just as it would do under battle-field conditions. Their place was taken by the 262nd Station Hospital (T/O 30 Officers, 1 Warrant Officer, 56 nurses and 307 men) who arrived on the twenty-fourth, taking on the care of 230 patients. By the end of the month another 167 cases were admitted, mainly of disease rather than injury and 766 outpatients cared for.

Photo: Carmarthen Hospital. #13LocC4-30 PRS (UKUS28) 2 MARCH 1944. NAW MED. 1468 (Lib No's 4409). Courtesy: WAG Aerial Photographic Unit. Aerial oblique photo looking from roughly North to South. Carmarthen town to the right of the photograph. River Towy visible to top right and A40 Carmarthen to Llandeilo road runs from picture right to top left corner.

Many lessons had been learnt by the hospital units, especially the 12th Evacuation. Clearly it would be advantageous for engineers to be on site 3 to 4 weeks ahead of the hospital and prepare the site, followed by an advance party to erect tents and set up equipment. Desirable but not one the Army could guarantee; if a hospital was needed somewhere quickly, then the 'hospital unit' had to be prepared to get on with it. Enlisted men trained as Medics were getting used to be engineers as well as soldiers. The 1944 Medical Report also included recommendations that nurses were not needed "until proper accommodations, messing facilities and a functioning hospital are organized."

There was praise all round for the various units involved in the experimental project. The previous month, the new Commanding Officer of the 95th E (GS) R., Lt. Col. Edward J. Finnell received a letter from the C/O Western Base Section detailing that:

> 2. *The excellent performance by one of your battalions on the construction of the Carmarthen Hospital has been brought to my attention*
> Unit History of the 95th Engineers.

Down in the Channel two more 'Liberties', this time from the biggest Halifax convoy to date with HX282 mustering 96 miscellaneous cargo ships brought US Army goods into Cardiff and Newport respectively with the arrival of the *Clinton Kelly* and the *Francis C Harrington* on the twenty-first. Both ships had special significance as they would not simply return to the US with the next scheduled ON convoy, but would be the first to be removed from regular transatlantic service in preparation for their role in the invasion. The *Clinton Kelly* remained in Cardiff for conversion into a MTV (motor transport vessel) which meant the forward holds (1,2 and 3) would be cleaned, ballasted with sand and then timber planked to create flat level bases to receive vehicles. The rear holds (4 and 5) were converted into troop quarters with the installation of companionways, ablutions and bunks for around 480 men. The 863rd Ordnance troops at G-40 were involved as well, as it was they who manufactured the prefabricated toilet cubicles for the Bristol Channel Ports newly converted MTV's. The *Harrington* transferred to the Clyde for her similar conversion and two other ships from the same convoy were held back at their unloading port for conversion, namely the *Ephraim Brevard* on the Clyde and the *Robert Lansing* elsewhere. Gradually over the next couple of months conversions would be carried out to selected Liberty ships, with more specialised extensive alterations and conversions taking place to some vessels in the United States.

Camp Bulwark at Chepstow welcomed the 987th FA Battalion which had arrived at Greenock on the former liner *Ile De France* before travelling by rail to Monmouthshire on March 22nd. The battalion strength of 30 Officers and 550 men was slightly larger than most USA FA units due to its armament of M12 self propelled 155mm guns. These long barrelled guns mounted on M3 Lee or M4 Sherman tank chassis' were open to the rear with the equivalent of a bull-dozer blade to stabilize recoil. Classed as heavy artillery, and as only 74 were available for ETO use, they were to be in high demand. The SP guns could carry only 10 rounds of ammunition, so they were supported by M30 carriers. Based at Bulwark for only three weeks, the 987th transferred to Clacton-on-Sea, Essex where they continued training but uniquely with the British 50th Northumbrian Division scheduled to assault GOLD beach on 5th June. This they did, although not until the 7th, loaded on 4 LST's of Force 'L' from Felixstowe.

Concurrent with the 1st Battalion's work at Carmarthen, the 2/372nd E (GS) R moved east to Barry to take over the work of the 2/373rd Battalion on 22 March with Company 'D' on roads, Company 'E' on drainage and Company 'F' railroads. Two dump truck companies were now attached with the 419th joining the 420th and the extra 'tippers' were being increased to 150. Such extensive work heralded the arrival of even more Service of Supply troops to the already large depot and by the middle of the month the roster of units at G-40 was as follows:

G-40 DEPOT, BARRY

183rd Ordnance Battalion
816th Ordnance Base Depot Company.
3529th Ordnance (Medium Automotive Maintenance) Company
863rd Ordnance (Heavy Automotive Maintenance) Company
64th Quartermaster Battalion.
953rd Quartermaster Service Company*
961st Quartermaster Service Company*
965th Quartermaster Service Company*
966th Quartermaster Service Company*
240th Quartermaster Depot Company 3rd platoon
3036th Quartermaster (Mobile) Bakery Company
1231st Quartermaster Engineer Fire Fighting Section
782nd Base Depot Company (TC) Det. 'A'.
13th Chemical Maintenance Company
59th Chemical Maintenance Company
61st Chemical Depot Company
111th Chemical Process Company
710th Engineer Base Depot Company
713th Engineer Depot Company
614th Engineer Base Equipment Company Det. 'C'
1302nd Engineer General Service Regiment Company 'B'
131st Army Post Unit
134th Army Post Unit

Later there would be major changes in personnel as units were attached to invasion forces and new organisations arrived to take their place.
6th Engineer Special Brigade (Attachment)
517th Port Battalion (TC) - 797th, 798th, 799th, 800th Port Companies
11th Major Port of Embarkation (Attachments)
554th Quartermaster Battalion
509th Port Battalion (TC)* - 306th, 307th, 308th, 309th Port Companies*

The enlarged open-air Engineer Storage Facility required the employment of the 1199th Engineer Base Depot Group and additional MP's drafted in from Scotland, the 294th MP Company Det 'A' to guard it. Other new arrivals would include the 16th Medical Depot Company Det. 'A', the 599th Port Company (TC) and the 513th Port Battalion* with the 322nd, 323rd, 324th and 325th Port Companies. Most of t he 373rd Engineers were at last free of their construction jobs and would now be able to start training for their mission on the continent.

Photo: RAF 22801 Oblique 25 April 1944(?) Courtesy of the Welsh Office. Looking west the extensive open air storage expansion bases served by both road and rail lie to the north of the Sully road. To the south are the raised banks covering the underground fuel storage facility. Further west the depot stretches away into the distance and to the north (not in picture). Trees separate the tented camps south of the road from the civilian Sully Hospital. Coal hoists surround the Dock (top of picture) served by the sweeping railway sidings.

Back on 14 March the 373rd had closed in at Clytha Park near Usk with the Headquarters in the main house, the First Battalion on the estates East Slope and the Second Battalion on the West. Formal training began on the following day concentrating on demolition, explosives, mines and booby traps, bailey bridging, heavy rigging, dock and railroad construction and camouflage with crew served weapons training including anti-tank defence and field forts. (This was the period when extensive felling of the massive redwood trees that Clytha was renowned for, to facilitate training and also to provide timber for use following the invasion when Engineers would require large amounts for wharf reconstruction at Cherbourg etc.)

More and more work was being taken on in the dockyards of the United Kingdom as many ships were getting worn out with the constant heavy demand being placed on them. When the 22 ships of CU17 arrived around the 23rd March the British *HMT Moreton Bay* having landed her cargo and troops in Cardiff, had to have another 14 days of repairs carried out. She had made the crossing unscathed unlike the Avonmouth bound 11,300 ton tanker *SS Seakay* carrying 14,000 tons of vapour oil and 14 aircraft (P.17's and P.51 Lightning's) as deck cargo, which was sunk by a torpedo from U-311. She had made a number of CU and UC return crossings and was only one of the few to have been lost. The now familiar *Powder River* made it safely to Swansea, as did another 6 tankers to Avonmouth. Many of the newer Liberty's were getting altered rather than repaired although there were a rising number of concerns regarding their all-weld construction rather than the conventional riveting found in older vessels. Three ships had been lost through major structural failure, the earliest in March '43 and two others only ten days apart in January '44.

Another 'Liberty' was effectively lost on 24th March sailing down the Irish Sea. A regular visitor to the Bristol Channel ports, the *Artemus Ward* had left New York with HX 280 back in February, but had straggled and waited at Ponta Del Garda in the Azores to join another UK bound convoy. On 15 March she left with convoy MKS-42 from the Mediterranean, the *Ward* bound for Barry, but was hit in the Irish Sea by the T2 tanker *SS Manassas* which apparently cut straight through the convoy during the night. Severely damaged, the *Ward* managed to gain the safety of Milford Haven and beached stern first at Angle Bay. Unfortunately part of the cargo aboard was highly secret – it even had its own security guard aboard mounted by a 40 strong detachment from Company 'B' of the 526th Armored Infantry Battalion. They were from the unit that was earmarked to travel and protect and work with the specialised armour called CDL tanks (Canal Defence Light) being the odd title attributed to the weapons of 6 separate battalions of specialized armour of the 9th and 10th Armoured Groups. Due for training on the Preseli Mountains of North Pembrokeshire with more to follow in the coming weeks, the authorities were keen to keep the unfortunate incident under wraps. On site repair was carried out – it was rumoured that the hole in the side of the *Ward* was big enough to drive several tanks through, as indeed had happened – and when complete she was refloated and made her way to Barry. Once all the valuable cargo had been offloaded, the *Artemus Ward* was taken over by the US Navy and went through further examination which would result in another specialized role for the hard working vessel. To prepare for the tank battalions that would work with the 526th, the 373rd E (GS) R Company 'E' first platoon was despatched to set up a bivouac camp at 'Quarry' near Mynachlogddu on the 25th, returning to Clytha ten days later.

From HX283 the *Edward W Scripps* docked in Swansea, unloaded, then transferred to the Clyde for conversion, the *Robert L Vann* with stores and a couple of locomotives on deck remained in Barry for MTV conversion following unloading and the *George E Pickett* also arrived on the same day on the Clyde for clearance before transferring to Newport for conversion. Sixty-two ships had made up this convoy, with just three carrying only US Army cargo. Ships that would have a high profile in the forthcoming invasion (which only a few knew anything about) were beginning to appear occasionally at BC ports. The Attack Transport *AKA 53 Achernar* from CU18 brought 400 or so men into Swansea on the thirtieth and she would become the General Omar Bradley's First Army Headquarters ship for the assault. The *SS Robin Tuxford* also landed a similar number again at Swansea and the T2 tanker *Kenesaw Mountain* delivered her cargo of fuel in to the Queens Dock. *SS Warrior* put cargo into Barry and the *SS Santa Margarita* debarked approximately 500 at Newport. Transportation Corps was able to report that the Bristol Channel Port Command had received and landed over 16,000 troops and 638,062 tons of Army stores in the month.

From now on the following months would see the establishment of the three key phase operation:

OVERLORD MOUNTING PLAN

April – CONCENTRATION
Bringing together in their respective areas the Invasion Forces with an emphasis on re-equipping and supply.

May – MARSHALLING
Ordering units to camps near embarkation ports, waterproofing of vehicles, breaking down into boat loads, sealing-in under strict guard starting around the 24th of the month, issuing of foreign currency, briefings and final preparations.

June – EMBARKATION
Pre-loading of armour, artillery and vehicles, movement either by foot, road transport or rail to embarkation ports and troop loading.

To provide the necessary support for the invasion forces, there would be a requirement of a large number of static troops for a short period of time. Further south in Devon and Cornwall virtually the entire 5th Armored Division (minus its tanks and artillery) plus the 29th Infantry Regiment and the 6th Tank Destroyer Group would be used to provide the extra manpower the SOS needed.

In the Western Base Section XXIX District a total of 24 Marshalling and 4 Residue Camps would be required (see appendix list) with an Operational Headquarters set up at Newport involving the whole range of service troops undertaking specific static duties. Signals, Quartermaster, Engineer, Transportation, Medical, Ordnance, Provost Marshall, Special Services, Postal, and Fiscal sections with a total strength of 8,122 soldiers. Command of the OPS HQ would rest with Col. Harold T. Weber as District Commander, with the C/O of the 17th Major Port Lt. Col. Crothers assisting, but it would take until the middle of the April before facilities could be provided and assigned personnel gathered from around the country. The 17th Major Port was new to the area and had taken over the administration of the Bristol Channel ports from the 11th Major Port when the unit was assigned to support the Provisional Engineer Special Brigade Group.

Photo: A heavily laden unnamed Liberty ship of 7,200 tons at anchor.

They were experienced in port operations, but all activity of the 17th Major Port in the past had been concerned with the reception of incoming troops and the handling of cargo. Scrutiny of one particular convoy received in March indicates the enormous volume of cargo that was arriving from the United States every week for the port battalions and dockers to handle. There were 18 army cargo vessels fully loaded and another twenty-four commercial ships with part loads for the US

Army. The inventory included 1,500 wheeled and tracked vehicles including tanks, 2,000 cased vehicles, 200 aircraft and gliders, and 50,000 tons of supplies.

> 'All this cargo had to be discharged within about 8 days, the planned interval between convoys. The prompt clearance of this cargo from the ports involved the running of 75 special trains with 10,000 loaded cars and the movement by highway of large numbers of wheeled and cased vehicles and aircraft'
>
> Logistical Support of the Armies Vol. 1. - Ruppental.

Coming from the Clyde, the 17th Port were well used to large numbers of troop arrivals but out loading a back-up force was a different matter with the extra ramifications of security etc. Rumours abounded that officers said they could cope, but that they continually sought help from their British counterparts. The change of unit, although necessary to allow the 11th Port to prepare for its Provisional Engineer Special Brigade Group role, definitely did concern a certain British Army Officer in London, the overall British Port Commander, Col T.J. Breen, O.B.E., who had been a regular visitor to the Bristol Channel ports wrote from Quartermaster General House:-

> 'I am seriously alarmed that anyone, either American or British, can be so misguided as to imagine that the Americans can cope with the task at present envisaged for the Bristol Channel.
> No. 11 Port H.Q. with whom we have worked happily since July 1943 are now in process of packing up and No. 17 Port H.Q. are taking over. Their new Commander, who I met yesterday, is Colonel Crothers who has been Yeo's opposite number at Glasgow. He takes over a completely "green" staff; doubtless by the time the big job takes place they will have learned something. Meanwhile I am keeping in touch with Crothers who said yesterday that he would require all the assistance possible from my staff and myself.'

History would show that through close co-operation between American and their British counterparts' disaster would be avoided. But just who were these men, where did they come from, what units were they part of that created a task causing the Colonel such concern?

From the time back in January, it had been decided that the Normandy Landings had to increase in size and on a broader front than just the original three beaches to ensure any sort of success. The addition on UTAH beach on the Contentin peninsular immediately offered a doubling of potentially available troop and equipment build-up zones once the assaulting divisions had secured sufficient ground. Now two Infantry Divisions, not just one, could follow on in immediate support and be drawn from two different Corps, making Bradleys First Army Command much more controllable. Moreover transport would also now have to be provided to include seaborne elements of not just one but two Airborne Divisions plus attachments to the 1st Engineer Special Brigade and VII Corps troops. The whole of the South coast of England was already designated for the Assault Task Forces so it naturally fell to the Bristol Channel and Severn Estuary ports as the next nearest locations to provide the build up force for the Americans. Distance from the beachheads meant that the Western Force troops required preloading, no trans-Atlantic crossings this time such as those that were tried for Operation TORCH.

The 90th Division now selected as the immediate follow-up force to the 4th Division on UTAH beach, although not a regular army division, was to create a distinguished history after a less than illustrious start. A National Guard Division formed with a cadre from the 6th Infantry Division, it was inducted into Federal Service on March 25, 1942 at Camp Barkeley, near Abeline in Texas. It was a typical triangular division with a Headquarters and HQ Company and Band, consisting of three Regiments each of three battalions comprised of three rifle companies and one heavy weapons company. Breaking down further, each company had three rifle platoons and one weapons platoon, each platoon having three squads. Armaments for the Heavy Weapons Company were 81mm mortars and .30-caliber water cooled machine guns, Rifle Company weapons platoon firing 60mm mortars and air-cooled machine guns. A rifle squad led by a Sergeant with a Corporal in support had a two man Browning Automatic Rifle team and eight riflemen. Direct support Artillery battalions of 105mm howitzers plus a 155mm general support battalion and what were termed 'special troops' were the additional units including an Engineer and a Medical Battalion, a Reconnaissance Troop, with Signal, Ordnance and Quartermaster companies plus MP platoon.   Authorised strength was 14,000 men to which the usual dedicated attachments included separate Tank, Tank Destroyer and Anti Aircraft Artillery Battalions that would be added and utilised as the Division Commander saw fit.

Early in 1943 the Division had taken part in the Louisiana Manoeuvres, ill-equipped, and many men remembered the period as one of continuing to dig holes in which to hide, use as a latrine, or bury garbage*. Further training back at camp and then they were off to the heat of the Californian Mojave Desert Training Center in September for more 'digging holes, marching about, and staging attacks', this time with live ammunition. By December they were ordered to Fort Dix, New Jersey to prepare for overseas movement, leaving for Camp Kilmer at the beginning of the month and then arriving at New York for embarkation on 22 March.

The 2nd Division ('Second To None') being a regular army formation had a much more distinguished history. The oldest unit, the 9th Regiment, could trace its origin back to 1798, although soon to be disbanded, it was re-established in 1812

Footnote: The words of their later Third Army Commander Gen. George Patton delivered to the 2nd Division in Armagh spring to mind here, but can be found elsewhere!

to take part in the war of the same name earning battle honours up in New York State. Periods in limbo, just like the next oldest Regiment, the 23rd Infantry, saw battle honours awarded to both for the Mexican War, Civil War and Boxer Rebellion over in China. Following more success in the final year of The Great War, the Division returned home and Fort Sam Houston, Texas, then followed by Camp Travis* for the next 23 years.

Reorganisation of divisions saw the Fourth Brigade (Marines) leave with the 38th Infantry taking their place and the 'Indianheads' became the first triangular division. Participation in both Texas and Louisiana Manoeuvres and defence of the eastern seaboard of the United Sates occupied much of their time. Providing cadres for the establishment of the 85th and 102nd Infantry Divisions resulted in more promotions and training until in October 1942 they were ordered to permanently change station to Camp McCoy, Michigan. Intense winter warfare training under Major-General Walter Robertson and Michigan Manoeuvres took the division through into the following year, with elements of one regiment being utilised to restore order in Detroit following early summer race riots. All through continual skills and fitness training was ongoing until with POM's taking place, the 2nd Division finally received the order to move to Camp Shanks, New York at the end of September. In company with the 28th Division they had sailed to the UK, and whilst the Pennsylvania 'Keystone' Division made SouthWales home for the next six months, the 2nd Division, by enlarge, endeared themselves to the people Northern Ireland.

The vast majority of the 1st Engineer Special Brigade would land during D-Day itself sailing from the English south coast, only the attached port battalion troops aboard coasters and MTV's coming in as part of the BCPLBU Force. Parts of the Airborne Divisions would be similarly split up, due to insufficient lift capacity, only half their total strength to be in the air assault with some glider infantry paired up as additional reinforcement to the 4th Division in the seaborne assault with the two 359th Infantry Regiment battalions from the 90th Division. The third echelons including more parachute and glider field artillery therefore would sail from South Wales.

March had seen 16,447 servicemen landed at the Bristol Channel Ports with the UK cumulative total now at 1,345,848. Army cargo previously detailed continued to rise peaking by the end of the following month.

Now changes were about to take place and in Armagh, Northern Ireland, 'Blood and Guts' Patton arrived to address the 2nd Division whilst 'Ike' did likewise in South Wales with the 28th Division.

*****

Footnote: Named after the Colonel in command of the legendary defence of the Alamo Mission at San Antonio in 1836.

Chapter IX

APRIL '44 - CONCENTRATION

April 1st dawned and Margam Park camp was buzzing as troops from the 28th Division's 109th Regiment assembled to be addressed by a visiting VIP. Turned out this was a special day as who should step up onto the bonnet of a jeep to speak but the main man – General Dwight D. Eisenhower himself – the ETO Supreme Commander. Accompanied by V Corps Commander Major-General Leonard T Gerow, Ike addressed the troops in his own warm inimitable manner, stepping down to talk to men individually. Continuing on to address the 112th in Carmarthen and the 110th in Pembrokeshire, Eisenhower left the 'citizen soldiers' very ready to speculate what was behind the sudden interest in them by the Allied High Command. They had been visited only a few days before by Lt. General E.C.A.Schreiber CB, DSO, and Chief of the British Western Command. A week later their commanders would find out what was going on and why.

Whilst these high powered visits were going on, the 741st Tank Battalion Company 'B' was completing its two week live-fire training down at the Castlemartin Tank Range, following on from the 744th which had been there for the previous two weeks. The next scheduled unit, the 749th Tank Battalion from VIII Corps would have the range to themselves for the last three weeks of April.

Back along the coast the 5th Engineer Special Brigade was holding the biggest of its own exercises with all three Beach Groups participating over a three day period. Exercise LION would be the last occasion that they trained together, for as soon as it was over they were back in their respective camps preparing for final departure to the English south coast. Exercises would continue, getting bigger and bigger all the time. The ill-fated Exercise TIGER in late April didn't involve any of the engineer troops from the South Wales based and OMAHA bound 5th ESB, as it was for the UTAH beach 1st ESB and associated troops.

Meanwhile the ports of the Bristol Channel had been getting close to overcrowding for months, but nothing would compare to the concentration of vessels, both troopers and freighters in April. This was the month that also saw the first phase of the operation that would culminate in the biggest amphibious invasion in history. Field forces had to be first 'Concentrated', 'Marshalled' and finally 'Embarked' in Operation NEPTUNE, the naval part of OVERLORD.

The experienced unit that had been such an important part of the Bristol Channel Port Headquarters and had been responsible for the reception of troops and cargos was now on the move and with a new commander. Col. Richard S. Whitcombe 11th Major Port C/O vacated his billet in the 'Tredegar Arms' Caerleon on the 6th transferring to his units concentration area in the Cynon Valley. Both Whitcombe and his aide, Colonel Juzek were to enjoy some special hosting as they were welcomed into the home of the High Constable Gwillym Williams at Compton House, Victoria Square, Aberdare. Being an Auctioneer and County

Valuer for Glamorgan County Council, Mr Williams was able to advise the local constabulary and the Billeting Officer for the 11th Port Headquarters in finding suitable accommodation for his Officers and men. Concentration had in many respects been ongoing ever since the first units requested by Eisenhower and Montgomery arrived back in the UK from the Mediterranean theatre, but the first scene of the final act brought the two divisions that would immediately follow the Assault troops onto OMAHA and UTAH beaches.

Photo; 90th Division troops arrive at Liverpool. (IWM. H37390).

Direct from the United States came the 90th Texas/Oklahoma National Guard Division under the command of Brigadier-General Jay Kelvie. Nicknamed 'Tough 'Ombres' from their title, they would take a beating on the Cotentin Peninsula with lacklustre leadership, but would ultimately become one of the best divisions in Patton's Third Army. But that was all to come in the future. For now they were pleased to be ashore in England arriving as part of UT10 on a misty Liverpool morning onboard the Australian 27,000 ton Shaw Saville liner now serving as a troopship *QSMV Dominion Monarch*, together with *HMT Athlone*

Castle and a few days later by the *SS John Ericsson*, repaired after breaking down and able to join CU19 and docking by the ninth of the month. Then it was on the train and away to the newly built camps in Shropshire plus two Herefordshire camps at Stannage Park and Berrington Park near Leominster, with Division Headquarters located at King Edward's School in Birmingham.

This 26 ship UT10 convoy had split in the usual manner into Belfast, Clyde and Mersey sections with 11 vessels carrying on down the Irish Sea and through St. Georges Channel before gaining their respective Bristol Channel ports. The *SS Exchange, SS Ocean Mail* and *SS Shooting Star* debarking 4,000 men at Swansea, with the usual couple of escorts in for R&R, this time the DD *USS Mervine* and the DE665 *USS Jenks*. The *XAP 77 Thurston* and *SS African Sun* debarked 1,200 men at Cardiff, the *USAT James Parker* and *XAP 76 Anne Arundel* another 4,000 troops at Newport and the *SS Santa Rosa* and *SS Marine Eagle* almost 5,000 at Avonmouth. Both US Navy XAP's were now in UK waters ready for exercises and their assault role in FORCE 'O'.

But if any ship watchers thought they were going to be able to go down to the coast to see or photograph these vessels, they were going to be disappointed. Newspapers were reporting that coastal areas were to be 'regulated'. From Yorkshire around to Land's End and in the Bristol Channel security was increasing all the while.

> *'From Saturday, "a coastal strip along the whole of the south coast of Wales and round the Bristol Channel as far as Portishead" is included in extensive new areas becoming "regulated" under by-laws made by the War Secretary. In these regulated areas all persons over 16 must carry identity cards and produce them on demand. Only persons belonging to certain exempted classes (Royal Observer Corps, raid spotters and the crews of ships) may, when their duty requires it , use binoculars or telescopes within the regulated areas without a special permit, and the use of cameras will continue to be governed by the Control of Photograph Orders.'*

The South Wales Evening Post. Thursday April 6th 1944.

That morning a conference had been arranged for the special committee members from military and civilian organisations at Swansea regarding OVERLORD planning. In attendance and playing a major role were Colonels Crothers and Fritchler of the US Army, who would be responsible for the marshalling of the Bristol Channel Pre-loaded Build-up Force. Actual embarkation at Swansea would be under British Movement Control, but there were now so many other factors to consider and plan for, that the month would see a continual increase in the number of senior officers visiting the port for closely guarded secret meetings. Barry, Cardiff and Newport docks were witnessing similar activity. Colonel Naylor at the British BCP HQ at Raglan Barracks in Newport was scarcely at his desk through escorting senior officers on inspection visits.

More 'Liberty' ships were depositing their US Army supplies before receiving orders taking them away from Atlantic convoy duty and being converted to MTV's. No less than forty-two of the seventy-seven freighters that made up HX284 arriving on the seventh were US registered 'Liberties' with eighteen being retained or diverted for fitting out. The Bristol Channel contingent included the *Amos G Throop* at Barry, the *Collis P Huntingdon* at Cardiff, the *Clara Barton, John Hay* and *Charles Morgan* at Newport and the *Jedediah S Smith* at Avonmouth. The *Charles Morgan* was one of the very few that were to be bombed off the Normandy beaches with Port Company troops on board.

The Easter weekend was highlighted by Sunday Services all over the country, but none could have been more impressive than the two 'sunrise' services that took place simultaneously in 'blitzed' Swansea. No service at the roofless St. Mary's, nor at the big Wesley Chapel flattened during the February 1941 'blitz'. Some of the roads in the centre of the bomb damaged town had been cleared by US soldiers but there was no rebuilding yet. During those dark hours just before dawn, troop carrying trucks from outlying camps brought in servicemen to attend either Catholic or Protestant services organised by the Special Services detachment. The Brangwyn Hall played host to Communion led by Captain Morris McEldowney, the 336th ECB Protestant Chaplain. The Swansea Clerk had earlier minuted:

> *"The Mayor read a letter from the Commanding Officer of the 5th Engineer Special Brigade stationed in Swansea, extending on behalf of the American troops a cordial invitation to the Mayor, the Members of the Council and the members of Parliament to be guests at a Sunrise Easter Service to be held in the Brangwyn Hall on Easter Sunday the 9th of April 1944 at 7.30am."*

The *South Wales Evening Post* reported on the following day;

> *'The service was led by Chaplains McEldowney, Haga and Grim and the Mayor of Swansea and Col. W.D. Bridges took part in reading the lessons. The Brangwyn Hall Orchestra had played as a voluntary the Pastoral Symphony from Handel's "Messiah". Most of the music except the hymns was taken from the "Messiah". There was one dramatic moment when Chaplain McEldowney announced that Eva Turner would sing the Easter Hymn from "Cavalieria Rusticana". With the orchestra and the choir dressed in their outdoor clothes there was a sense of realism of an early Easter morning that removed the famous "Rejoice that the Lord has Arisen" from all its theatrical associations. Eva Turner sang brilliantly with an intensity that eclipsed her performance at a concert on the same platform not many hours before. Her voice soared above the choir and orchestra with a thrill that she can rarely have attained in any opera house'*

The South Wales Evening Post. Monday April 10th 1944

St. Helens Rugby and Cricket Ground held a two hour missa cantata with an impressive altar facing the front of the grandstand. The Mass was conducted by Captain John G. Schultz, the Catholic Chaplain of the 336th ECB based at Camp Mynydd Lliw, with the Rev'd Canon Louis Moody of St Joseph's assisting.

There was no rejoicing for some, however, as sudden news broke for the Pennsylvanian National Guardsmen. The 28th 'Keystone' Division was being pulled out of V Corps First Army and being transferred to XX Corps Third US Army under the command of General George Patton. The Division Officers were given the reason that their role had been changed quite simply because Patton's Army did not possess an amphibious assault trained division, and if Normandy didn't go well, such a division was going to be of great importance if Patton had to take on a beach assault elsewhere. When word got out to the men, rumours started that although praised by the High Command, the commander of another National Guard division resented the 28th pivotal role and undermined its credibility. Back in the days of the Louisiana and Tennessee Manoeuvres, it was obvious that there was no love lost between various National Guard Commanders, some of which attempted to make 'their candles shine brighter by attempting to snuff out others'! There may have been some truth in that, in as much that the 28th Division had done what had been asked of it and done it well. Right from the start of their deployment to the ETO they had been praised and their subsequent amphibious training was lauded. The embarkation of the Pennsylvanian National Guard Division at Boston had been reported thus:

"The 28th Infantry Division has just completed its staging and embarkation at this port. During the period of its stay ... and during its embarkation, it set the highest record for discipline and control ever observed here. Their morale is of the highest and the ready and willing cooperation of all officers and men were outstanding. The staging of this unit and its embarkation was conducted with precision and dispatch due entirely to the ready response of all officers and men to the requirements of this phase of troop movement. Commander Boston POE.

Letter to the War Department, Washington.

What was possibly nearer the truth lay undisclosed for decades until the full details of the massive Allied deception Operation entitled FORTITUDE were revealed some fifty years later.

There were many, many parts to this Operation but the element that so affected the 28th Infantry Division role was centred on FORTITUDE SOUTH, the deception that created the fictitious FUSAG – First US Army Group located in the south-east of England. Under Command of 'Blood and Guts' Patton (which the planners guessed would make the enemy take more note perhaps), the deception would see the creation of imaginary commands, phantom divisions and mythical locations of existing US and British divisions, even including some still on the Atlantic, together with other Allied formations. Feeding information to the

Abwehr (German Intelligence Police) via double agents – Garbo and the like – the plan was to tie up and keep as many Wehrmacht and SS Divisions around the Pas de Calais due to the imminent threat of attack across the Straits of Dover, whilst a feint landing operation took place further west in the Bay of the Seine. Using decoy radio transmissions spreading what would turn out to be false information coupled with minor correct information that would be of little consequence, the Signal squadrons of both the British and US Armies (3103rd Signal Service Battalion) were successful in confusing the German High Command, buying time for Montgomery (21st Army Group) to gain that all important foothold in Normandy. All this was yet to come, but for now the 28th Division had its part to play, albeit in a way they had never expected.

> *"At the same time the 2nd Infantry Division was ordered to move from Northern Ireland and replace the 28th Infantry Division in V Corps, First US Army. This order was issued in London on the night of April 8, 1944. Movement by advance detachments was initiated 11 April. In connection with this move the attached Air Support Party, Order of Battle Team, Photo Interpretation Team, Military Intelligence Team, Signal Photo Detachment, Prisoner of War Interrogation Team and parts of the Civil Affairs and CIC detachments were transferred to the 2nd Infantry Division. The 28th Infantry Division acted as reception party for the 2nd Infantry Division which replaced it in Wales, taking over identical billeting arrangements."*
>
> '28th Infantry Division History'.

The 'Keystone' men had to provide for their own reception facilities at their new location around Swindon and with the assistance of a truck company from the 89th Quartermaster Battalion in Cardiff managed the move by utilizing its own motor pools in three shuttles by the 19th. Importantly all this was to be done in secret. FORTITUDE transmissions reported that the division 'keystone' patch had been seen on troops in the Folkestone area and as the 28th Division Headquarters had left Pembrokeshire then that's where they must have ended up – with Patton and ready to invade the Pas De Calais!

Whilst this was going on, down at the ports troops and cargo were still flowing in, the 26 ship CU19 had arrived on the eighth, no tanker for Swansea this time but seven scheduled for Avonmouth with *SS Mormacmoon* and *HMT Esperance Bay* landing men there as well. The *'Bay'*, like her sister ships, needed 12 days of repairs before setting out again. The *Hellas* also docked at Cardiff having transferred from Southampton for MTV conversion and yet more ships arrived with HX285 on the fourteenth, the SS *North King* and the SS *Mormacswan* to Swansea, whilst the *Abiel Foster* and *Charles C Jones* unloaded at Barry and the *Francis Asbury* and *Jim Bridger* in Cardiff, all four then undergoing MTV conversion. Back ashore the 863rd Ordnance Company at G-40 Barry were getting busier and busier, but not just on the vehicle repair side. Lt. Specter and his team of six enlisted men had been doing the rounds of units in the XXIX District on detached service, carrying out inspections of Class I and II vehicle maintenance which was so successful that the 224th Ordnance Base Group decided to run courses at the Depot. The mechanics' reputation in the water-proofing field also resulted in another team being despatched to Camp St. Mary's Hill to carry out training and instruction. Their services were so much in demand that they were placed on detached service down at Weymouth supervising work to FORCE 'O' vehicles, not returning to Barry until after D-Day.

Over the other side of the Irish Sea there were more Liberties and troopers setting out for Wales, not as one convoy, but staggered so as to not cause extra interest or congestion at already busy ports. First to leave Belfast independently and in advance - no convoy to draw unwanted attention - was the *USAT James Parker* on April 12th arriving at Newport overnight. She was followed on the 15th by the *Robert L Vann*, *Lou Gehrig*, *Ephraim Brevard*, *Robert Lansing* and *Francis C. Harrington*, all already converted to MTV use and sailing again independently, spreading their arrival between the four South Wales ports with Swansea taking the *Vann* and *Gehrig* with Barry, Cardiff and Newport with their unrecorded cargo of the Division artillery and equipment taking the others. Over the next few days the other troopships slipped out of Belfast Lough with no fuss, the *SS Exchange* going to Swansea on the seventeenth, the C4 *SS Marine Raven* to Newport on the 18th and the *SS Santa Rosa* to Cardiff on the 19th. The infantry, artillery and leading elements of 2nd 'Indianhead' Division was now in Wales.

More and more Engineer Regiments were completing or simply being released from their construction jobs in order that extensive training could be undertaken in specific roles. The task of rebuilding ports on the continent may have seemed a project well into the future but planning was already well in hand and centred at Porthcawl. The South Wales resort town boasted a number of good sized accommodations including the Seabank Hotel and guest houses with suitable internal instruction lecture venues and external training locations. The 398th E (GS) R was very familiar with the similar Woolacombe Bay Hotel having constructed the Assault Training Centre camp at nearby Braunton. On April 15th they departed Camp Crowcombe in North Devon, home for the best part of the past year and set off by train for Porthcawl to receive detailed training in port construction and repair work under the expert tutelage of the 1057th Port Construction and Repair Group. There had been training going on at Porthcawl for over a month with other Engineer PC&RG's training elements of regiments, the 355th with 'D' company from both the 342nd and 351st E (GS) R's. This would continue with the 1053rd, 1056th, 1057th and 1058th PC&RG's taking schools. Most men found the experience to be a bit of a 'holiday' after months of strenuous construction work. Down by the seaside with the Coney Beach Amusement Park and towns, pubs and girls what could be better! Even training and crawling about in the nearby dunes wasn't too bad. Throwing up Bailey Bridges and tearing them down again, digging foxholes and filling them in again was ok. But soon they wanted to get on with what they were there for.... continental rebuilding.

A late addition to the 5th Engineer Special Brigade was the 6th Naval Beach Battalion better known certainly by its men as 'Carusi's 400 Thieves'. NBB's were in that difficult position where they may have been in the Navy but they were organised and kitted out as if they were in the Army! Consequently they always seemed to be at the bottom of the pile when it came to securing anything like equipment, uniform, weapons or stores. Their opposite numbers from the 7th NNB attached to the 6th ESB fared the same, but kept clear of any similar sobriquet.

Commander Eugene Carusi with Headquarters and three additional Companies had sailed on the *Mauretania* from New York and were based at Camp Singleton where they took part in all the exercises at Caswell, Oxwich and Port Eynon, Company 'A' attached to the 348th Beach Group, 'B' to the 366th and 'C' to the 37th which would be assisting the 16th RCT in the assault. Crucially duties included communications with off shore vessels, Beach Masters and assistants directing incoming craft, and providing medical care with doctors and corpsmen.

Photo: Commander Eugene Carusi inspecting his 6th Naval Beach Battalion.

Two engineer units had to interrupt their training plans however to literally cater for the troops that were going to be marshalled in S. Wales. On 13th April the 360th E (GS) R moved out of their Stonewall Jackson bivouac in the Nantmor Valley near Bedgellert heading south by truck for their East Wales assigned Marshalling Camps. They were to primarily look after the 90th Division that would be bound for UTAH beach. Simultaneously the 373rd had to interrupt its training schedule at Clytha Park, near Abergavenny, and moved west to be housekeepers for the 2nd ID scheduled for OMAHA beach.

A ship that had its own schedule interrupted was being towed in to Barry, minus some of her cargo that had been lost in the collision or had been transferred in Angle Bay and trying not to cause too much interest, was the damaged *Artemus Ward* due for inspection and further repair. Sadly her cargo carrying days were over as the Navy decided to release her for yet another style of conversion, this time becoming a block ship and a member of the 'Corn Cob' fleet. Her cargo which had included some of those secret CDL tanks that had been lost in the Irish Sea were finally transferred ashore for checking out and storing. The 526th Infantry Battalion guard detachment went to the Brynhill Golf Course Camp.

By the middle of the month yet another and the last troop convoy to bear the UT designation, steamed in over the horizon with UT11 bringing the 79th and 83rd Infantry Divisions. The eleven UT convoys had carried 592,041troops in all, averaging nearly 54,000 per convoy. The two divisions were highlighted in FORTITUDE transmissions as going to the far south-east of England. In fact they were going to camps around North Wales and Staffordshire for the time being. Thousands of other troops were aboard as well. Going into Greenock were the remaining men of the 526th Armored Infantry Battalion who would join their comrades at Barry before transferring to Rosebush in the Preseli Mountains of Pembrokeshire at the end of the month in company with the CDL 'Gismo' Tank Battalions. Eleven ships were scheduled for BC ports with the *USAT Lakehurst, AP 72 Susan B. Anthony* and *SS Orpheus* due at Swansea, the *SS White Squall* for Barry, the *USAT Seatrain Texas* and *SS Santa Teresa* docked at Cardiff, the *SS Sea Porpoise* and *SS Robin Sherwood* at Newport and the regular *HMT Highland Brigade* again at Avonmouth. All in all, about 9,000 troops from this one convoy came into Bristol Channel Ports. Two destroyer escorts *USS Burrows* and *USS Cates* were fortunate to have ten days in Swansea before sailing again on the 28th. Troop and fast cargo convoys would be combined the following month and designated TCU for those eastbound, UC for westbound. Also docking at Cardiff was the *SS Exchequer* carrying, amongst others, the urgently required 299th Engineer Combat Battalion earmarked for specialized under water demolition training at the ATC at Woolacombe. Following instruction at Camp Gordon Johnston in Florida, the unit had embarked in New York on 4th April firmly convinced that this was just yet another dry-run in their ever changing routine. How wrong could they be! Unknown to them, whilst at sea, a letter from Maj. Gen. Leonard T Gerow, V Corps Commander charged with the assault on Omaha Beach, was penned to Brig. Gen. William Kean, US First Army Chief of Staff.

Gerow had been worried ever since Christmas about how he could ensure the safe beaching of landing craft. The discovery of an ever increasing number of obstacles – steel 'Belgian gates', mined stakes and the like – being installed along the beaches of northern France could devastate the best of plans. The 299th Engineer Combat Battalion were part of the answer and would be the only unit that would be split between both OMAHA and UTAH beach providing underwater demolition boat teams in the multi-service Special Engineer Task Force.

He wrote;

> *"I am rather concerned about progress being made on training in connection with the removal of underwater obstacles. The time is short – to cite specific matters of concern to me, I find that the engineer battalion specifically trained in the US for work of this character has not arrived in the UK. Furthermore, no information is available as to its state of training or equipment"*
>
> 'Omaha Beach' - Joseph Balkowski.

He need not have worried for even now, armed with newly provided toilet kits courtesy of the American Red Cross and a booklet entitled 'Life in the British Isles' they were looking down on the scene unfolding below on Cardiff's dockside. Already the events of an eleven day voyage were fading in the memory, although many men would remember a spectacular Easter morning service in Mid Atlantic.

> *'Services were held by the ship's chaplain at the ship's stern. It was one of the most impressive services ever attended by men of the 299th Engineers. The deep blue green of the ocean, in all directions, a trail of spinning white foam following in the wake of the ship , cool salty breezes blowing gently and caressing the flag on the staff, the sound of men's voices singing hymns made an unforgettable setting for the traditional Easter worship.'*
>
> 299th Engineer Combat Battalion History.

Docking in Cardiff overnight of the 16th afforded great interest for the troops by watching cargo being off loaded the following day. The men were amused at the size of the British railway cars (wagons) and laughed outright when they saw a train man push a car by hand. That day, in two echelons, it was off to Ilfracombe. Advance parties had been busy and the seriousness of the Battalion's future role became evident with the appearance of their Commanding Officer Lt. Colonel Jewett who had been flow over by air following conference calls. The *SS Exchequer* would return to Boston ready to make one more troop carrying crossing in May before becoming part of the BCPLBUF.

The OPERATION HEADQUARTERS was steadily preparing for June and while invasion troops were being concentrated, so too were the men who would look after them. The 811th Signal Port Service Company was backed by a section from 810th Battalion at WBS Headquarters in Chester plus detachments from the 4th Armored Division Signals and from the Signal Depot S-800 in Bury St. Edmunds. There were even 6 men from the 979th Motor Messenger Co. at SOS HQ in Priors Park, Cheltenham to run messages.

Petrol, Oil and Lubricants had to be readily available at camps and on embarkation routes and POL stations were provided adjacent to Cefn Tilla Court near Usk and at Pontlliw, Pontardulais. The US Navy also had a POL Depot at Thornhill, just to the north of Cardiff. Manpower came from the 3916th QM Gas Supply Company at Port Talbot and the 3915th at the Eardisley Q-303 Depot, near Hereford.

Quartermaster supplies were handled by the 561st Railhead Company at the Barry Depot, and by the 577th at Pontardulais Sub Depot. The 557th Railhead Company withdrawn from the 1st ESB would eventually be transferred to Cardiff for similar duty once replacements had joined, as they would lose 69 men on one of the LST's torpedoed on the night of 27-28th April by E-boats during TIGER.

Engineers were the principal 'housekeepers' at the camps with the detachments of the 360th and 373rd E (GS) R's at each and every one and there would be other engineer units on standby including the 438th Engineer Dump Truck Company in Llandaff Fields and central to the whole marshalling area a Maintenance Company, the 954th and the 1214th Fire Fighting Platoon at Camp Island Farm, Bridgend. The 1512th Engineer Water Supply Company was also nearby at Cowbridge.

Transportation Corps naturally would have a formidable task ahead of them and quite apart from the number of GWR trains required, the number of troop carrying trucks would need to be increased and be bolstered by civilian contractors. Lt. Col. Joseph Fleisher commanding the 89th QM Battalion (Mobile) at Maindy Barracks had a number of truck companies under orders and due to the way the command structure was organised, he could attach any number of additional companies. They were spread across South Wales with the 3345th QM Truck Company at Mumbles, the 131st at Bridgend, the 3632nd and the 3883rd at Cardiff, 3552nd and the 3326th at Risca and the 4012th at Abergavenny.

Ordnance Depot O-635 was already in operation at Tredegar Park near Newport and another was to be set up on Llantrisant Common with the 187th and 980th Ordnance Depot Companies. The 607th Ordnance Ammunition Battalion with headquarters in Gowerton was to provide detachments at Field Service Points that were to be placed at strategic spots on the road network. Also certain FSP's were to have vehicle repair detachments provided by a Company of the 957th Ordnance HAM Battalion based at Crick in Monmouthshire. These Field Service Points were to be manned by detachments of the 627th Ordnance Ammunition Company and 515th Ordnance HAM Co. and located at:-

No.1.   Clytha Park, Abergavenny for Sub-area 'U'.
No.2.   Admiralty Road, for Sub-area 'V'
No.3.   Cowbridge Common, for Sub-area 'W'.
No.4.   Margam Park, for Sub-area 'X' (east)
No.5.   Gorseinon. For Sub-area 'X' (west)

The 205 men of the 858th Ordnance Heavy Automotive Maintenance Company were also based at Miskin Manor in reserve.

Military Police were to be drawn in from as far afield as Hereford, Preston, Glasgow and Kirkby with four companies, 258th, 286th, 294th and 295th given security and escort duties at Griffithstown, Swansea, Cardiff and Swansea. These were in addition to the 159 'Snowdrops' of the 793rd Battalion Company 'D' at Llandaff whose men already covered the marshalling area.

Medical emergency and possible hospitalization had been covered, even though the assigned Field Hospital was still crossing the Atlantic. The Transient Field Hospitals would have the 571st Ambulance Company attached for the movement to Embarkation Ports. All 30 ambulances had been distributed to area camps but once they were 'sealed', the ambulances would be transferred and grouped accordingly. Another transfer, albeit temporary, affected 40 men from the 366th E (GS) R who were placed on detached service to the 5th Armored Division which was to provide housekeeping duties to invasion forces in Southern England. Mess sergeants, cooks and assistants left on the 16th April and wouldn't return to their respective companies until mid August. It seemed that every small detail had been thought about even down to issuing foreign currency for the troops – when they would get to spend any of it was open to discussion. The 15th Special Service Company would also provide cinema projector teams to all camps for entertainment to keep up morale. There were however two aspects regarding Quartermaster supplies that would cause problems, namely food and blankets.

Convoy CU20 arrived on the seventeenth with just two cargo and personnel ships coming south with the *SS Surprise* unloading cargo at Cardiff and *HMT Tamaroa* 600 troops and cargo at Avonmouth followed by 14 days of repair. Seven tankers continued on to Avonmouth and two days later the T2 *Four Lakes* was arriving at Queens Dock Swansea after part transferring her cargo on the Mersey ports. Convoy HX286 more than made up for any shortage three days later arriving at the North Channel with no less than 85 ships and 21 escorts. Nine Liberty ships laden with US Army cargo carried on south to all the Bristol Channel ports, *Elihu Root, George G Whitefield* and *James B Weaver* to Swansea, *James I McKay* to Barry *George E Badger, Harry Percy* and *Jesse Applegate* to Cardiff, *George G Crawford* and *David Star Jordan* to Newport prior to transfer to Barry for MTV conversion and *Stanford H King* to Avonmouth. The turnaround of vessels at ports with the Port Battalion troops working alongside the local dockers was speeding up despite the notoriously slow steam winches of the Liberty ships. Dockside and Floating cranes were working flat out as well.

April 22nd dawned with the arrival of a convoy at the Mumbles anchorage consisting of 22 Royal Navy Landing Ship Tanks, chock-a-block with American equipment. However US troops were noticeably absent, although the curious bystander wouldn't have noticed, unless anyone overheard any orders or conversation. For this was General Leclerc's Free French 2nd Armoured Division en route from Oran in North Africa to take station in the northern UK as part of Patton's Third US Army. Over the next few weeks three more convoys with the local prefix of Naphill (28, 30 and 33) would be part of initially MKS convoys from Gibraltar which would join with the SL convoys coming up from West Africa en route to the UK. Many of the ships of Naphill 26 also carried Italian POW's plus their British Army guard detachment and these 15 LST's docked in Swansea with the remaining 7 berthing and off-loading in Port Talbot.

Movement Control was already pretty stretched with the escalating number of incoming troops and cargo, but had gained considerable experience at handling large numbers of men and equipment at short notice. Constant liaison with civilian organisations especially the GWR ensured rapid clearance of quays, roads and railway stations. So it was for the 2,649 Free Frenchmen, 890 Italian prisoners and their British Army guards, however there was one complication this time.

Photo: LST's moored awaiting the tide increase before being able to enter Kings Dock at Swansea. (Courtesy of the South Wales Evening Post.)

Troops were normally fed on board before off-loading, but this was not possible on this occasion so an additional duty placed on Colonel Bevan and his staff was provision of two sandwiches plus a slice of cake and a packet of biscuits per man, but no liquids! Suitably fed the POW's were marched off via The Strand to High Street Station where 3 trains awaited. The French troops were expected to depart from nearby St Thomas Station or entrain at the dockside. Those fortunate to be outside the dock gates were supplied with tea by many local residents who took pity on these somewhat scruffy colonial troops – a gesture that was highlighted in a letter of appreciation from Colonel Langlade, Commandant of Detachment 'A' 2eme D.B to Col. Naylor in BCP HQ Newport. General Leclerc did likewise, with Col. Bevan ensuring The Mayor of Swansea got a copy. A further 9 LST's in Naphill 28 would dock in early May and by 3 June, 5,194 Free French troops with 1,916 vehicles had arrived in Swansea for forward movement to England.

Leaving New York on the twelfth, HX287 consisted of another 71 vessels plus 17 escorts arriving on 27 April, *Jane Long* and *John R Park* to Swansea, accommodation ships *Thomas B Robertson* and *Eleazor Wheelock* carrying 400 troops each with the *James Wolfe* to Barry, *Florence Crittenton, James Caldwell,*

John Merrick and *Joseph Pullitzer* to Cardiff, *Cyrus H McCormick, G W Goethals* and *Jeremiah O'Brien* to Newport. Finally, the *Henry S Lane* and *HMT Mataroa* bearing 600 troops docked in Avonmouth and 21 days of much needed repair. There were now so many troops arriving in South Wales that it seemed the camps would just not be big enough. Similarly the whole of the Western Base Section appeared overloaded and many units especially from Third Army had to be moved out of the proposed Marshalling Camps – and quickly. On the 24 April, 'Charlie' Company 95th Engineers (GS) Regiment in Llanelwedd was pulled off its training schedules for an emergency job and sent back up country with the 'little' task of providing a tented bivouac camp on Ludlow Racecourse - for 10,000 men! Even as they were setting up, troops were arriving from camps near Abergavenny and Newport. The 514th Heavy Maintenance Field Artillery Company of the 41st Ordnance Battalion departed Llangattock Park arriving at Ludlow and their battalion comrades of the 116th Medium Maintenance Company travelled west to Llandovery. They would be servicing units attending the Sennybridge range.

The day before, the main elements of the 5th ESB were on the move as well, not to the north, but the opposite way to the 'D' Marshalling Camps inland from Weymouth. Their training on Gower was now over and soon a distant memory as they took part in the various and bigger exercises including FABIUS I on the South Coast of England. The 37th ECB left their Camp Singleton on the 23rd April for the last time entraining at Swansea station for Dorchester, with the 348th and 336th doing the same 24 hours later. Many vehicles went by sea with the US *LST 325* being one of several calling into Swansea on the 26th to load en route to Falmouth having completed engine repairs at USNAAB Penarth. There was one driver of the 348th ESB who was very sad to leave and was well known by the Italian fish 'n chips shop community of South Wales, being a regular guest at their Sunday dinner tables. To them he was simply Pvt. Rocco Marchegnamo. He had got into trouble one night in a Wind Street 'bodega' when he got into a brawl and was nearly arrested after apparently Aussie soldiers picked on him. He knocked out three of them. Next thing he was in a South Wales miner's pub, swapping blows with a Welsh miner who Rocco described "as big as Tommy Farr". 'This time MP's, the 'Snowdrops' were on the scene and he faced a court martial. His Commanding Officer pleaded with court that he'd be short of a driver (for D-Day) and a solution was arrived at. He was ordered to take up amateur boxing in the clubs around Swansea. At the end of the war, back in Brockton, Massachusetts, the boot repairer gave up his job, changed his name and turned professional. The legend that was Rocky Marciano was born and it all started in Swansea.*

A final Gower exercise named CELLOPHANE began on 28th April, a Services of Supply test at Oxwich designed to demonstrate skid loading techniques to First Army staff. It included skid-load palleting and loose cargo loading to

---

Footnote: Taibach boxing club in Port Talbot hosted soldier boxers from the 95th Engineers on several occasions, giving youngsters, including a certain Richard Thomas (Burton), instruction in the noble art.

coasters at ports, offloading at beachheads into DUKWs and LCTs, transfer of cargo to trucks at beach transfer points, discharging direct from DUKWs to dumps and off-loading LCT's to trucks for direct transfer to dumps. The lessons of this exercise were not appreciated immediately, but the exercise did point the way to beach transfer points as they were eventually used on both US beaches. Another fact learned early on was that clear roadways were essential to enable rapid transfer of supplies material. The narrow road through Port Eynon village to the beach became congested despite the one-way system which had been introduced with an additional roadway cut through fields directly to the west and down to the beach. During all the months of training the 5th ESB troops rotated through the Training Camp often on a weekly basis from their stations at Singleton Park, Manselton, Mynydd Lliw and Penllergaer. It was quite common for units to road march to or from the camps covering 18 miles as fitness training. That would continue down on the English south coast.

Yet another fast cargo convoy was also in the Irish Sea by the twenty-eighth, CU21's last three mixed cargo and troops freighters, the *SS Flying Eagle*, *SS Santa Barbara* and *SS African Dawn* speeding south to Swansea, Barry and Cardiff. Stock demands of fuel in Swansea resulted in three T2 tankers also tying up in Queens Dock, *Powder River*, *Santiago* and *Sappa Creek* leaving their nine sisters to voyage on to Avonmouth. Simultaneously down in Start Bay another Slapton Sands Exercise was taking place as previously referred to, involving the 1st Engineer Special Brigade. A convoy of eight fully loaded LST's with a single Royal Navy leading escort, *HMS Azalea,* was off Portland at 5 knots heading for the beachhead when it came under attack from marauding German E-Boats. Exercise TIGER resulted in the loss of two LST's and the official death toll of 639 soldiers and sailors. Keeping the tragedy a secret was paramount in the authorities' view; casualties, of which there were at least three hundred, were despatched to many different US Army and Navy hospitals so as not to raise alarm. The much bigger series of FABIUS exercises involving all assault forces were to follow immediately afterwards and it was a bad omen. Many years later that original figure would be revised to give an overall death toll of 946 servicemen from both the US Army and the Navy.

The month of April had seen 28,388 troops arrive in the Bristol Channel ports. Overall the UK had taken in one and a half million US troops into the country, with the 6 counties of South Wales being home to 68,885 American servicemen and women.

Monmouthshire	15,121	Carmarthenshire	4,265
Glamorgan	33,403	Cardiganshire	1,316
Brecknock	8,322	Pembrokeshire	6,458

Those figures would continue to increase as D-Day approached. Army cargo continued to rise at 240,997 long tons with 496,384 into the UK.

Appendix D to FORTITUDE SOUTH II - Outline Plan for Special Means
Phased programme for identification and grouping of military forces
1st May to NEPTUNE D DAY - US Army

Serial	Unit	Location	Concentration	Command	Remarks
3	1 US Army	Bristol		21 Army Gp.	
4	V Corps	Taunton	Norton Manor	1 Br Army.	
5	1 Inf. Div.	Dorchester	Slapton	No grouping	No mention
6	2 Inf. Div.	N. Ireland		No grouping	ditto
7	29 Inf. Div.	Tavistock	Tavistock	V (US) Cps.	Less often
8	VII Corps	Braemore	Braemore	1 (US) Army	
9	4 Inf. Div.	Tiverton	Tiverton	VII (US) Cps	No stressing
10	9 Inf. Div.		Winchester	No grouping	FOYNES
11	90 Inf. Div.	Birmingham	should not be mentioned in period		
12	XIX Corps	Warminster	should not be mentioned in period		
13	30 Inf. Div.	Chichester	Chesham	No grouping	
14	2 Arm. Div.	Tidworth	Tidworth	No grouping	Salisbury Plain Tr.
15	3 Arm. Div.	Wincanton	Wincanton	1 (US) Army	Less often
16	82 AB Div.	Leicester	should not be mentioned in period		
17	101 AB Div.	Newbury	Newbury	No grouping	Continue reports
18 – 46	British and Canadian Units				
48	VIII Corps	Marbury	Folkestone	1 Cdn Army	(wireless traffic)
49	79 Inf. Div.	Northwich	Heathfield	VIII Corps	
50	28 Inf. Div.	Tenby	Tenterden	VIII Corps	Assault trained.
51	83 Inf. Div.	Staffs.	Eltham	VIII Corps	(wireless traffic)
52	3 US Army	Mobberley	Chelmsford	FUSAG	
53	XII Corps	Bewdley	Chelmsford	3 US Army	
54	80 Inf. Div.		Hadleigh	XII Corps	
55	7 Arm. Div.		Hatfield Peverel	XII Corps	(wireless traffic)
56	35 Inf. Div.		Brentwood	XII Corps	(ditto)
57	XX Corps	Marlborough	Bury St Edmunds	3 US Army	
58	4 Arm. Div.	Chippenham	Bury St Edmunds	XX Corps	(wireless traffic)
59	5 Arm. Div.	Chisledon	East Derham	XX Corps	(ditto)
60	6 Arm. Div.	Batsford	Woodbridge		(ditto)

Appendix E to FORTITUDE SOUTH II - Outline Plan for Special Means
Moves to Concentration and Other Related Troop Movements - US Army

Serial	Unit	Location	Concentration	Command	Remarks
1	14 US Army	Mobberley	Little Waltham		Notional formation
2	XXXIII Corps	Marbury	Bury St Edmunds		ditto
3	11 Inf. Div.	Northwich	Bury St Edmunds		ditto
4	48 Inf Div.	N'castle-u-Lyme	Woodbridge		ditto
5	25 Arm. Div.	Wincanton	East Derham		ditto
6	17 Inf. Div.	Birmingham	Hatfield Peverel		ditto

*****

Chapter X

MAY '44 - MARSHALLING

More work was assigned to the 366th Engineer (GS) Regiment following their training period that had concluded with a Regimental Review and March past. Penybont Camp needed attention, the Ross-on-Wye Camp required kitchen improvements, Govilon Hospital was to benefit from covered walkways and in Herefordshire the Foxley Hospital needed sanitation improvements and a Hereford camp needed new water towers.

The night before the "Salute the Soldier Week" began, the New Drill Hall in Bridgend featured an 'All American Dance Band' together with a 'running buffet' for the princely sum of 10/6d, proceeds to be added to the Bridgend target of £200,000. The town and district actually raised £335,000 reckoned to be enough to equip and maintain a Base Hospital for a year. The 'week' was between 6th and 13th of May and in Monmouth a parade on the sixth included the 1st Battalion Headquarters and Co's 'C' and 'E' from the 366th E (GS) R. Barry targeted £250,000. Aberdare looked to raise £150,000 but actually totalled £264,000 whilst Pontypridd aimed for £200,000 and raised £337,788. Col. Harold E Bonar C/O 517th Port Battalion raised the target indicator and took the opportunity to thank the people for their hospitality. (The following month Col. James A Crothers C/O 17th Major Port would raise the target indicator at Cardiff showing £2,878,935. Bridgend figure was then up to £345,887.11s.4d. Maesteg has risen to £100,000 and Port Talbot had aimed for £275,000 but achieved £320,000)

Highly secret CDL Tank Battalions began arriving in Wales for training and exercises up in the Preseli Hills. Under control of the 9th Armored Group based at their Headquarters down at Sodston Manor just outside Narberth, the 736th and the 748th Tank Battalions were the first in, camping around the perimeters of fields to the north and west of Trefach Manor and Capel-y-Fem in Mynachloddu parish. They were followed by the 701st and the 738th Battalions setting up their tent camps around Puncheston fields. The units and including the 526th Armored Infantry had the services of the 538th Ordnance Heavy Maintenance Tank Company assigned, registered as occupying a camp quite simply called 'Quarry' that had been prepared for them.. Could have been anywhere! The 50th Ordnance Ammunition Company was also not too far away at Cilgwyn Manor, near Newcastle Emlyn. Training would carry on with mixed success as the rock-strewn terrain was not really suitable for the type of warfare envisioned by the designers. The M3 Grant tanks retained their 37mm guns in the side sponson but the main turret 105mm had disappeared and been replaced with a million candle power arc light capable of totally blinding any opposing enemy infantry. The accompanying 526th Armored Infantry troops would then move forward with the 'Gizmo's mopping up the blinded enemy infantry. That was the plan, but what may have worked in the Desert Training Center at Bouse, Arizona, didn't work so well in mountainous Wales. Two more Tank Battalions, the 739th and 740th would be added to those already in Pembrokeshire and would continue training for a couple of months. The 10th Armoured Group joined this top secret organisation to provide additional Headquarters capability and control. Training continued until well after the Normandy Landings had taken place, with tank units not leaving for France from Swansea until July and August.

Individual assignments of static service troops got under way early in the month. The acknowledged experts in Ordnance supply, waterproofing and vehicle maintenance resulted in officers of the 863rd Ordnance HAM Company being placed on detached service to the two Infantry Divisions marshalling in the area. Lt. Specter as Liaison Officer for the 2nd ID and Lt. Smith likewise for the 90th.

The first week in May saw the arrival of HX288 containing an unprecedented number of ships in one convoy - 99 merchantmen with 24 escorts - entering the North Channel on the 4 May. Significantly, this convoy also included some of the last and newest LST's making their maiden voyages across the North Atlantic. All of the 15 'large slow targets' were ballasted with fuel oil for delivery to the UK (nine going to Milford Haven) and also included a variety of cargo, mainly AFV's on their tank deck and some with LCT's on the top deck, such as the Londonderry bound *LST 980* and *983* carrying *LCT 654* and *659* respectably. *LST 981* and *982* were scheduled for Swansea where the crews greatly enjoyed their time ashore before onward sailing to Plymouth and ultimately Tilbury to join Force 'L'. The *LST 543* crew, having been built in Evansville, Indiana in one of those 'cornfield' shipyards in the headwaters of the Mississippi must have felt just as much as home, too. Swansea also received 4 other ships plus the tanker *SS Thorshav*, with another 3 plus a tanker, fleet oiler *Maja* docking in Barry; Four ships arrived at Cardiff with another two going to Newport and two more tankers and two freighters including the accommodation ship *Bernard Carter* docking at Avonmouth transferring her 976 servicemen ashore before leaving for Barry.

Convoys arriving included CU22 from New York coming in on the sixth with the *SS Mormacswan* taking cargo into Swansea, and two T2 tankers *Millspring* and *Cayuse* berthing in Queens Dock. It turned out that much of the cargo from the *Mormacswan* was not supposed to be in Swansea at all and the port authorities certainly didn't want the huge number of wooden telegraph poles that had arrived. They were scheduled for the G-22 Moreton-on-Lugg Depot near Hereford and needed no fewer than 232 railway trucks to shift them from the Cross Bank Sidings area where they had been dumped, for want of space. Meanwhile the *SS Santa Cecelia* sailed into Cardiff to unload cargo plus her 250 troops, the Dutch registered *SS Java* unloading her cargo at Newport and the *SS Hegra* doing likewise at Avonmouth, in company with five T2 fuel tankers.

The independent *HMT Lancashire* entered the Bristol Channel bringing, among others, the 644th Tank Destroyer Battalion from Belfast and docked at Newport on the thirteenth. She would leave light, voyaging north all around the British Isles before arriving at Tilbury ready to take her part in Force 'L', the follow-up armada to transport and land British troops from the 51st Highland and

7th Armoured Divisions on GOLD beach during Operation NEPTUNE.

The Advance Echelon of the 90th Infantry Division Headquarters was the first to move on 9 May from Shropshire to Camp Llangattock Park and the last would be the 382nd Medical Collection Company (53rd Medical Battalion of V Corps) travelling from Higher Barracks, Exeter to Camp Wenvoe arriving as late as 2 June. Arriving at Camp Cwrt-y-Gollen on May 11th, the 2/359th Infantry Battalion with the divisional 915th FA on the 14th, were joined by the Headquarters with 'A' & 'B' Batteries of the 321st and 907th GFA battalions and the 426th Quartermaster Company from the 101st 'Screaming Eagles' on the 17th. Finally an advanced Headquarters Detachment of the 9th Infantry Division follow-up unit to the 90th Infantry Division from their base around Winchester completed the roster, all being cared for and supplied by the troops of the 360th E (GS R detachment.

Photo: USAT Excelsior which would be one of the BCPLBU Force troopships.

On 12 May the entire 358th Infantry Regiment left Bewdley rail station, detraining at Severn Tunnel Junction and was trucked to Llanmartin, being the only US Regiment complete in one camp. For the next 3 weeks the 'Tough 'Ombres' were to be brought up to peak fitness through all sorts of exercise including 12 mile endurance marches in full invasion kit. Up until the end of the month passes were allowed to give some free time, mostly on Sundays. Sadly pubs, cinemas and amusement centres were closed although people were friendly! All three battalions of the 357th Infantry Regiment arrived at Camp Racecourse on the following day, HQ and HQ Company arriving separately at Camp Sedbury, with others being quartered at Camp Bulwark with the 343rd and 344th FA Battalions and their 105mm howitzers plus Company 'A' and 'B' 315 ECB arrived for Marshalling under a 360th E (GS) R platoon care on May 14th. 300 vehicles left for loading on

MT Liberty ships at Newport on 31 May, drivers returning to camp before 1,296 men marched to Chepstow Station on the 3 and 4th June.

All the usual fitness training, equipping and vehicle waterproofing was carried out during the few weeks that the troops spent in Chepstow, although furloughs were permitted to primarily Newport, Cardiff and Chepstow of course. The ancient site at Tintern Abbey proved of great interest to many, some men from the southern states never having seen a monastic ruin before, the 'Alamo' in San Antonio, Texas, probably being the exception. Sadly they contributed to the condition of the nearby mansion of Piercefield using it for target practice!

Camp Heath in Cardiff, designed for 84 Officers and 1,750 men was the ideal location to serve as Marshalling Advance Headquarters for the 90th 'Texas/Oklahoma' Division which had been selected as the immediate follow-up division for VII Corps assault on UTAH beach. The individual RCT's were marshalled elsewhere so it was the Divisional troops who arrived in two groups on 13th and 14th May with the Advance Headquarters Echelon of 267 men preceding them in their rightful place on the 9th. Using their own transport, the 'Tough Hombres' journeyed from their Shropshire tented camps being delighted to find the best berths that they had experienced since landing in the UK in March.

Meanwhile the Rhondda had been preparing for the 'Yanks' to arrive for a couple of months and apart from an MP platoon setting up a wired detention centre in Porth, nothing had really happened. The usual noises of a mining valley didn't turn any heads, but just occasionally something unusual did.

'However, this was a different sound and coming from the direction of Pontypridd, a steady drone growing more audible every minute. Curious surface workers moved to the colliery gate entrance and were joined by the families from the houses opposite who came out onto their doorsteps. It was the residents of Bryn Eirw, a terrace of houses higher up the mountainside who first saw the source of the noise. Between the gaps in the houses below lorries could be seen. Around the bend of Coed Cae Road, a jeep appeared bearing a red flag followed closely by a convoy of army trucks. Each huge olive-green truck bore a white five-pointed star and was laden with petrol cans, ropes, canvas bags and a deep treaded spare wheel. Most of the trucks carried troops. The convoy over a hundred strong was interspersed with a few squat weapons carriers and Dodge ambulances. It moved on to Porth and assembled on Llwyncelyn Field.'

'A Moment in History' – Bryan Morse

The 517th Port Battalion had arrived carried by the 'deuce and a halves' of the Cardiff based 89th Quartermaster Truck Battalion. The black American unit had been and would be convoying thousands of men over the next few weeks. The Port battalion had been based at Barry unloading ships with one company detached to Cardiff. The companies were rotated through the Amphibious Training Centre in North Devon or the Transportation School on Gower, near Swansea as they had a role to play with the 6th Engineer Special Brigade in the invasion. They were to be spread in billets throughout the Rhondda Fach with 797th and 798th around Porth, 799th in Penygraig and the 800th in Ferndale. Headquarters was at Porth House with Lt. Col Harold E. Bonar in command.

Camp Malpas had been home to the 487th Port Battalion since the beginning of the year when they took up the duties of unloading cargos at Newport Docks. Brief training interludes at the ATC in Woolacombe and the Transportation Training School at Mumbles interrupted this work as individual companies rotated. But now assigned to the 5th ESB they arrived by train at Pontypridd before being trucked to their billets in the Rhondda Fawr. The famous valleys were proving popular with the US Army longshoremen. Headquarters was the Thistle Hotel in Tonypandy, Lt. Col. Montgomery C. Jackson in command, with the men in private homes stretching from Tonypandy through Llwynapia, Gelli, Ystrad, Ton Pentre, Treorchy right up to Treherbert. More billets had been required for the 487th Battalion as at the beginning of the previous month the unit had been augmented by two more stevedore companies, the 282nd and the 283rd bringing the total unit strength up to 33 Officers and 1,406 men.

Marshalling began on 13th May at Camp Pontllanfraith under 360th E(GS)R control with men and material of Collins VII Corps arriving from all over Western Britain – Sherborne, Cattistock, Fordingbridge, Banbury, Newbury, Pangbourne, Faringdon and Bromyard saw troops leaving for assembly at Camp 94 destined for UTAH beach. The Headquarters and HQ Company 1120th Engineer Combat Group including the 294th ECB were attached in support of the 4th Infantry Division and the 87th Armored FA Battalion with their 105mm 'Priests' (tracked self-propelled artillery US equivalents to the British 'Sextons') were back-up to the 101st Airborne many of whom including parts of the 326th A/B Engineer Battalion, also staged in Pontllanfraith. In addition the 42nd Field Hospital - one of the last units to arrive in camp but one of the first Hospitals to land and operate in France – brought the camp occupation numbers up to the maximum.

14 May was one of those days when it seemed everyone in uniform was either packing or actually on the move to new locations. Around the coast 13 escorts including the heavy cruiser USS Cincinatti plus the carrier USS Ariel in convoy TCU23 brought 51 ships to the UK including nine 'troopers' carrying almost 35,000 soldiers. The T2 tanker Waggon Box put into Swansea together with a new ship of distinctive design, mooring off Mumbles being the landing ship dock HMS Oceanway. With loaded LCM's aboard they shuttled back and forth to the dockside landing army cargo before departing. She would take part in the invasion with each of her 20 LCM's carrying a Sherman Tank of the 745th Tank Bn. onto OMAHA beach during June 6 afternoon. The SS Exanthia and the SS Exhibitor unloaded at Cardiff with the USAT Henry Gibbons and HMT Highland Monarch both debarking 1,900 troops at Avonmouth by the 18th. The Monarch crew had a welcome break as she had 14 days of repairs carried out just like her sister ships. Among the 5,400 troops aboard the USAT Gen. William Mitchell anchoring at Gourock was the 29th Field Hospital which had already been on Pacific Theatre

active service in the Aleutian Islands and had provided a hospital at the Kiska Island assault. Now they were a late arrival but would set up potentially important although small field hospitals. First call was to the Provisional Medical Training Area at Llandudno in North Wales.

Organisation of Field Hospitals at this time meant they could set up three 100 bed hospitals at different locations independently. The First Hospitalization Unit (or platoon) set up an Air Holding Station for Prestwick Airport at Westfield House with 90 beds and a 10 bed Dispensary for the evacuation of patients back to the United States. The Second and Third HU's were to provide Transient Hospitals under tents in the S. Wales Marshalling Area. Second HU set up on Malpas Cricket Field right next to the main arterial road running from the Sub-area 'U' camps around Abergavenny to the Embarkation Port of Newport. A Headquarters Section and Third HU moved west to Morriston setting up a 100 bed tented Hospital at Glyn Collen near the new permanent Morriston Hospital to serve Sub-area 'X' camps and embarkation routes to Swansea. Sub-Area 'V' was served by another specialised Transient Hospital at Llandaff Castle provided by the Medical Section of the 360th E(GS)R and named the '360th Provisional Field Hospital'(reverently referred to as the 'Barkesdale Memorial Hospital' after their Regiment C/O Lt. Col Barkesdale!) to serve Cardiff Embarkation Area. Sub Area 'W' with its Embarkation Port of Barry not loading any large troopships was possibly deemed to not require an additional hospital unit. The presence of the 42nd Field Hospital on the loading registers may have been seen to provide medical assistance if required, perhaps. These additional emergency Transient Hospitals were set up to cover the final stage of the mounting operation i.e. movement from camps to ports, and in addition they were provided with vehicles of the 571st Medical Ambulance Company. Ten ambulances were kept as a reserve at the 279th Station Hospital at Govilon with the remaining twenty distributed, eight to Llandaff, nine to Glyn Collen and three to Malpas. The Tidworth Ordnance Depot O-640 released a further fifteen ambulances on request and they were sent to bolster those already there with five going to the 29th at Malpas and five to Swansea with a further five going west to the 232nd Station Hospital in Carmarthen, thereby ensuring good overall coverage. With over 40,000 men being moved, the Medical Corps had to be prepared and the permanent US Army Station Hospitals at Govilon, Rhyd Lafar & Carmarthen were already busy.

The US Navy Hospital at Milford was also gearing up and enlarging in anticipation of casualties. They had already received a number of Naval wounded in late April as a result of the surprise attacks on the US LST's down in Start Bay during Exercise TIGER. Two had been sunk and another severely damaged. Part of the highly secret cover-up at the time was the far and wide distribution of the wounded servicemen to hospitals throughout the country so that there was no large influx at any one spot. Equally the 800 or so dead *(figures are still disputed 75 years on)* were gathered and transported by a dedicated QM Truck Company charged with the gruesome task of delivery to a number of special mortuaries run by a QM Graves Registration Company. It turned out that Quartermaster unit was the 146th Truck Company which was alerted with its 48 trucks to join with another two other companies to perform a secret 'hush hush' assignment on midnight 28th April. Under command of an SOS Major the trucks arrived at Weymouth and loaded large numbers of former servicemen, one Sergeant noting he had 540 corpses aboard his trucks. The silent and secret convoy complete with MP motor cycle escorts travelled unhindered to Brookwood Cemetery where the authorities took charge of the truck company cargo's with all due necessary respect. It was a very sombre bunch of drivers who returned to their bases on the twenty-ninth, sworn to secrecy.

The Dispensary or Hospital at Milford had three admin units, four surgical wards, four medical wards, and one ward each for isolation, G.U., S.O.Q., N.P., convalescent and receiving. There were two operating rooms, one eye and E.N.T. clinic, separate buildings for dentistry, physiotherapy, laboratory, pharmacy, X-Ray, store and a store/morgue. There were also 3 mess halls plus buildings for the galley, bake-house, linen, laundry, shop (PX) and generator room. Additions enabled the 220 bed facility to be massively increased by 600 more beds; personnel rose with the inclusion of two M.O's, one Dental Officer and 70 Corpsmen.

May 15 was to be a significant day in 1944. This was the day that such preparations that could be revealed for the OVERLORD/NEPTUNE operation were presented to HM King George VI, the Prime Minister Winston Churchill and all the top 'brass' of the United States, the United Kingdom and Canada. Gathered in the main lecture hall of St. Pauls School, 21st Army Group Headquarters, on the banks of the Thames, Montgomery as Ground Commander had laid out on the floor a huge map of Normandy. The gravity of the undertaking was dawning in the minds of many but Eisenhower in his usual warm style of speaking seemed to dispel any potential doubts in his opening remarks. Montgomery and the heads of all three services spoke and the true scale and complexity of the operation became apparent. Starting at 0900hrs, the briefing went on until 1415hrs, at the end of which Churchill, who had been so anxious over the past months having told Ike that he could see 'tides running red with blood' was now very much on board and 'hardening towards this enterprise'.

It was also 'gloves off' down in Carmarthen of the 15 May, but in a totally different and more conventional way. The end of the month would see many camps sealed under strict security so entertainment and the social round were in full swing all over the country. But a 'Grand Boxing Tournament' organised by the Special Services was taking place at the Market Hall, and would feature American boxers now in uniform including Pvt. Phelix Rayes (from New London), and Pvt. John Ameto (New Haven). There would be exhibition bouts by and including the famous Master Sgt. Keen Simmons, winner of the 1940 New York Golden Glove and who had also trained with Joe Louis. Narberth Victoria Hall had an 'All American Concert' for the first time in its history with a whole range of troops providing music, dance and comedy spots organised by T/5 Sonnie Honor.

Whilst the new arrivals to the UK were getting their shore legs back and being mostly entrained for destinations all around the country, they were not part of the Invasion Force being primarily Third Army and other Corps troops. However the thousands of troops that were scheduled and had been 'concentrated' in the west and had not actually started to move were now setting off by road and rail to their various marshalling area camps.

These areas stretched from the Wash around Norfolk, Suffolk, Essex and down around the Thames Estuary, Kent, East and West Sussex and Hampshire for the British and Canadians Forces to 'SWORD', 'JUNO' and 'GOLD', with Follow-up 'FORCE L' for all three beaches. Then Dorset, Devon and Cornwall for the Americans 'OMAHA', 'UTAH' and Follow-Up 'FORCE B', finishing up with Somerset, Gloucestershire, Monmouthshire and Glamorganshire for the Bristol Channel Pre-Loaded Build-Up Force - the 'BCPLBUF' as it became known. The sheer volume of military traffic, incidentally not all going one way at this time, was something to behold. Parts of units not slated for D-Day but for D-Day+1 had to separate from their parent formations and move to the marshalling areas devoted to follow-up forces, thereby travelling in the opposite direction to those that were! Marshalling was fortunately spread over a several weeks and the South Wales area followed along the same lines as elsewhere.

There were a number of units already in their correct camp in South Wales. Unlike elsewhere the US Army was able to use the same camps for marshalling as had been built or re-assessed and improved during the previous months. Elsewhere saw the creation of the infamous roadside 'sausage camps' each one for 200 men as close as was reasonable to the Embarkation Ports of the South Coast. The same formula for providing static troop manpower for camp 'hospitality' based on 200 strong units was adhered to and the two Engineer GS Regiments (373rd and 360th) whose job it was to look after the BCPLBU Force did just that.

VII Corps support troops to be marshalled at Camp 131 St. Mary's Hill arrived between the 15th and 18th and included the 988th Engineer Treadway Company, 649th Medical Clearing Co., 92nd Ordnance Medium Maintenance Co. and HQ sections of 692nd Quartermaster Battalion, and 3rd Tank Destroyer Group. Also on the 15th May the 2nd Ordnance Medium Maintenance Company from VII Corps arrived at Camp St. Mellons and was the only UTAH beach bound unit there. Two days later the bulk of the occupants – 38th Infantry Regiment Second & Third Battalions (2nd Indianhead' Division) arrived from their concentration area around Carmarthen, the St. Mellons Marshalling Camp being well placed to provide access to either Cardiff or Newport docks via the A48 or from the nearby Marshfield Railway Station on the main GWR line for embarkation elsewhere.

V Corps troops for OMAHA arrived for marshalling hospitality at Camp Margam Park. The 383rd Collection and the 684th Clearing Company's of the 53rd Medical Battalion (Motorized) with their ambulances came from Exeter on 14th May (the 382nd Company was in advance with Force B). 582nd Ordnance Ammunition and 463rd Evacuation Company's were in on the 15th and shared with the 17th and 21st Ordnance Bomb Disposal Squads.

On the same day 1,400 troops of the 6th ESB including the 203rd Engineer Combat Battalion, arrived at Camp Dan-y-Parc, being joined by 300 men of the 5th

ESB. All told, 270 vehicles were prepared for loading at the ports travelling out on the 29th May, drivers returning to camp. All 'passes' were stopped, the camp sealed and final preparations carried out. Troops departed on the 1st and 3rd June, some by road to Newport, others like the 203rd ECB by rail to Swansea.

Photo: Familiar sight of mess lines in camps all over marshalling areas. (IWM)

Those deemed non-essential troops of the 1st Infantry Division with 203 vehicles arrived from their bases on the English south coast at Camp Llantarnum, Newport. Whilst the veterans of the 'Big Red One' would have said <u>all</u> their men were essential, certain elements clearly did not have an immediate role in the Invasion of Normandy and OMAHA beach in particular. The 156 strong Recce Troop with their M8 Armoured Cars would be heavily involved once the First Army had confirmed a consolidated beachhead, but until then they had to wait. The Quartermaster Co. and part of the 701st Ordnance Light Maintenance Co. were with them as were the remnants of all three Division Infantry Regiments. Vehicles from the Heavy Weapons Companies of the 16th Infantry ('D', 'H' & 'M') and from the Cannon and Anti-Tank Co's were present together with those from every company in the 18th RCT. Although the 26th RCT was to be aboard the LST's of 'Force B' voyaging from Cornwall and due to land on D-Day afternoon, parts of the HQ. and Service Companies were also at Llantarnum. 1 ECB troops and Medics of the Divisional Medical Battalion meant there were almost 500 men from Gen. Omar Bradleys' principal OMAHA assault division in South Wales. However this contingent would be outnumbered by the stevedores and longshoremen of the 494th Port Battalion who journeyed south from their duties in Liverpool and Manchester Docks at short notice, arriving on May 31st. As part of the 6th Engineer Special

Brigade (just like the 519th who were arriving at Island Farm Marshalling Camp at the same time) they would undertake cargo unloading and beach operations on the western end of OMAHA. The 239th, 240th, 241st and 242nd arrived just as the 1st Division drivers marched back into camp, their vehicles now at the Docks.

Elements of the 29th 'Blue and Gray' Infantry Division arrived at Camp Singleton being looked after by Lt. Joseph W. Wheeler and 3rd Platoon Co. 'C' 372nd E (GS) R. These men were the 20% 'over strength' reserves of the 115th and 175th Infantry Regiments and 110th Field Artillery Battalion. Not with them were reserves of the assaulting 116th Regiment as they were with Force 'O'. All told some 650 men of the other OMAHA assault unit, Gerhardt's' 29th 'Blue and Gray' Infantry Division were in the Swansea camp.

Marshalling began at Camp Mynydd Lliw as well on this day with more of the 20% 'over strength' detachments, this time of the 224th and 227th FA Artillery Battalions from the same Infantry Division together with 99 men of that Divisions 121st ECB arriving from Cornwall. From the 2nd Division Headquarters sections of all the companies of the 9th and 38th Infantry Regiments turned in on the 16th, plus the First Battalion of the 23rd Infantry Regiment, the Second and Third Battalions being marshalled out at Scurlage on Gower. Large elements of the 2nd ECB and 2nd Medical Battalion were also present together with the entire 23rd RCT Cannon and Anti-tank Companies. All in all 1,235 troops to be catered for by Lt Powell with his Headquarters troops of the 373rd E (GS) R and part of 'B' Company.

SECOND INFANTRY DIVISION HEADQUARTERS STAFF

Photo: 2nd ID Headquarters Staff outside the Belgrave Hotel, Tenby. Second Division in World War II. ISBN: 0-89839-017-6. The Battery Press.

The lead Regimental Combat Team of the 2nd 'Indianhead' Division, the 9th Infantry Regiment under their Commander Lt.-Colonel Chester J. Hirschfelder, arrived at Camp Barry on 16th May. Scheduled to be the first follow-up unit immediately behind the assaulting 1st Division onto OMAHA beach, they had to be ready to 'Keep Up The Fire', their appropriate motto. Their composition was:

Regt. HQ/Hq Co., Anti-Tank, Cannon & Service Co's plus Medical Detachment;
1st Bn. HQ/Hq Co. 'A' 'B' 'C' and 'D' (H/W) Companies & Medics;
2nd Bn. HQ/Hq Co. 'E', 'F', 'G' & 'H' (H/W) Co. & Medics; 'A' Co.2nd Med. Bn.
15th FA Bn. HQ/Hq. Battery, 'A' 'B' 'C' Battery's, Service Company & Medics.

The Headquarters staff of the 2nd Infantry Division had been concentrated at the Belgrave Hotel in Tenby following their arrival from Northern Ireland but was now assembled at Camp St. Donats to make final preparations. Other Divisional troops plus the Headquarters Divisional Artillery with the 12th FA Battalion arrived on 17 May including the Recce Troop, MP platoon, and teams from Military Intelligence, POW Interrogation, and Civil Affairs. Units had been broken down into craft loads and serials with no one unit to embark totally on the same ship. The Reconnaissance Troop would board the *Louis Kossuth* and *Hellas* with 12th FA 'A' Battery, and 'C' with the Service Battery also on the *Kossuth,* others on the *John Hay,* all waiting their arrival for embarkation at Barry docks.

Nearby, over at Camp Wenvoe with Headquarters plus 3 Platoon from Company 'D' 373 E (GS) R in control, the 9th RCT reserve battalion, the 3rd plus the division other direct support artillery of the 38th FA battalion duly arrived on the 16th and 17th May, followed by the attached 447th AAA Automatic Weapons Battalion up from Cornwall with an additional battery attached from the 535th AAA AW Battalion on the 22nd. A complete Quartermaster truck company on attachment to the 82nd Airborne Division (3809th) rolled up on the 25th with their trucks packed with paratroopers' kit and supplies, the camp finally being full with a late arrival on 2 June of 382nd Collection Company of V Corps 53rd Medical Battalion from Exeter. Units were being separated sometimes for 'combat loading', grouped by priority or so that not all were gathered on the same ship should disaster strike. For example, on May 16th the 2nd ECB left Abermarlais for their Marshalling Camps near the South Wales coast ports with HQ/Hq Service Company plus the Medical Detachment trucking to Mynydd Lliw, 'A' Company to Wenvoe, 'B' Company to Scurlage and residues to Bournemouth for later transfer. On the same day as 'C' Company arrived at Camp Kenfig Burrows, a detail of V Corps 56th Signal Battalion arrived from Devon, followed on the 18th by the 38th Infantry and support troops. Regimental Headquarters boosted by 'G' Company, Anti-Tank, Cannon, Service Companies, and Medical Detachment with the entire 1/38th Infantry Battalion started with making preparations for departure to France. Company 'C' of the 2nd Medical Battalion together with Divisional Signal and MP platoons brought the compliment up to strength and with the final last minute arrival of the 252nd Ordnance Medium Maintenance Company detachment, the camp surrounded by the infamous barbed wire, was sealed. They were to join their respective division Regimental Combat Teams bound for OMAHA Beach, Normandy in June. The 2nd ECB were slightly under-strength as 90 men had been detached to augment the Special Engineer Task Force that had been set up with both Army and Navy Boat Teams to deal with the various and many mined obstacles that covered the assault beaches.

Camp Manselton, Swansea was designated a Reserve Marshalling Camp for the Sub-Area 'X' lift of over 1,100 VII Corps and Airborne Division troops. The 101st Airborne residues began arriving on the 17th with similar from the 82nd Airborne later on the 25th. 517th Port Battalion and 3 of its companies were in on the 31st and either marched to Swansea Docks, or were trucked further afield or taken by rail to Barry to join their ships. Late arrivals of the 90th Infantry Division over the River Wye from Chepstow at Sedbury were the Regimental Headquarters of the 357th Infantry Regiment together with the regimental support elements, Service, Cannon and Anti-tank companies and Medical detail. Camp Llanover Park greeted 1,400 officers and men plus heavy equipment from the 820th and 834th Engineer Aviation Battalions ready to ship out to Normandy. Travelling by road from their base at Great Barrington near Burford, Oxon on the 20th May, they found the camp already in occupation by the TAC men who would operate the potential airfield(s). Signal and communication detachments, air control and command sections, a detachment from the 21 Weather Squadron, the 327th Fighter Control Squadron and even the 2029th Fire-Fighting Platoon with their fire-engines were preparing for the off. Even before them, army, navy and air force elements of the Beach Control and 5th ESB had arrived, preceded by the stevedores of the 502nd Port Battalion, down from an unloading assignment in Glasgow.

Also on the move into and within the South Wales Marshalling Area was the 490th Port Battalion attached to the 1st Engineer Special Brigade who would be supporting the UTAH assault. The 227th Company, following their training at the Transportation School in Mumbles were joined by the 228th Company fresh from exercises with the 1st ESB at Par in Cornwall, arriving at Penarth to load ammunition aboard coasters, several of which they would also unload on UTAH. By the 18th, the work was done and they set off for Harpton Court, New Radnor which would be home for two weeks whilst they prepared for the Invasion. They were joined by Battalion Headquarters and the 228th and 229th Companies from the Seamills Camp, near Bristol. Being so far away, 90 miles to the nearest embarkation port, perhaps it was not surprising that they never received enough gas-impregnated protective clothing. Thankfully it would not be required anyway.

Paratrooper and air landing troops of the 82nd 'All American' Airborne Division not able to fly due to unavailability of transport or not being required for early assault were among the late arrivals in South Wales. Camp St. Mary's Hill had some 1,500 airborne troops to get to France, many being trucked to Glamorgan on 25th May. Three Batteries of the 80th A/B FA Battalion and two of 456th A/B

PFA Bn., plus the HQ and Service Companies of the 319th & 320th FA Battalions were ready to go but there were still more of the support echelons unable to fly. The Camp Heronston compliment of 360 men and 76 vehicles of the Division Headquarters teams and special troops arrived on the previous day as well from their Leicestershire bases that had been home since returning from Italy.

On the 31st May (D-5) troops arrived at Reserve Marshalling Camp Island Farm, Bridgend for final preparations. Two Port Battalions (518th and 519th) were attached to the 1st Engineer Special Brigade whose task was the unloading ships and organising the UTAH beach maintenance area. These army stevedores, 'Long shore Soldiers' had been working in Crookstown (Glasgow) and Avonmouth Docks respectively and were to provide the hatch gangs aboard the MTV's and coasters. Divided up across all South Wales Embarkation Ports and including Avonmouth plus Southampton they were among the last men to arrive in the marshalling area. Likewise the 517th Port Battalion, part of the 6th ESB, arrived at Camp Singleton, ready to march to Swansea docks with the 29th ID reserves.

All through the month OPERATION HEADQUARTERS had come across supply problems. The two infantry divisions had equipped themselves relatively well during the concentration period but some other units didn't fare so well, the Commander of one Port Battalion would turn up at the Operation Supply office three days before the Invasion date only having just received orders to report to the marshalling area. They had been on port duties unloading ships for a considerable time, never expecting to get the call. Fortunately the Supply Section had managed to get help since the formation of the Operation Headquarters and had become used to such eventualities, even getting the required ammunition passed over after the gang-plank had been raised! The 164th QM Battalion commander at Newport had contacted his opposite numbers at the neighbouring depots at Thatcham, Moreton-on-Lugg and Wem and the 64th, 272nd and 562nd QM Battalions loaned their supply sections to help the one warrant Officer, one sergeant and one clerk of the 164th QMB. When demands for supplies escalated and with extra phone lines, orders were resourced and met. On this occasion First Army decreed that impregnated clothing had to be worn over wool clothing; 15,000 of the larger leggings would be required! Eventually after continuous phone calls gaining authority and depot stock checks, the order was met taking the entire stock of 2 depots and part of a third.

There were huge demands placed on the Laundry Service as well, but much of that was by choice. Three QM Laundry Companies were assigned to provide service to the troops being marshalled in South Wales. A Lieutenant of the Caerphilly based 634th Company was placed in overall charge with facilities spread across the area; the 'Bubble Boys' were ready. His duty was to contact the Marshalling Camp Area Supply Officer and arrange the schedule for the three mobile Laundry Companies (his own plus the third and fourth platoons of the 633rd Laundry Company at Sophia Gardens, Cardiff and the 600th Laundry Co. at Aberglasney House, Llandeilo). He reported that the Laundry Companies could do more than the limited bundle per man per week (normally just socks and underwear), and that they were willing to take field jackets and denims, if permitted, and to work their equipment around the clock if necessary. This 'service before self' was typical of many SOS Quartermaster units, whether they were Railhead or POL or Bakery companies. The later, as part of the morale drive were charged with providing white bread instead of the usual British brown 'stuff', which was not popular.

> *'It was hoped to improve troop morale by feeding them white bread while in the Marshalling Area instead of the bread baked from the darker British National wheat flour. And further to give them the best send-off possible, it was planned to provide coffee and white bread steak sandwiches at the Embarkation Points. The white bread rations appeared to be sufficient in the Marshalling Areas, but when it came to making sandwiches, the Commanding Officer, 360th Engineers reported that there wasn't any way he could slice the ration allowance of bread thin enough to make the required number of sandwiches. This fact was reported to SOS Food Service at Cheltenham and at the same time, ten pounds extra per hundred men was ordered by the Operational Supply Officer for sandwiches'.*
> 'Supply Operations in the Bristol Channel Area'. Lt. Col. F. Deisher.

There was some hilarity at Operation Headquarters apparently when a ration expert arrived from SOS Headquarters in Cheltenham to advise on sandwich making! Two-thirds of the troops had already been loaded and sandwiches made. It seemed that the extra 4,400 loaves had upset their calculations.

There were some pretty strange supply requests as well with some troops not entirely satisfied with the free PX rations. An Engineer Supply Officer in a 90th Division camp in Monmouthshire received an order for '200 cans of Copenhagen Snuff, 500 plugs of chewing tobacco and 1,000 cigars' as recorded by Lt. Col. Deisher. Amazingly one Battalion duly received these 'combat supplies'!

A couple of valleys away to the west and locomotives were starting to fill another set of sidings above Caerphilly. These weren't the 2-8-0 'Boleros', their ever increasing numbers were now going to Cadoxton as Penrhos and Tonteg were full. These were the smaller 0-6-0's tank engines. After the usual checks, greasing and trial steam run from Ebbw Junction and back following their trans-Atlantic crossing, they followed the tracks of their big sisters along the old Brecon and Merthyr line out through Basseleg to Machen, but instead of branching off towards the Rhymey line at Caerphilly continued for another 11 miles or so passing Bedwas pit to Dyffryn Isaf. Here were more of the redundant exchange sidings for the old Barry Railway, but these where the line joined the B&M Railway next to the remains of the mighty Llanbradach Viaduct (demolished in 1937) that had carried the line from Barry over the Rhymney River. The line had already soared over the River Taff on that other massive Walnut Tree Viaduct at Tongwynlais on its way through Penrhos to the eastern valleys. One or two 'shunters' were out on loan in the yard, but otherwise around 70 or so were stored here. The 0-4-4-0 Diesel Electric loco's which had also arrived over a period of months were stored primarily at Ebbw Junction with 6 of the 65 brought over stored to the west at Llanelly Sheds. There were very few GWR men experienced on diesels; consequently they remained in storage until shipped to France with just one trial run before mothballing, with an unnamed GWR driver (Payroll No. 20) sharing the footplate with a 756th RSB sergeant.

Other units not part of the immediate Invasion plans were still arriving in the country and although being accommodated in WBS camps further north they still needed to access ranges for training and checking newly supplied weapons. The 561st FA Battalion from VIII Corps with their 155mm 'long toms' were scheduled for exercises and weapon calibration on the Sennybridge Artillery Range. On Friday 19 May they trucked from their Doddington Camp in Cheshire to Llandovery and set up a bivouac camp. The journey was not without incident as five vehicles got lost in the Welsh mountains, delaying arrival by one and a half hours. The tent camp a mile or so to the south of the town at a location known locally as Llwyn Jack on Mr Thomas's meadow was near a lovely little clear stream. This was home for the next ten days with daily runs up to the range. The original plan was for half the battalion to carry out training and calibration returning to Cheshire and then bring down the remainder with the other 6 guns. However as the weather worsened then orders were cancelled and the entire unit got back together. They were not alone as their sister battalion from VIII Corps, the 559th FA was on station for the same reason. It seemed that it rained for the best part of a week up on Mynydd Eppynt so there was only two full days of live firing. However the all important calibrations were done and both battalions left for Cheshire on Monday 29th May. The men got the impression that someone didn't want them to go, as the prime movers and guns got bogged down and it took a borrowed M4 recovery tractor to get everyone out onto the roadway. Finally they were away 559 in the lead with the Executive Officer of the 561st Major A James Gordon as Convoy Commander.

The day before one US Navy ship that would have a significant role in the forthcoming invasion docked independently at Avonmouth on the 18th. Having offloaded trans-Atlantic cargo, the *AKA 53 Achernar* began loading the 1st Army Headquarters equipment from Clifton School which had been their base since arriving in the UK. The Navy Attack Freighter had been selected to be Gen. Omar Bradley's amphibious headquarters for the assault and would sail with Force 'B' from Plymouth to arrive off OMAHA during the early afternoon of D-Day.

Such were the demands on all types of fuel now in S. Wales that the largest number of T2 tankers unloaded simultaneously at Queens Dock Swansea. TCU24 like its predecessor consisted of 44 vessels, but with more tankers numbering 21 in total. The *Beaver Dam, Lyons Creek* and *Esso Portland* all arrived on the same tide on 24 May with the *Cerro Gordo* from TCU24B berthing in Queens Dock the following day. Dock space had really reached bursting point, but still ships were arriving, many laden with troops that had to get ashore and away to their new stations. Anchoring in roadways was beginning to be a regular feature over the forthcoming last week in May and the first week in June 1944.

An US naval commander who would earn distinction in the assault on Southern France in August had an unfortunate experience in the Bristol Channel on 24 May. John Bulkley, Captain of the Gleaves class destroyer *USS Endicott* had the misfortune of colliding with the much larger freighter *SS Exhibitor* which had just left Cardiff. Dry-dock inspection revealed so much damage that the *Endicott* had to be removed from duty in NEPTUNE, being replaced by the *USS Eamonns*.

Towards the end of the month the first of the preloaded coasters left the Bristol Channel on the 30 May bound for the Solent for mooring. They were;

Port	Ship/Owner		Cargo	Tons/Year	Mooring	B	Date
Swansea	*MoWT Bidassoa* (ex Fr.)			558 / 01	3N/b5	'O'	6th
"	*Edle* (Norwegian)			654 / 16	3N/b7	'O'	"
"	*Mari* (Norwegian)			565 / 25	3N/b4	'O'	"
"	*Sarnia* (Dorey)			711 / 23	3N/b9	'O'	"
"	*Skarv* (Norwegian)			852 / 23	3N/b3	'O'	"
"	*The President* (Hay)			926 / 36	3N/b8	'O'	"
Port Talbot	*MoWT Empire Cape*	(CP)		872 / 41	3N/b2	'O'	"
"	*Lottie R* (S & R)	"		972 / 37	3N/b11	'O'	"
Penarth	*Heien* (Norwegian)	A		995 / 26	3N/b9	'U'	"
Sharpness	*Cameo* (Robertson)	(CP)		946 / 37	3N/b1	'U'	"
"	*Starkenborgh* (Dutch)	"		878 / 41	3N/d10	'U'	"
Penarth	*MoWT Valborg* (D)	(A)		844 / 14	broke down		
Swansea	*Moelfre Rose* (Hughes)	(A)		631 / 31	4/d1	'O'	7th
"	*Rockleaze* (O&Wallis)	A		486 / 24	4/e3	'O'	"
Port Talbot	*Erna* (Dutch)	(CP)		361 / 40	4/e1	'O'	"
Barry	*Crewhill* (Kelly)			695 / 23	4/d2	'O'	"
Penarth	*Wallace Rose* (Hughes)	(A)		632 / 31	4/d6	'U'	"
Sharpness	*Hawarden Br.* (Sum's)	(CP)		297 / 40	4/e2	'U'	"
Portishead	*Cushendun* (Longstaff)			646 / 04	4/d4	'U'	"
"	*Gem* (Robertson)			640 / 24	4/d3	'U'	"
Avonmouth	*Fluor* (Robertson)	(A)		914 / 25	4/d7	WTF	"
?	*Chemong* (Collier)	(C)		?	4/d5	WTF	"

Abbreviations; A Ammunition. CP *Cased Petro.* **C** Coal. (*probable cargo*).

They would remain fully loaded until their Port Battalion hatch gangs joined them a week later. Certain ports in the Bristol Channel were dedicated to particular cargos, Port Talbot and Sharpness for cased petrol, Penarth and Swansea for ammunition. In the days to come these 22 coasters sailing up the English Channel from the west would be joined by another 33 from the east for final assembly prior to leaving as part of the initial assault convoys. Small, some old and of shallow draught, many would be beached in France for unloading, but

SOLENT ANCHORAGE FOR FORCE 'G' and COASTERS

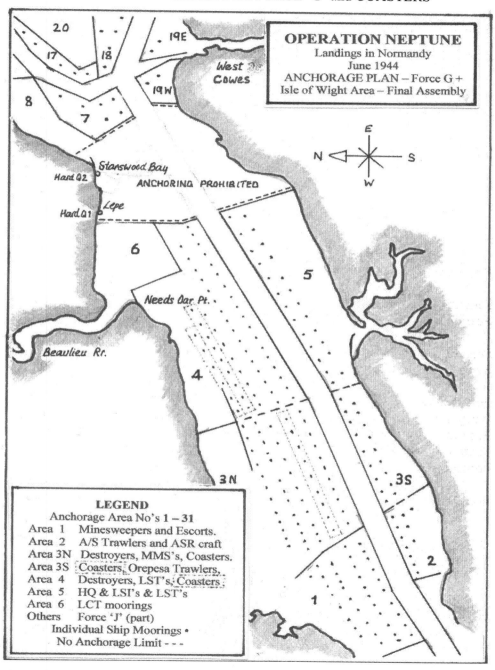

OPERATION NEPTUNE
Landings in Normandy
June 1944
ANCHORAGE PLAN – Force G +
Isle of Wight Area – Final Assembly

LEGEND
Anchorage Area No's 1 – 31
Area 1   Minesweepers and Escorts.
Area 2   A/S Trawlers and ASR craft
Area 3N   Destroyers, MMS's, Coasters.
Area 3S   Coasters, Orepesa Trawlers.
Area 4   Destroyers, LST's, Coasters
Area 5   HQ & LSI's & LST's
Area 6   LCT moorings
Others   Force 'J' (part)
Individual Ship Moorings •
No Anchorage Limit - - -

Note. Orientation has been altered for ease of viewing with true North to the left of the page rather than the convention generally used of north at the top of the page.

for now formed part of the armada of over 500 ships anchored between Hurst Castle in the west and Bembridge, Isle of Wight, in the east. How the vast anchorage of the Solent together with Spithead and Southampton Water containing so many ships was never attacked by the enemy remains not so much a mystery, but certainly amazing. Any enemy reconnaissance aircraft were kept well away by the squadrons of the RAF, Fleet Air Arm and the USAAC and the batteries of anti-aircraft artillery in the area. The odd Luftwaffe sortie was seen further west but the skies around Southampton and Portsmouth were kept clear. Likewise the navies kept the waters free of marauding E-boats and U-Boats, mindful of the disasters that befell the LST's in Exercise TIGER, only a few weeks previously.

Most coasters would return to their Bristol Channel departure ports for repeat cargos including more cased petrol from Llanelly. Here some 5,000 tons of aviation spirit had been stored by the American Armed forces and although some had been moved away an even bigger amount was stored prior to D-Day. A dump of 12,000 tons of cased petrol from nearby Llandarcy Refinery where there had been a loading facility for quite some time, was stockpiled right alongside North Dock. Forty-four coasters would be loaded up to August, when the Dock then specialised in ammunition loadings of barges. Shipping left on time, as well.

Photo: The former 'SS Oriente' then renamed the USAT Thomas H. Barry, another regular bringing troops into the Bristol Channel Ports. US Army Ships and Watercraft of World War II - Courtesy of Naval Institute Press

The size of the operation that Movement Control had to manage was becoming more and more evident especially at Swansea with the large number of troops that had to be out-loaded to Normandy. Meetings and dock site visits involving more and more senior officers were taking place, Lt. General Watson, General Officer Commanding Western Command together with Major General Halstead arrived on the 24th and two days later the US Army Service of Supply Commander for the ETO Major-General Lee turned up to see preparations for himself. Lt. Colonel Bevan was able to show how well prepared they were – even surprises such as the huge pile of unscheduled telegraph poles from the *Moremacswan* that had caused problems were loaded aboard 223 railway trucks ready for departure to Laybourne.

Another visitor to Swansea on the 27th was the American built but Royal Navy operated Landing Ship Dock *HMS Eastway*. Already a Mediterranean veteran, she demonstrated her carrying capacity when she offloaded various smaller LCT's and LCS whilst offshore, all craft making their way into the docks before reloading. Trials of these revolutionary 10,000 gross ton vessels as a LCT Repair Ship were not entirely successful but as semi-submergible landing ships they proved their worth with safe off loading of DUKW's and small craft, eventually evolving into the bigger amphibious assault ships of later years.

The second of the big combined trans-Atlantic convoys TCU24, this one bringing the 35th 'Santa Fe' Infantry Division had arrived on the twenty-fourth with over half the division coming in through Avonmouth. Aboard the *AP 111 General A E Anderson* were 5,000 troops glad to get ashore well in advance of their 3,587 comrades aboard the *USAT Thomas H Barry* which docked the following day having been held overnight at Barry Roads such was the congestion in the ports. *USAT Seatrain Texas* also docked and unloaded in Cardiff, closely followed by the *SS Examiner* on the twenty-eighth which had sailed independently from Belfast having deposited part of her cargo there. Seven of the nine troopships that were to be part of the BCPLBU Force came to the UK in this convoy: *Bienville, Borinquen, Excelsior, Exchequer, Explorer, George S Simonds* and the *Susan B. Anthony*. The *USAT George W. Goethals* had been in UK waters doing short troop transfer trips around the Irish Sea since arriving in mid April and the newest vessel, the C4 *SS Marine Raven* was yet to return following departure to New York with the TU11 convoy which docked 'stateside' on the 1 May.

Following a brief stopover in their UK arrival ports of Gourock and Liverpool, the ships masters received their sealed orders instructing them to proceed south to the Bristol Channel ports of Swansea, Cardiff and Newport and prepare for loading and embarkation of troops for another destination.

Having been freed of the 2,000 troops that she had transported to Liverpool the *Excelsior* called in at Milford Haven for victualing on the way around to her next destination, arriving at Newport on the 30 May. The next time she left port it would be for Normandy, France. All troop ships were selected at relatively short notice with possibly the exception being the *AP 72 Susan B Anthony*. Captain Gray and his crew, as experienced in assault landings as any, was classed as a reserve assault transport and could be transferred at very short notice away from the Bristol Channel to either Force 'O' or 'U'. Although not boasting of anywhere near as many LVCP's as those APA's and XAP's previously selected, the 'Susie B' and her 8 craft could certainly make up any sudden shortfall.

Photo: An 11,500 ton C4 troopship possibly the 'SS Marine Raven.'
(Courtesy of US Merchant Marine.)

Meanwhile other new-comers to Pontypridd were the men of the 94th Medical Gas Treatment Battalion under their commander William C. Bury from Pittsburgh, Pennsylvania. An advanced detachment had been working with the local constabulary in securing billets since their arrival from Bewdley in early May, but on the 25th the whole unit arrived by train. Travelling from the States aboard the *SS Uruguay* to Liverpool they were delighted to find that their homes for the next 10 weeks would be with individual Welsh families around Cilfynydd, Pontypridd and surrounding villages. Headquarters and Mess was set up in the Royal British Legion Hall which possessed a large hard standing nearby for the 55 vehicles that the unit had secured. An adjacent church provided a suitable venue for meetings as well. The unit was not part of Bradleys First Army, but became the designated Medical Holding Station for Patton's Third Army.

US Army cargo into the UK reached the dizzy height of 601,615 long tons during the incredibly busy month with the Bristol Channel Ports offloading 171,665 tons. Added to that and by the end of May there were another 13,814 troops landed in the Bristol Channel Port area despite the volume of shipping being assembled for out loading invasion troops, equipment and stores. The UK had now reached the total of being home to 1,671,010 US servicemen and women - less those of the USAAC and others who had lost their lives in the service of their country. Many, many more were to follow in both respects.

*****

Sub-Area 'U' Camps

All under control for the purposes of Marshalling by the Officer commanding the static detachment drawn from the 360th E (GS) Regiment.

Camp Racecourse
Chepstow, Mon. WBS XXIX District No. 40. Map Ref. VO 970160

Photo: 3472 CPE/UK/2081.19MAY47.F20"//16,400' 82SQDN. (WAGAPU).

A large camp with a capacity approaching 2,800 men with buildings adjoining the western side of the racecourse (pictured top left) further utilised. Built as a 'winter' tented camp, it was subsequently enlarged for its marshalling role with a summer camp extension on the high ground on the eastern side. Requiring major sewage and drainage work leave alone the usual Nissen huts and no less than 184 concrete bases; the work was carried out by the 366th E (GS) R, a black two battalion unit based there following their arrival on 10th October 1943. Their primary mission, as per WBS instructions, was camp expansion, reassessments and general construction with the 438th Engineer Dump Truck Company and their 55 tippers attached, until the completion of works in the middle of March '44. A notable achievement was linking the camp to the Sewage Treatment Works involving excavating and laying a 5,000 foot run of 6" pipe and building a pumping station for a waterborne flow over a 58' rise.

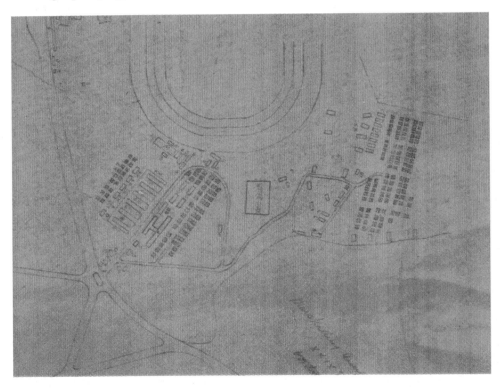

Plan: AHC/HS, ETOUSA. WBCE/Diag's/CL's. ADM 603-0/3. Courtesy of Fold3

Sunrise 4th June and serried ranks of infantry were drawn up ready for the road march to Chepstow Railway Station – all 244 vehicles preloaded. Second Battalion Surgeon William M. McConahey MD and other medics of the accompanying 315th Medical Battalion had already seen that heat exhaustion could be a problem but the men were aided by the coolness of the morning and marched in silence through the streets of Chepstow – any civilian early risers not surprised any more by tramping boots. Cardiff was the destination for the 2,710 troops and the S*S Explorer* and S*S Bienville*. Breakfast of hot coffee and doughnuts on the dockside beckoned! Chepstow Racecourse has thrived since the war, unlike Piercefield Park which overlooked the camp, the house suffering further ruin as it provided useful target practice for the 90th Infantry Division troops.

Camp Bulwark
Chepstow, Mon. WBS XXIX District No. 41. Map Ref. VO978135

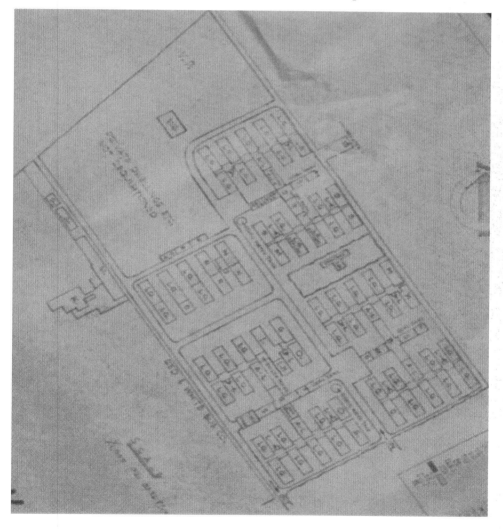

Plan: AHC/HS, ETOUSA. WBCE/Diag's/CL's. ADM 603-0/4. Courtesy of Fold3

A former British Army base converted into a camp for 1,300 Officers and men in a residential area accessed from Heol Alpha off Bulwark Road that runs from a junction on the notoriously steep A48 Hardwick hill west of Chepstow. Entirely hutted but requiring work by the 366th E (GS) R including hard-standing works being completed by 4th December '43. Units including the 174th FA Group HQ from VIII Corps and 26th Ordnance Battalion took station in early 1944, moving out by April. The 987th Field Artillery was here before being transferred right across the country to Clacton-on-Sea to work with the British 50th 'Tyne Tees' Infantry Division. Two of the 90th Division FA Battalions were marshalled here and today the camp is a mix of housing and light industry.

Camp Sedbury
Sedbury, Glos. WBS XXIX District No. 42. Map Ref. VO995153

Photo:3003UK/1997.3.APR.47.F20"//MULTIWBS4.16,400'58SQDN. (WAGAPU)

The smallest of all the South Wales Marshalling camps, entirely hutted similar to Bulwark and located at the end of a rural civilian street on the opposite bank of the River Wye to Chepstow, accessed via Tutshill on the A48. A limited amount of camp expansion and re-assessment work was carried out by the 366th E (GS) R between November '43 and end of January '44. The 690th FA Battalion and 187th FA Group Headquarters were based here before being moved out in April to allow the camp to be used for marshalling elements of the BCPLBU Force.

The three 357th battalions were well into their POM (Preparation for Overseas Movement) down in the Racecourse Camp before the Regimental Headquarters and support troops moved into Sedbury on the 20th having cleared the divisions' previous camps in Shropshire. Cardiff was to be their destination where the 483 men and 119 vehicles would link up with the rest of the Regiment for the voyage to UTAH beach.

Camp Llanmartin
Nr. Newport, Mon. WBS XXIX District No. 66 Map Ref. VO829098

Photo: Part 1044 CPE/UK 1828 4 November 1946. (Courtesy of WAGAPU).

Constructed around the same time as the similar camp at Cwrt-y-Gollen, Llanmartin was utilised as an incoming transit base for European Theatre of Operations United States Army (ETOUSA) troops prior to assignment to designated US Armies or Corps. Whereas some camps received a mixture of units, Llanmartin contained anti-aircraft units especially those with Automatic Weapons. By March various units had come and gone. However there were still a number (391st, 398th, 465th, 776th and 777th AAA AW Battalions) that would need new locations to enable the camp to be used for marshalling the BCPLBU Force.

One ack-ack unit though would remain until mid May before transferring to Selsey and have a special role. The 397th AAA AW revised its title and became the 397th Provisional Machine Gun Battalion, Batteries 'A' and 'B' being augmented by men from many different AAA battalions including Lt. John Sheehan and two sergeants of the 462nd Battalion, based at East Blockhouse, Pembs. They would be up front for the assault on OMAHA utilizing 50 calibre machine guns in both support and air defence roles. The other two batteries would man the AA guns on the US Mulberry Harbour 'A' Phoenix caissons. The 320 vehicles of the 358th Infantry Regiment were taken for loading on 1 June, drivers returning for final preparations. An advance detail of HQ and Battalion Officers went ahead on 3 June to the docks to prepare for their arrival of their men with other 90th Division troops. Then on the fourth, now divided into 33 boat groups, the battalions boarded trains at Magor, 1st and 2nd travelling to Newport and the *USAT Excelsior* and the 3/358th detraining at Cardiff to march to the *SS Bienville*.

Camp Llanover
Abergavenny, Mon. WBS XXIX District No.71 Map Ref. VO763300

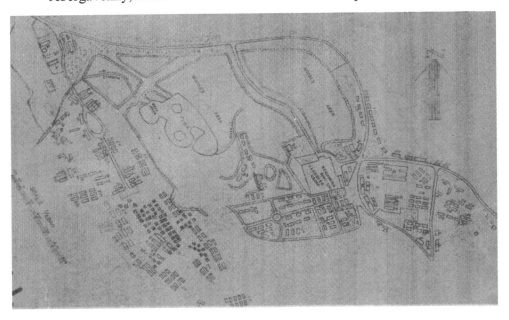

Plan: AHC/HS, ETOUSA. WBCE/Diag's/CL's. ADM 603-0/7. Courtesy of Fold3

The 200 acre gardens and estate were requisitioned for wartime use with only a small part of the original Hall in use, the 3 storey remainder having been demolished in 1936. Home to Lady Llanover, wife of Sir Benjamin Hall after whom 'Big Ben' is supposed to have been named, she was devoted to the use and retention of the Welsh language and culture and would probably been unimpressed with the changes to her lifetime home in the 20th century. The camp could accommodate over 3,000 troops with main gate access from the Pontypool to Abergavenny road with extensive hard-standings available surrounding the drive.

US Army occupation began with the establishment of the 164th Army Post Unit, there being only a small number of others in South Wales chiefly at Newport (516th) and Barry (134th). Mid '43 and with BOLERO getting under way units, chiefly anti-aircraft battalion's, began arriving prior to dispositions around the country. The 113th AA Group HQ was followed by the 481st, 601st and 863rd AAA AW battalions plus the advance party of the 128th AAA Gun battalion. All except the 113th Group, the 481st and Company 'B' 347th E (GS) R who had been carrying out expansion work left by the end of April. In their place came the 360th E (GS) R section to prepare for the biggest camp marshalling duty in the South Wales area.

Serial	Unit Name / Description	Men	Veh's
80	555th Signal Aviation Battalion (Type II)	119	31
81	834th Engineer Aviation Battalion	561	75
82	816th Engineer Aviation Bn. Recce Party	9	2
83	2029th Engineer Fire Fighting Platoon	22	7
84	332nd Signal Company HQ (Detachment)	15	3
85	926th Signal Battalion ASC Co. A (Det HQ Ops)	15	3
86	RAF Naval Land Section	11	2
87	327th Fighter Control Squadron A Ech.	109	31
88	555th Signal Aviation Battalion A Ech.	61	11
89	820th Engineer Aviation Battalion (less Recce)	687	100
90	HQ Engineer Command (Adv HQ Det)	22	5
91	395th Signal Company Aviation (Comms Plat)	15	3
92	8th Air Force Intransit Dept. (Ops Beach Party)	106	15
93	394th Signal Company Aviation (Ops Plat. AFSC)	15	3
94	1923rd Quartermaster Truck Company Aviation.	152	56
95	21st Weather Squadron Det. EE	15	3
96	40th Mb Com Squad Det. EE	12	4
97	HQ IX TASC Advance Detail.	54	10
98	8th Air Support Command	22	9
99	392nd Signal Control AF Detachment	14	3
100	3rd VHF Radio (Squadron Mob. Ops Plat)	40	8
101	900th Signal Depot Company (Mob Radio Team)	6	3
	502nd Port Battalion HQ/Det. & 270/1/2/3rd Co's.	928	

Llanover Park would be filled to overflowing mainly with USAAC troops of the IX Engineer Command whose task would be to prepare as soon as possible airfields immediately behind OMAHA beach for operation by the Tactical Air Command. None of the units had been based in this part of the country having trucked across England. The listing of the units by serial number indicates by their titles how much preparation work was to be carried out on the far shore as soon as the beach head was secure. The camp was bursting at the seams with almost 400 vehicles and over 3,000 men. Two-thirds marched to Penpergwm Station to go for embarkation, the remainder being trucked to Newport Docks for loading.

Not surprisingly Llanover became a POW Camp until 1946 when it was returned to its owner and is now privately owned again.

Camp Llantarnum
Newport, Mon. WBS XXIX District No. 74 Map Ref. VO752142

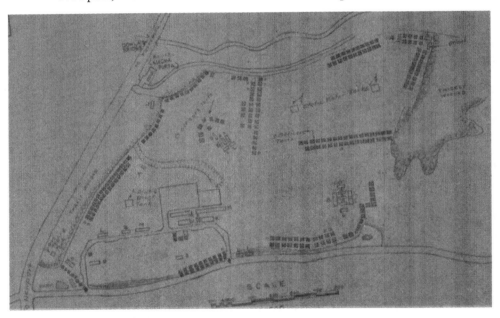

Plan: AHC/HS, ETOUSA. WBCE/Diag's/CL's. ADM 603-0/8. Courtesy of Fold3

A camp for 56 Officers and 1,240 men serving the needs of the 372nd E (GS)R HQ since mid March '44 having been built by 'Fox' Company with a section of the 418th Engineer Dump Truck Company before they were moved to the Barry expansion project.. Located on the main Newport to Pontypool thoroughfare at the Malthouse Road junction behind a screen of dense woodland, the camp was constructed on land previously requisitioned in 1941 from the Llantarnum Abbey estate. Lying south of the Magma Porta Gate and driveway to the Abbey, it was nicely secure behind a crenulated estate stone wall. Utilising both the 'company street' layout and edging the camp boundaries, the plan details officer tents towards the centre and a one way road around the Nissen hut mess's to the hard standing. Perhaps hard to believe that large numbers of troops from the 'Big Red One' Division were to be shipped to Normandy from South Wales, but it was inevitable that some like the Reconnaissance Troop would have a major role once the landing was secure, but not before. During the first few days of June 500 of the 1,374 troops that marched down the Newport Road to their ships were from the 16th Infantry Regiment and 1st ID men, the remainder being Port Battalion troops of the 6th Engineer Special Brigade. At the end of World War II, Camp Llantarnum was returned to its owners and became part of the original Abbey grounds, now extensive pastureland sandwiched between Newport Road and the new A4042. What was the entry and exit gates in the wall of the farm on Malthouse Road for trucks to the hard standings can still be seen, but the woods have gone.

Camp Cwrt-y-Gollen

Crickhowell, Mon. WBS XXIX District, No. 87 Map Ref. VO680380

Photo: Part 1084 106G/UK652 11JULY46 F/36"//MULTI (5) 540 SQDN. Courtesy of the Welsh Assembly Government Aerial Photographic Unit.

A beautifully clear image of the camp adjacent to the A40 with the River Usk visible bottom left. Requisitioned in the early part of the war with quadruple Maycrete prefab hut groupings familiar in this part of Wales, Cwrt-y-Gollen was designed as a Brigade Depot with a capacity of 112 Officers and 3,000 troops, making it the same size as both Llanover on the other side of Abergavenny and Llanmartin to the south near Newport. Only a small number of extra tents were erected for the marshalling role. A number of the existing British Army camps in Monmouthshire were used in 1943 to house the Advance Detachments of incoming US Forces prior to the arrival of entire battalions as part of the Operation BOLERO. The 744th Tank Battalion, the 258th FA Group and the 258th, 174th and 991st FA Battalions all passed through carrying out local fitness training and artillery 'zero-ing' new weapons on the Sennybridge Range. April came and with the camp needed for marshalling the incoming 90th Division, the units left for the 10,000 man Ludlow bivouac camp. Gen. Collins ordered Barton's 4th Infantry Division (the 'Ivy Leaves') to lead the way onto the Cotentin Peninsular beach at UTAH with the 90th Division to follow, so he attached the 1/359th & 3/359th Battalions with a ship-borne Glider Airborne Battalion from the 101st Airborne Division as back-up.

The 2/359th therefore found itself and its supportive elements with the less essential parts of the Regiment including HQ as part of the Bristol Channel Pre-Load Build-Up Force. Waterproofing, equipment checks and re-supply continued with all personnel confined to base by the end of May, then they were off, 2,800 men with 600 vehicles in advance, most marching to Abergavenny rail station to get to their ill-fated 8,100 ton troopship *AP 72 Susan B. Anthony* or the 10 MTV 'Liberty's in Newport Docks. Meanwhile the First and Third Battalions aboard LCI (L)'s were setting off from the South coast of England.

Cwrt-y-Gollen was converted into a Prisoner of War camp later, and then after the war the site became the British Army Junior Leaders Camp in the 1960's. More changes occurred and the camp became the 160th Brigade Depot covering Wales. Now part of it is the 'Robert Jones VC' Army Cadet Training Centre and the remainder sold off as a housing development.

Camp Dan-y-Parc

Gilwern, Mon. WBS, XXIX District, No. 89 Map Ref. VO670365

Requisitioned to create a camp on the southern and western side of the Harcourt family home and accessed from the Gilwern / Crickhowell A4077, the gardens had been landscaped in the 19th century by a new owner, the Beaufort Ironworks magnate Edward Kendall. Keen to emulate the country lifestyle of his business purchaser Sir Joseph Bailey (a Crawshay), Kendall created a spectacular addition to the estates of the Usk valley, rivalling Llanover, Glanusk, Llangattock Parks plus Cwrt-y-Gollen just across the river (see photo top right corner). Ownership passed to the Sandeman branch of the family who witnessed their idyllic landscape disappearance under concrete and tin, the damaged mansion (in trees at the right) being demolished in the 1950's.

Photo: Part 1084 106G/UK652 11JULY46 F/36"//MULTI (5) 540 SQDN.
Courtesy of the Welsh Assembly Government Aerial Photographic Unit.

The photograph taken early in the morning clearly defines the quadruple grouping of Nissen hut messes, offices, ablutions and stores for the accommodation of 1,600 officers and men. Marshalling of invasion troops began under the care of the men of the 360th E (GS) R in May. The two ESB's under the command of the Provisional Engineer Special Brigade Group had specific roles to play in the OMAHA beach part of NEPTUNE. The 5th ESB attached to the 1st ID had a loading priority over the 6th ESB (attached 29th ID), so the reserves from South Wales reflected that situation. Therefore both ESB's had troops at Dan-y-Parc for shipment.

Some 1,700 men would leave camp between the 1st and 3rd June, all 270 vehicles having gone for pre-loading a couple of days earlier. Most would be trucked to Newport, although the entire 203rd ECB of the 6th ESB which had come up from their Paignton camp would entrain at Abergavenny to journey to the Kings Dock in Swansea to board the *SS Marine Raven*.

The camp returned to private ownership following use as emergency accommodation for civilian displaced persons.

Camp Llangattock Park
Crickhowell, Mon. WBS XXIX District No. 91. Map Ref. VO657388

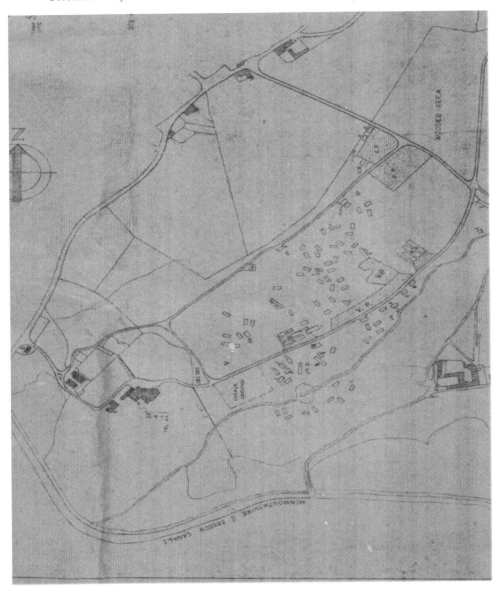

Plan: AHC/HS, ETOUSA. WBCE/Diag's/CL's. ADM 603-0/12. Courtesy of Fold3

The valley of the River Usk contained a number of beautiful estates and mansions built during the later part of the 19th century including Llangattock Park. Not as big as many but notable as the summer residence and hunting lodge of the

Duke of Beaufort. Much work was carried out in the requisitioned park by the 366th E (GS) R troops during the winter of !943/44 to bring the camp up to the standard required by the Western Base Section XXIV District Headquarters at nearby Abergavenny. Cook-houses, Nissen huts, water towers, latrines, ablutions, roads, hard-standings and 3,500 feet of water and drainage systems were installed. The 360 E (GS) R static detachment found the camp ready and waiting.

A Reserve camp containing troops scheduled for both OMAHA and UTAH beaches. First to arrive on the 14th and 15th May were the tail-ends of some of the Infantry Regiments that made up the 29th Infantry Division including those of the ill-fated 116th Regiment which was attached to the First Division for the actual assault. and men of the 115th Regiment and Headquarters Battery 227th FA Battalion, their 155mm firing batteries all being aboard the LST's of Force 'B' sailing from Cornwall. Divisional troops not required for the Invasion included the 29th Reconnaissance Squadron, the MP Platoon and 104th Medical Battalion, plus the 17th Field Observation Battalion from V Corps. The UTAH bound contingent entered camp by the 18th when the 90th Division Reconnaissance Squadron arrived with Company 'C' 315th Medical Battalion. Over 400 men would leave in three separate echelons between the 1st and 3rd June, some being trucked to Abergavenny Station, and others going by road to Newport Docks.

Photo: Llangattock Park, Crickhowell. (Courtesy of Peter Davis Collection.)

Following the war Llangattock Park Camp returned to being part of the estate.

Camp Glanusk Park
Crickhowell, Mon. WBS XXIX District No. 93. Map Ref. VO640420

Built in 1862 by Sir Joseph Bailey with the fortune created by the Richard Crawshay of Cyfartha Ironworks in Merthyr Tydfil and set amidst beautiful parkland bordering the River Usk, Glanusk became a camp in the early part of

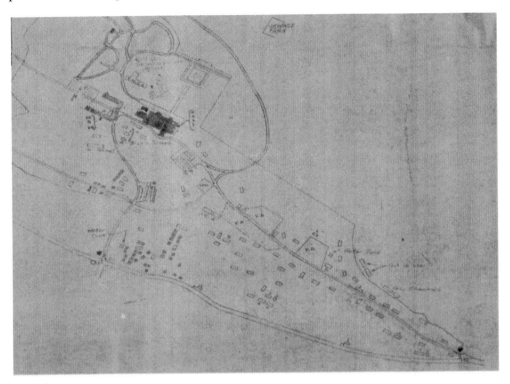

Plan: AHC/HS, ETOUSA. WBCE/Diag's/CL's. ADM 603-0/13. Courtesy of Fold3

the war but had few of the hallmarks of others in the area as the mansion and stables housed Headquarters and various other sections of occupying troops. Some huts immediately adjacent on the north side of the main house were of British Army origin and not used by US Forces, accommodations being provided in widely spaced Nissen huts adjoining the access from the B4558 Cwm Crawnon Road. The original main entrance through the Gate House (now called the Tower) bridge over the River Usk to the north was also not used. Later pyramid tents were added by the 1/366th E (GS) R which also installed a new electrical system for the entire camp together with extensive vehicle hard-standings and roads between November '43 and April '44. Initially home to the Norwegian-American 99th Infantry Battalion, they were gone by the first day of May, with the 360th E (GS) R detachment arriving for marshalling duty. Some of General Collins VII Corps soldiers arrived two weeks later including Troop 'B' & 'C' of the 4th Cavalry Squadron, Company 'B' 507th MP Battalion and the 574th Medical Ambulance Company. Finally the 187th Port Company (attached to 494th Battalion) arrived from their Rhondda Fawr billets on the 16th; all men would entrain at Abergavenny Railway Station to ship out from Newport destined for UTAH beach.

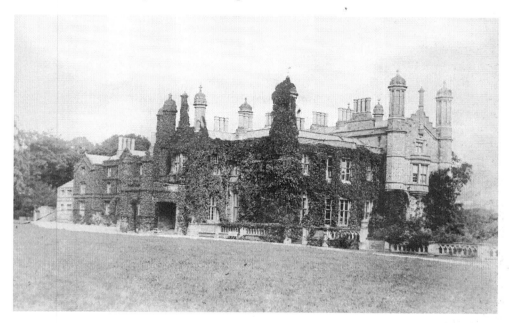

Photo: Glanusk Park. Courtesy of Glanusk Park Estate.

Bailey's grand and badly damaged Glanusk Park House was demolished after the war but the estate has been returned to its former glory.

The area contained the largest number of Marshalling Camps in South Wales and was also home to a number of sub-depots set up to support the exodus of invasion build up units. Ordnance Sub-depot 0-635 at Tredegar House, just outside Newport came under control of G-40 at Barry and handled large numbers of vehicles from its site to the rear of the Main House. Leading up to D-Day, storage areas include the dual carriageway Forge Lane approaching Bassaleg which had the carriageways closed to traffic and was full of heavily laden trucks ready for loading and embarkation at Newport docks. At Abergavenny a Quartermaster Distribution sub-depot was created by the 366th E (GS) R to provide basic Class 1 supplies and across near Lord Raglans' Cefn-Tilla Court, a Petrol, Oil and Lubricants sub-depot provided the vehicular requirements on part of a field that is now the Usk Agricultural Show Ground.

*****

Sub-Area 'V' Camps

Camp Heath
Cardiff, Glam. WBS, XXIX District, No. 98 Map Ref. VO 623013

A totally hutted camp constructed for the British Army in the early part of the war on the requisitioned Heath Park Estate. Before US troops arrived, extensive air raid precautions had been carried out with the installation of bunkers around the site, the War Department continuing to have use of the facilities. The US 36th Replacement Battalion was in occupation by 1944, looking after guard duties and the Casual Detachment No.5 from the First Field Force Replacement Depot at Llandaff. By the middle of May they were off to Braunton at the now quiet ATC.

Photo: Heath, Cardiff 4021 G/UK.1502. 13 MAY.46F20"//541SQDN. (WAGAPU).

Advance Headquarters of the 90th Infantry Division made their final preparations with the advance echelon arriving on 9 May followed by over 1,700 men on the 14th. The Quartermasters were kept busy ensuring all troops were fully equipped with their personal equipment and dress, most men being pleased to be in a regular barracks rather than the more usual tents. General Sam Williams, deputy division commander and Advance Headquarters staff would not be marching down to Cardiff Docks unlike the rest of the men at Heath. Instead they would go to Newport to board the *AP72 Susan B. Anthony* ready to get ashore quickly and get the 90th to support the 4th Infantry Division as per orders.

Camp St. Mellons

Nr Cardiff, Glamorgan. WBS, XXIX District, No. 88. Map Ref. VT685033

Constructed by 372nd 2 Engineer (GS) Regiment Company 'B' during late '43 on St. Mellons Golf Club south of the A48 Cardiff /Newport road (visible top left). The slightly 'fuzzy' aerial photo still reveals a typical fairly spacious arrangement of tented 'company streets' for 56 Officers & 1,550 men grouped around the central core of Nissen hut facilities with truck parking to the west adjoining the lane that would become Vaendre Close. Main Gate with Guardhouse and Headquarters was naturally near the main road, but there was an additional gate off the lane down at the south and downhill end of the vehicle parks. Company 'F' completed the work before preparations began for full occupation with the arrival of a platoon from the 360th E (GS) R, assigned to undertake 'hospitality'

Photo: St. Mellons.3031.106G/UK1509.13MAY.46F/20"//541 SQDN. (WAGAPU).

duties in the 15 camps of the Eastern part of S. Wales just like the 373rd EGSR were doing in the 11 to the west. Senior Officers from both the First Army and SOS Headquarters in Cheltenham undertook moral boosting visits to the troops during the lead-up to the Normandy Invasion and Eisenhower's Deputy Commander of the ETO Major-General Lee inspected Heath Camp (90th Div HQ) and St. Mellons (2nd Div) on 21st May. On 3 June 1,331 troops would march out, the two 38th Battalions taking the train from Marshfield to Swansea on 3rd June bound for their troopship, USAT *Gen. George S. Simonds* and OMAHA beach, the balance of 362 troops and 213 vehicles off by road for embarkation elsewhere. After the war the camp reverted to a golf course before house development started.

Camp Pontllanfraith
Pontllanfraith, Glam. WBS, XXIX District, No. 94 Map Ref. VO 623170

Photo: Pontllanfraith. 3G/TUD/T193AUG.45.F/6" (154.7)//38SQDN. (WAGAPU).

An unusual location for a camp in many ways, up above the Rhymney and Sirhowy valleys and adjoining Penllyn housing estate. Constructed by the 2/372 E (GS) R, the extensive site was designed for 2,500 men with options for enlargement if necessary. First US troops in occupation during early '44 were artillery units fresh from the States with the advance detail of the 204th FA Battalion and the entire 270th FA Battalion of the Third Army minus their 240mm howitzers. Continual improvement works were attempted to combat the ever present mud which continued to be a problem right up through the concentration period. Strongest memories were of the ever pervading smell of coal smoke and the presence of clinging mud. Despite hard-standings, over 400 vehicles including tracked artillery on site and 2,300 troops, it was always going to be messy.

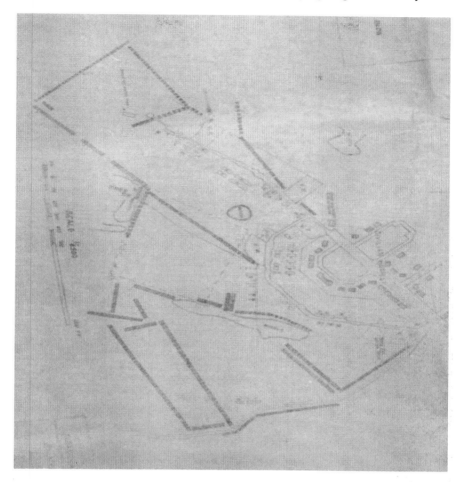

Plan: AHC/HS, ETOUSA. WBCE/Diag's/CL's. ADM 603-0/14. Courtesy of Fold3

Whilst mechanics were kept busy waterproofing vehicles and extending vertical exhausts, many men were bored sick. Confined behind barbed wire with foul weather most of the time, many were glad when they were finally on their way. Vehicles would leave for loading aboard the MTV's in Cardiff and Newport, so in 3 increments on 2 June troops entrained at the nearby railway station.

The 42nd Field Hospital platoons they were trucked to Newport where the Second Platoon boarded the *AP72* with the others loading at Barry. The 294th ECB had already lost 29 men in an accident during training on March 20th and it certainly seemed fate was against them, for they were also loaded on the *AP72 Susan B Anthony*. The 'Susie B' was the only troopship to be lost by the Americans during the assault period. The area is now housing with some common land remaining.

Camp St. Mary's Hill

Nr. Bridgend, Glam. WBS, XXIX District, No. 131 Map Ref. VO 4002

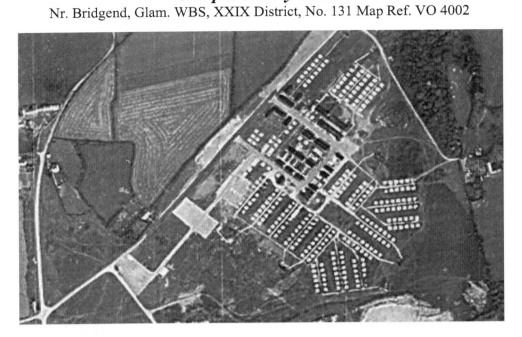

Photo: St. Mary Hill 3059 106g/uk/844.25 SEP45 F/20"//541SQDN (WAGAPU)

The 1/372nd Engineer (GS) Regiment from their base at the former munitions worker hostel at Island Farm, Bridgend began work in September on an open moorland site of Mynydd Ruthin, later found to be of strategic importance. Rapid construction, aggregate available from the nearby quarry (see bottom of picture) enabled the engineers to move on to other sites, leaving the camp occupied by the 50th Replacement Battalion and 21st PRS. Once complete the hutted facilities and pyramid tents and extensive parking/assembly plots for troop carrying trucks surrounded by double fences, St. Mary's Hill housed 1,500 men with ease. Company 'streets' of tents on concrete bases with good pathways made for a dry, but windy winter camp, one of 5 camps in Sub-area 'V' serving EA Cardiff.

Outside the camp to the north-west the widened road provided further truck parking with the junction to the north/south road within a matter of yards – visible in the bottom left corner of the photo. Travelling south to the village of Pentre Meyrick, convoys could access the main A48 to Cardiff. Troops marshalled at Camp 131 were destined for 'UTAH' beach as part of Collins VII Corps or 82nd Airborne. The most significant element were airborne troops who had to travel by sea either because there was insufficient aircraft 'lift' capability or they were held back as a reserve element. The 'All-American' parachute & glider troops flew from their East Midlands airfields on the night of 5 June with some PFA. RAF Llandow was nearby if aircraft came available! The site is now common land.

Camp Heronston
Bridgend, Glam. WBS, XXIX District, No. 137 Map Ref. VT350998

Another completely new camp built by the 2/372 Engineer (General Service) Regiment in the autumn of 1943 on ground immediately adjacent to the GWR rail line south of Bridgend. Not particularly large as it would only have accommodation for 750 officers and men and appeared to have had limited numbers of concreted tent bases for winter occupation, the majority of 'squares' being already quite faded by 1946. Limited land availability between the railway

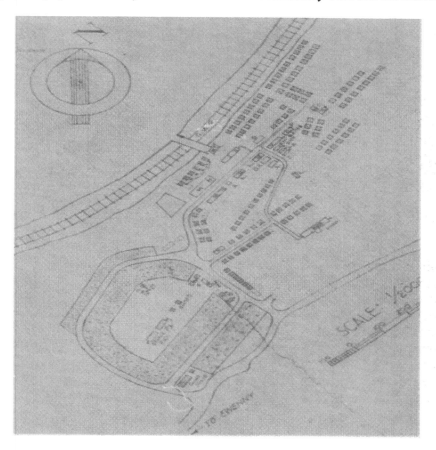

Plan: AHC/HS, ETOUSA. WBCE/Diag's/CL's. ADM 603-0/22. Courtesy of Fold3

and Heronston Lane resulted in the hard-standings being located to the south near the main gate. Heronston for several months was only home to the 455th and 456th Replacement Companies from the 79th Replacement Battalion HQ at Kenfig Burrows. However that meant they could carry out their duties of training the Detachment No 8 from the First Field Force Depot at Llandaff. Constant incoming and rotation of replacements in the ETO was necessary as preparations for the invasion gathered place. All assault infantry and artillery units were enlarged to 20% over-strength to cover losses. Captain George W. Cearly CE and part of his Company 'E' 373rd E(GS)R arrived on 15 April to undertake marshalling duties for both Officers of the 82nd Airborne Divisional and Artillery HQ's that were here with the greater part of the Medical, Service and Quartermaster Company's.

Photo: Part 3018. 541/5:6.5.48:F20"//16,600. (WAGAPU)

The 782nd Ordnance Co. and the 325th Glider Infantry Regiment Service Company were present and the attached Fourth Platoon of the 603rd Quartermaster Graves Registration Company. Finally making up the total group was the MP platoon. Marshalling Area 'V' embarkation port was Cardiff and on the 3 June most troops would march out to entrain at Bridgend Station.

*****

Sub-Area 'W' Camps

Camp St Donats Castle
Llantwit Major, Glam. WBS, XXIX District, No. 133 Map Ref. VT375898

One of the grandest of locations for US troops in South Wales was the old home of Randolph Hearst, newspaper magnate and philanthropist. Renowned for legendary parties in the thirties with Hollywood stars a-plenty, there were many young officers who found themselves occupying rooms of mind boggling splendour albeit slightly more sparse by the time they arrived. The surrounding camp comprised Nissens, pyramid tents, and wood prefab huts built by the British for 28 Officers & 692 men.

2nd Infantry Division Insignia.   *St. Donats Castle facing south to the sea.*

In October '43 half of the Third Battalion 109th Infantry Regiment of the 28th 'Keystone' Division arrived with their HQ and HQ Company plus 'I' and 'K' companies and part of the Service Company, the remainder being nearby at St. Athens and the Miners Rest Camp. Come April and they were off to Wiltshire exchanging places with their opposite numbers from the 9th Infantry. They in turn marshalled elsewhere and 'F' Co of 373rd E (GS) R under Lt. Warren L. Downs CE moved in on the 15th to take on the camps new role. St. Donats was to be the Marshalling HQ for the 2nd ID under the 'two star' Maj.-General Walter M Robertson. Movement orders were received and on the 3rd and 4th the troops would march out to Llantwit Major Railway Station bound for Barry, Cardiff and Swansea to board the *SS Marine Raven*. During the early hours, in full battledress, the men marched to the train station arriving in their respective Embarkation Ports as dawn broke, ready to go. St. Donat's continues today as Atlantic College.

Camp Wenvoe
Nr. Barry, Glam. WBS, XXIX District, No. 111. Map Ref. VT565925

Another golf course disappeared in late '43 under tin, tarpaulin, canvas and concrete, Wenvoe being built by 372nd E (GS) R Company E. No sooner than it was complete and occupied, then WBS decided to expand it as BOLERO got into full swing and NEPTUNE/OVERLORD was enlarged. Pentrecoed Woods opposite provided a good location for an assault course which was heavily used.

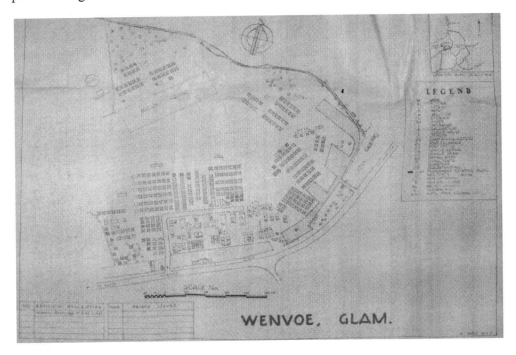

Plan: AHC/HS, ETOUSA. WBCE/Diag's/CL's. ADM 603-0/18. Courtesy of Fold3

Home to the 771st Tank Destroyer battalion and replacements, they were gone by mid April as Concentration and Marshalling for the Invasion began. The 3rd Battalion 9th RCT with their 'A' Company 2nd Engineers and 38th FA Battalion were into camp by mid May together with attendant detachments and Corps troops, including the 447th AAA AW Battalion and a Battery of the 535 Battalion. Almost 300 vehicles and 2,200 troops were at Wenvoe ready for embarkation when they were joined by the 82nd Airborne Division attached truck Company of 130 men and 56 deuce and a halves loaded with kit. Very late arrivals, in fact on the day of departure, was the 382nd Medical Collection Company (53rd Medical Battalion) up from Exeter with their ambulances. The Infantry and Artillery left for Swansea by train from Wenvoe Station with the Artillery troops (weapons already aboard ship) marching to Barry Docks and a few being transported by trucks.

Camp Barry (Golf Course)
Barry, Glam. WBS, XXIX District, No. 112 Map Ref. VT555920

Covering part of the Brynmill Golf Course next to Port Road (the clubhouse being the largest dark coloured building) an extensive winter camp built by 'E' and 'F' companies 372nd E (GS) R with summer enlargement to eventually hold 56 Officers and 1,546 men. Layout of the camp illustrated that often two different

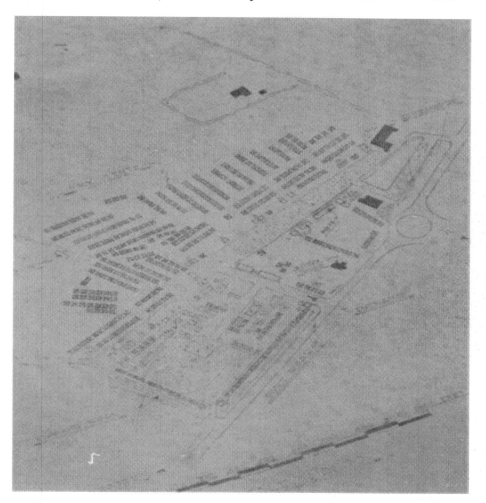

Plan: AHC/HS, ETOUSA. WBCE/Diag's/CL's. ADM 603-0/17. Courtesy of Fold3

Styles adopted by US Engineers were used on one site – peripheral tent accommodation on field edges and the more common 'company street' formations. By 1950, as the photo shows, many of the Nissen huts and tent bases had been removed. Lt. Leonard C. Welles CE with his First Platoon of Company 'D' 373rd E

(GS) R catered for the combat troopers with the 'Indianhead' shoulder patch that arrived on 16 May from their concentration at Margam and Kenfig Burrows. Organisation of this particular Marshalling Camp couldn't have been easier, apart from the continual re-supply of lost personal items. The entire camp was taken up by the 9th RCT which would lead the 2nd Division into action, with the Third Battalion plus 'A' Co 2nd ECB just up the road at Camp Wenvoe. They received a visit by First Army Commander Gen. Bradley prior to embarkation and then on June 3rd 1,888 men would leave for Wenvoe Station, all 285 vehicles plus 733 men going by road to embarkation points the day before. The Infantry were destined for Swansea and the *USAT George Goethals,* the artillery scheduled for loading among others onto the MTV *Charles Sumner* in Barry Docks

Photo: Composite provided by WAG Aerial Photographic Unit

The camp was quickly dismantled after the war, land requirement for housing.

Camp Kenfig Burrows
Kenfig Hill, Glam. WBS, XXIX District, No. 145 Map Ref. VT248020

The first camp constructed by 372nd Engineer (GS) Regiment during the autumn of '43 adjoining the 'P & K' golf course on the sandy 'burrows' close to the coast. The April '44 plan is confirmed by the May '47 photo although there appears to be one main difference. Either the two 'streets' of winter tent bases on the left (west) of the plan were proposed but never laid, or they were only for summer time use. Alternatively as there is nothing apparent, perhaps the legendary 'shifting sands' removed all trace! In late October the arrival 28th 'Keystone' Infantry Division in S. Wales saw the 1/109th Regiment take up residence, but

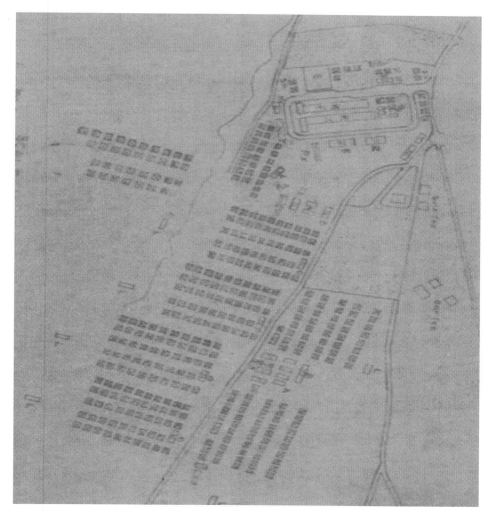

Plan: AHC/HS, ETOUSA. WBCE/Diag's/CL's. ADM 603-0/24. Courtesy of Fold3

following full RCT exercises and training at the ATC at Woolacombe in December they returned to a new camp at Penclawdd in north Gower. The 118th Infantry Regt. (Separate) Company 'H' and the Anti-tank Company which had various WBS and 1st Army LOC duties in the area remained with the 78 Replacement Battalion.

Photo: Kenfig Burrows 4061 CPE/UK2081.19MAY47.F20"/116.400'82SQDN. Courtesy of Welsh Assembly Government Aerial Photographic Unit.

The 'concentration' period began with the 28th Division departure and 2nd Division arrival. Chosen as a Marshalling Camp, further changes took place with all units being moved out. Third Platoon Company A. 373rd E (GS) R arrived as static 'housemaid' troops to provide for major elements of the 1/38th RCT, 'G' Company and Service, Cannon and Anti-tank Companies plus V Corps troops. On 3rd June 945 infantrymen would march out to the railhead at Pyle Station followed by another column on the 4th of 1,200 men.

Camp Island Farm
Bridgend, Glam. WBS, XXIX District, No. 139. Map Ref. VT345998

Built on farmland to house female workers employed at the Bridgend Munitions factory nearby, the barrack like conditions were unpopular, many women preferring to travel 20 to 30 miles from home. The camp therefore remained under care and maintenance until the US army arrived. Sited on the A48 Cardiff/Swansea main highway with access to training areas on the coast at Merthyr Mawr, the camp was ideally situated with accommodations eventually for 56 Officers and 1,500 men. October came and the 2/109th Infantry Regiment and the 108th FA Bn. (28th Infantry Division) fully occupied the camp. Happy times were had through Christmas and the New Year before the Division left for Chiseldon and the 'Indianhead's took their place.

Photo: Part 3018. 541/5:6.5.48:F20"//16,600. Courtesy WAGAPU.

First Platoon Co.'E' 372nd E (GS) R undertook static duties when Island Farm became an Area 'W' Marshalling Camp (Reserve) and was occupied by just the 518th and 519th Port Battalions of the 1st ESB. 1,400 men left the camp in two increments on 2nd and 3rd June, one third marching to the station to entrain, two thirds by truck. Later the camp became the celebrated POW Camp 198 Island Farm which witnessed a mass escape of German POW's. Senior Officers such as Field Marshall Von Rundstedt were held here prior to the Nuremberg War Trials. Now just the Chapel remains as a testimony to the events of bygone years.

Sub-Area 'X' Camps

Camp Margam Park
Port Talbot, Glam. WBS, XXIX District, No. 146/7. Map Ref. VO250080

The image below shows a full size plan of the double camp No.146 Margam Castle and 147 Margam Park created by the Engineer Section of the WBS dated 14 April 1944, being one of the series of plans of all proposed Marshalling Camps in South Wales. All existing buildings are blackened, the largest (right centre) being the main house with the long Orangery, Church and stables and recreation building surrounding the hard-standing (centre). Home of the Talbots, the entire estate was requisitioned with troop accommodation provided in existing buildings, just a few pyramid tents erected for static enlisted men north of the main house. There are also faint outlines of 'summer' tents along the driveway.

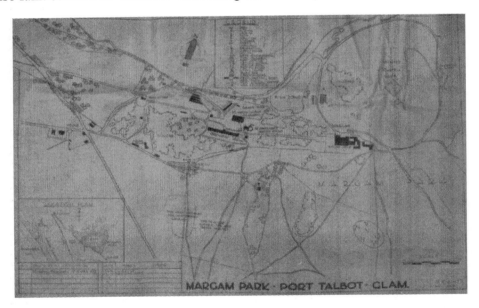

Plan: AHC/HS, ETOUSA. WBCE/Diag's/CL's. ADM 603-0/25. Courtesy of Fold3

Site of one of Eisenhower's celebrated visits on 1 April 1944 when he addressed troops whilst standing on a jeep, the double camp had extensive use but was by no means full for the marshalling duties provided by the 372nd E (GS) R Company 'A' 1st Platoon which greeted the troops, over 500 men with 100 vehicles leaving between 2nd and 4th June on foot and truck to embark on coasters in the shadow of the steelworks at Port Talbot. The 2nd QM Co. was aboard just one ship unusually and bedded down on deck beneath canvas! The estate including the Orangery is now a tourist & leisure amenity run by the City & County of Swansea.

Camp Manselton
Swansea, Glam. WBS. XXIX District, No. 170. Map Ref. VO 088132

A camp for the 5th ESB constructed by the 95th E (GS) R started on the 28th September 1943 on Manselton Golf Course. All camps were constructed to guideline plans provided by WBS District 29 Engineer - the enlarged extract shown below is an example of how detailed these overall plans were, although as this is a revision dated 18th May of the 14th April original, it would suggest it is an 'as built' plan. Three of the golf club 'greens' are shown to have been preserved - two of which probably suffered as they were adjoining vehicle parks! The usual 'winter camp' concrete tent bases appear on plan as crossed squares with the faded versions evidence of additional 'summer camp' provision. Main gate gave access from the south with Camp Headquarters immediately adjacent. A wet and windy location on Penylan Hill with a view over Swansea probably not appreciated!

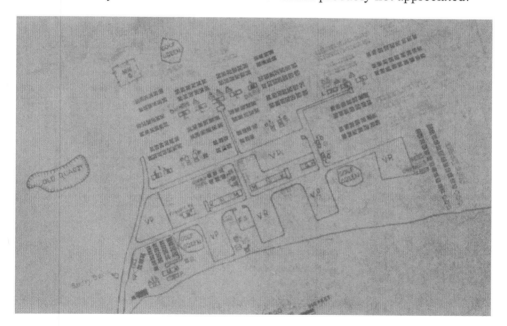

Plan: AHC/HS, ETOUSA. WBCE/Diag's/CL's. ADM 603-0/26. Courtesy of Fold3

Over 1,100 troops were looked after by Lt. Jack Power and Second Platoon Company B, 373rd Engineers prior to leaving by truck or marching to Swansea Station or the Docks for embarkation. Most destined for UTAH beach there were men from Collins VII Corps plus 82nd and 101st Airborne Divisions. OMAHA bound were the hatch gangs of the 517th Port Battalion of the 6th ESB.

Occupation of the site continued until dismantling after the war, with the ever increasing need for new housing resulting in the whole former camp disappearing as the land became part of the Penylan Estate.

Camp Singleton
Swansea, Glam. WBS, XXIX District, No. 174. Map Ref. VO 076140

The US Army extension to the original Transit Camp is clear on the Singleton site. Oystermouth Road, GWR and Mumbles Railway skirt the beach at the bottom right corner and Main Gate on Sketty Lane opposite King George V fields leads to truck parks surrounding the tree knoll.

Photo:Singleton5333/3G.TUD.UK109PARTIV1APR46.F12"//90 SQDN WAGAPU.

Camp construction had began on 28th September 1943 by the 95th Engineer General Service Regiment, but they were transferred to other works by the time the first resident troops arrived in October - the 37th ECB under Lt-Colonel Lionel F. Smith being bused from their troopship, the *USAT Borinquen* in the Docks on November 2nd to complete the work on their new home. Tents had been erected over concrete bases and a few Nissen huts put up, but after an Atlantic crossing it was hardly "dry land" – the site was a quagmire, inhabited only by the newly arrived 1119th Engineer Combat Group Headquarters Company. Three days later Company 'B' 348th ECB joined the fun plus 294th Joint Signal Company. Marshalling arrivals commenced on 15 May with the 517th Port Battalion Companies in on the 31st. The site plus adjoining land has been developed and is now part of the extensive grounds of Singleton Hospital and associated car parks.

Camp Mynydd Lliw No's. 1 & 2
Swansea, Glam. WBS, XXIX District, No. 180. Map Ref. VO 0411241

An extended large double camp with No. 1 to the north straddling Allt-y-Graban Road and No.2 to south. Bryn Lliw colliery and tip lies to the bottom left of the photograph and the storage area roadway for 'boxed' vehicles referred to in the text

Photo: Mynydd Lliw 4004 106GUK1419.15APR46.F20"//541SQDN. (WAGAPU)

is clearly visible. The 'halo' effect of the concrete tent bases makes them stand out from the faded patches of additional tents that can be seen near the colliery site at bottom left of the photograph. The camps were sandwiched between rail tracks, in a slightly un-populated and remote area given over to industrial waste, agriculture and scrubland. They comprised part of the 5th Engineer Special Brigade group of camps and the C/O of the 533rd Quartermaster Battalion based in No 1 camp became the Commandant and his troops plus those of the 61st Medical Battalion also in camp had been regulars on the training marches to Gower.

Use of the camps continued with less frequency until demolition, although the concrete 'winter' tent and Nissen hut bases can still be found in the undergrowth adjacent to Allt Y Graban road that links Pontlliw and Grovesend. The site is now crossed by the M4 running between Junctions 37 Swansea West and 38 Llanelli from bottom right to top left of photograph. The former landfill tip for the West Glamorgan County Council also covers part of Camp No.2 as well. The final act was about to take place. The men of the assaulting Divisions and support elements had been chosen; they had been concentrated in their respective areas, marshalled and kitted out. Next stop France.

Photo: US troops marching to the ships 'somewhere in Britain'. (IWM)

All over the south of the country columns of marching troops, convoys of truck-born soldiers and trainloads of infantry were heading to the ports for boarding. Lt Clement Powell with his HQ troops and part of Company 'B' 373rd E (GS) R provided housekeeping duties at both camps for the 2,100 troops of the 2nd Division. There were men of the 29th 'Blue and Gray' in camp as well with the over strengths reserves of the 224th and 227th FA Battalions plus the 121st ECB. Finally all and including 40 Division MP's left by train from Gorseinon.

Camp Corner House, Scurlage
Scurlage, Glam. WBS, XXIX District, No.192 Map Ref. VN 908907

Photo: Scurlage. US 7PH GP LOC 202 6-3-44 F24" SECRET. WAGAPU.

The invasion planning grew in size and intensity during early 1944, so much so that S.Wales had became a Marshalling Area in its own right to compliment those of Cornwall, Devon and others around the English south coast.

Camp Corner House, its amphibian role complete, became home to a number of SOS troops including HQ and part of Company 'C' 373rd Engineer General Service Regiment under Lt. John F Ritter CE whose responsibility was to ensure the incoming Field Service assault troops of the 2nd Infantry Division were well looked after and got everything they needed prior to leaving for France as part of the US First Army. Marshalling sub-area 'X' consisted therefore of 6 camps with Scurlage being the furthest from its embarkation port of Swansea.

One of the few aerial photographs of South Wales shot prior to D-Day included in this book is that taken by a USAAC F5 (Lightning) aircraft from a squadron of the US 7th Photographic Reconnaissance Group based at Mount Farm, Oxfordshire in March '44. The overview reveals a double camp layout plan not conforming to any other camp in South Wales. However it is uncannily similar to those of Sturt Common and Kinlet Park in Shropshire that were laid out in the last month of 1943 by the 373rd Engineer General Service Regiment under Western Base Section Engineer directives. The 95th Engineers had been transferred to relieve them and continued with building the camps and it could be that part of the reason was that they were already familiar with the design of these double sized camps having built the Amphibious Training site at Camp Corner House.

Residents at that time have memories of black US soldiers working in this area of Gower around the time although the Regimental History does not mention Scurlage by name. They were the only Engineer Regiment around based at the Clase Farm (Morriston) Camp from where they also began construction work at Mynydd Lliw. Although a housing development has covered part of the Corner House Camp adjoining the Rhossili road, the remainder looks much the same in 2019, less the tents and huts, of course. The Port Eynon Road is unchanged here, hedged with fertile meadows behind.

In summary it is worth taking an overall review of the size of the Swansea element that comprised the Bristol Channel Pre-Loaded Build-Up Force – the USAT's *George W. Goethals*, *Borinquen*, *George S. Simonds*, *Exchequer* and *SS Marine Raven*, providing seaborne lift for over 10,000 men. Another 22 coastal type MTV's were at the Prince of Wales Dock Tennant berths No's 1, 2, 3 and Rose, carrying a further total of 3,631 troops. The marshalling sub-area 'X' lift also comprised 3 more MTV's that loaded at the wharf in Port Talbot with V Corps troops marshalled at Margam Park, all in all 14,000 men and almost 1,000 vehicles.

All planning, concentration and marshalling was complete and Operation NEPTUNE was now underway. The British Army Movement Control was in charge of the embarkation of troops (with the assistance of the 17th Major Port personnel in South Wales) and then the Navy would take over under the Allied Naval Commander in Chief Admiral Bertrand H Ramsey.

*****

PART THREE
OPERATION NEPTUNE
(AND OVERLORD / BOLERO CONTINUED)

SPECIAL ORDER OF THE DAY

TO THE OFFICERS AND MEN OF THE

ALLIED NAVAL EXPEDITIONARY FORCE

It is to be our privilege to take part in the greatest amphibious operation in history – a necessary preliminary to the opening of the Western Front in Europe which in conjunction with the great Russian advance, will crush the fighting power of Germany.

This is the opportunity which we have long awaited and which must seized and pursued with relentless determination : the hopes and prayers of the free world and of the enslaved peoples of Europe will be with us and we cannot fail them.

Our task in conjunction with the Merchant Navies of the United Nations, and supported by the Allied Air Force, is to carry the Allied Expeditionary Force to the Continent, to establish it there in a secure Bridgehead and to build it up and maintain it at a rate which will outmatch that of the enemy.

Let no one underestimate the magnitude of this task.

The Germans are desperate and will resist fiercely until we out-manoeuvre and out fight them, which we can and will do. To every one of you will be given the opportunity to show by his determination and resource that dauntless spirit of resolution which individually strengthens and inspires and which collectively is irresistible.

I count on every man to do his utmost to ensure the success of this great enterprise which is the climax of the European war.

Good luck to you all and God speed.

B. H. Ramsay

ADMIRAL
ALLIED NAVAL COMMANDER IN CHIEF
EXPEDITIONARY FORCE

Chapter XI

JUNE '44 - EMBARKATION

Following the *Excelsior* the rest of the troopships that would make up the largest individual force to take part in Operation NEPTUNE began gathering in the South Wales ports. *AP 72 Susan B. Anthony* came down from the Clyde and berthed at Newport on the first of the month with the *SS Explorer* leaving Milford Haven having taken on victuals at the US Navy base, sailing for Cardiff to be joined by the *SS Bienville* from Liverpool. The SS *Exchequer* did likewise having come down from Glasgow but destined for Swansea where the *USAT George W Goethals* also berthed on 2 June. In addition the *SS Marine Raven,* one of the newest C4 type troopships and finally the *USAT Borinquen* and *USAT George S Simonds* also berthed at Swansea. All ships were victualled on the way in Milford Haven, and sailed independently. There was nothing special about these ships, their selection was down to their availability and carrying capacity. No doubt there were certain advantages as some masters and crew had carried elements of the 2nd Infantry Division before. Only the *'Susie B',* a veteran of previous Mediterranean Theatre landings and an US Navy 'Assault Personnel' transport complete with her own LCVP's, had been previously selected.

Amazingly, at this time, there were still even more cargo/passenger freighters due in from trans-Atlantic convoys, the Commodore of the thirty-nine ship TCU25 releasing the SS *Robin Sherwood* to unload cargo and 600 troops at Cardiff and the *SS Santa Teresa* 500 men with the *SS Aztec* at Avonmouth. All these transports were coming into ports already chock-a-block with Coasters and MTV's that had been loading over the previous week. In addition there were other freighters and merchantmen not associated with the invasion which had been earmarked back in the US to discharge at certain ports.

For the BCPLBU Force, a number of specialized carriers and accommodation ships also arrived with the *Bernard Carter, Thomas B Robertson* and *Eleazor Wheelock* docking in Barry on the third and the *George W Woodward* the following day before transferring to Cardiff. The United States Advanced Amphibious Base at Milford provided victuals and stores for the crews on the way, together with any minor repairs required.

The scheduled preloading of coasters and their subsequent sailing to the Solent anchorages had improved the availability of wharf space, as had been seen at the end of May. Twenty-two vessels left the Bristol Channel on June 2nd primarily loaded with ammunition and cased petrol, all destined for assembly around the Isle of Wight prior to their scheduled departure for Normandy. The coasters would remain in the Solent anchorage with their hatch gangs from the various companies of the Port Battalions already aboard, awaiting routing to Normandy in their designated convoy. The majority of these coasters were scheduled for UTAH beach as the earlier pre-loaded coasters that had left the

Bristol Channel at the end of May were ultimately destined for OMAHA with some earmarked for either beach, depending on requirements. All were escorted in convoy EBC1 to the Solent anchorage prior to onward routing.

Port	Ship / Owner	Cargo	Tons/Yr.	Convoy	Beach	Date
Swansea	*Monksville* (Monk)		599 / 21	EBC2W	'O'	8th
"	*Pebble* (Robertson)		597 / 25	"	'O'	"
"	*Vliestroom* (Dutch)		655 / 12	"	'O'	"
"	*Topaz* (Robertson)	(A)	577 / 20	"	'U'	"
Penarth	*Wheatcrop* (Spillers)	(A)	523 / 24	"	'U'	"
Avonmouth	*Westdale* (Ohlson)	A	424 / 11	"	'U'	"
Swansea	*Jargoon* (Robertson)		691 / 26	EBC3W	'O'	9th
Port Talbot	*Actinia* (Dutch) (CP)		352 / 37	"	'O'	"
"	*MoWT Empire Estuary*	"	319 / 40	"	'U'	"
"	*MoWT Empire Jonquil*	"	369 / 39	"	'U'	"
"	*Parknasilla* (Kelly)	"	846 / 32	"	'U'	"
"	*Saint Rule* (Gardner)	"	524 / 41	"	'U'	"
Avonmouth	*Beeston* (ICI)	(A)	466 / 22	"	'U'	"
"	*Joffre Rose* (Hughes)	"	715 / 15	"	'U'	"
"	*Porthrepta* (Care)	"	643 / 22	"	'U'	"
"	*MoWT Reuben Snow*	"	1,813 / 43	"	'U'	"
Sharpness	*Cairngorm* (Robertson) (CP)		394 / 38	"	'U'	"
"	*Oriole* (General Steam) CP		489 / 39	"	'U'	"
"	*Van Brake* (Dutch) (CP)		398 / 29	"	'U'	"
Portishead	*Cedarwood* (Constantine)		899 / 33	"	'U'	"
Penarth	*Coral* (Robertson)	(A)	638 / 19	"	'U'	"
"	*Gun* (Norwegian)	"	670 / 18	"	'U'	"

Embarkation schedules and ship manifests were organised in such a way as to ensure that not all of any one unit would be aboard just one vessel. 'Combat loading' also meant that some ships would have more or less room than another, especially the smaller MT coasters. In most cases ships would carry more troops that they were actually designed for, some of the MTV 'Liberties' as much as 50% more. Crucially, as the weather wasn't too bad at the start of the month, the period troops would have to spend time aboard was determined and there was no change to the timing and dates. That delay would come later.

Movement of troops to Embarkation Ports began on the first day of the month, vehicles and guns having gone before. This was a massive operation by foot, road and rail and not just in South Wales. One civilian lorry driver related his experiences. Bill Churchill of Penygraig encountered the huge convoys heading for the Channel ports. He was employed as a driver by the Ministry of Supply. His job involved transporting explosives and munitions from the Royal Ordnance

Factory in Bridgend to the various arsenals in the country. On June 1st 1944 he was returning from the Woolwich Arsenal when he met up with this great movement of military vehicles as he approached the Cotswolds. Military traffic had priority and there were many delays for civilian lorries. Mr Churchill recalls;

> *"I was forced to park on the side of the road many times to let this military traffic pass. There were trucks loaded with troops and equipment, jeeps, ambulances, weapons carriers, huge Diamond T breakdown trucks and giant tank transporters conveying tanks by the hundred. It was an unbelievable sight and one nobody would ever witness on such a scale again. From the area of the Cotswolds into South Wales was one unbroken column of military vehicles"*

'A Moment in History' - Brian Morse

Down in Dorset the men of the 5th ESB had been putting into practice the lessons and experiences that they had gained on the beaches of Gower. Exercise FABIUS 1 had further honed any rough edges, the planning and execution being so good that it had resulted in many men wondering if they had actually invaded a foreign shore! But they had returned to their various Force 'O' camps of D-6, D-11 Long Bredy, D-12A and D-12B, getting steadily bored as they went over time and time again what was going to be required of them, even though they didn't have any idea where they were going to go or when. When those elements scheduled for Force 'B' including the 336th ECB less the 331 men attached to the 348th Beach Group then had moved out, questions were asked but with no replies the men just kept wondering. In fact they had gone west to the Truro Marshalling Areas 'N' and 'O' Briefings would take place soon for those Officers who were BIGOTED' – few in number due to high levels of secrecy. Some wouldn't know until they were actually briefed on board ship during the passage.

But now most were moving to their embarkation 'hards' with the 37th ECB Beach Group to the fore loading at Portland together with the 348th Beach Group. The 2 platoons of the 61st Medical Battalion were to board the LSI *Empire Anvil* and *APA 45 Henrico* with the assault 16th Infantry Battalions, whilst the remainder voyaged aboard LST's of Force 'B'. Build-up elements of the Brigade remained in their camp until 7 June and those elements still in South Wales comprising the balances and reserves of equipment and trucks moved from Camp 89 Dan-Y-Parc to ports. The fifth and final group, the residue elements of the 5th ESB were at Tortworth Camp, Falfield near Bristol where they would remain, much to their distain and concern, due to a communication problem until 18 June!

Back in South Wales what did concern some was that actual time men would have to spend aboard ship. Due to the number of ships involved and especially the high rise and fall of Bristol Channel tides, it could mean vessels would have to complete loading, be locked out, and be anchored outside in the channel as much as three days before departure. During that time the men had to be fed. The old adage of 'an army marches on its stomach' was never so true, but for marching read 'sailing'. The XXIX Operation Supply Officer Lt. Col F. Deisher, queried which agency would provide embarkation supplies of food and blankets. Apparently the Navy would only take over responsibility for cargos including troops once under way. Before that the responsibility lay with the War Shipping Administration (administrators of many troopships). The situation was presented to the Western Base Section Quartermaster, who, after consulting with the Chief Quartermaster SOS directed three days of 10-in-1 rations and three blankets per man be placed aboard these vessels. It was explained that more would be needed, but to no avail. By direct contact with SOS Headquarters in Cheltenham, supplies were to be increased by two days. The resourceful C/O of the 164th Quartermaster Battalion also secured no less than 100,000 blankets required by scouring the sorting sheds, presumably at St. Mellons, as he couldn't get the various depots to release any of their already depleted stock.

Photo: 'William Tilghman' (MTV) at Southampton with black port battalion troops loading a 6x6 'Deuce and a Half' truck using the Liberty ships' own derrick winches with others being prepared on the dockside. Typical of what was happening at the end of May in Bristol Channel Ports as well. (IWM)

Troops generally were doing what so many did at this time. They hadn't been 'BIGOTED', the term used for those few officers who knew what this latest series of instructions and movements was about. 'Hurry Up and Stand Still' was the usual barked order that the 'GI' (or 'Tommy' for that matter) heard. This could be just another of those exercises that many had taken part in over previous months. None of them knew when they got to a Port of Embarkation what was happening elsewhere. Yes, they had foreign currency, but – so what? Some had only recently got used to pounds, shillings and pence. Francs and centimes were just more funny money! On arrival at the wharves and under tight security, for example there were 120 Military Police guarding the US cordoned off part of Swansea Docks perimeter, the troops began receiving briefings about what was happening, although where they were going was still a secret until aboard ship. Coffee and steak sandwiches and doughnuts? They were being fed well which worried most men as they hadn't been so well looked after for ages. The Army must be up to something was a common thought!

The ships were berthed at the quaysides and as the men boarded some of the 2nd Division troops even recognised that they had been on the same vessel before; perhaps they were going back to Belfast? Space aboard the MTV's left a lot to be desired but at least there were proper latrine cubicles installed by the 863rd Ordnance Company - one of the many extra jobs that they had been involved in at their G-40 workshops. Some of the smaller coasters had no such refinements with nothing more than troughs on the port and starboard rails flushed with a strategically aimed fire hose. Some men had no bunks at all, stretching out on palliases on deck under tarpaulins. Troopships and transports all possessed individual code numbers and were berthed with the ships name clearly visible together with its individual index number on high level boards to port and starboard. When offshore at Normandy, these identification signs were sometimes all the information that DUKW drivers and ship to shore ferry craft had and proved invaluable. The Transportation school at Mumbles and the additional training vessel that had been used in Penarth Docks for the Port Battalion troops showed their true worth. Shipping orders were straightforward for Masters using the destination initial O (Omaha), U (Utah) or W (Western Task Force Area) and convoy title abbreviations. The problems that did arise concerned unscheduled deck loading especially the highly volatile 5 gallon fuel cans for LCVP's, LCA's and miscellaneous ferry craft such as LCM's and DUKWs.

NEWPORT – Marshalling Sub-Area 'U' - EMBARKATION PORT

The 'Longshore Soldiers' related their experience.

'On June 2 the 519th Port Battalion left the marshalling area and arrived at Newport, Wales. The 303rd Port Company split from the rest of the battalion and embarked at Bristol and Southampton, England. The officers directed the men to their ships. "My sergeant was there to make sure you got on the boat. He'd call out your first name; you'd call out your second". Their packs were reviewed before boarding. "One guy had filled his gas mask with candy. He said it was his 'shaking-up material'! The battalion was divided among numerous waiting Liberty ships, freighters and coasters. They remained anchored until late in the evening of 5 June.'

The other companies split into their respective hatch gangs and boarded the MTV's, part of the 304th boarding the *Charles Morgan*. (Sadly she would be one of the few ships that were bombed off UTAH Beach on the morning of 10 June with the loss of 4 stevedores killed and six wounded from the Port Company.) The Service Section of the 186th Port Company 487th Battalion trucked down from Treherbert to board the *Francis Harrington*, the three other platoons left their trucks in Pontypridd and boarded the train for the marshalling area at Southampton where they would board the earlier pre-loaded coasters, wondering if they would join up again, no doubt. All companies were divided up in a similar fashion. The troops aboard the *'Susie B'* comprised elements of the 90th Division including General Sam Williams and the Advanced Headquarters, the 2/359th Regiment, the main body of 'C' Company 315th ECB, and the 535th AAA (AW) Battalion. The 82nd Airborne Division had elements of the 320th and 456th Parachute FA Battalions aboard as did the 101st Airborne Division with elements of 321st and the 907th Glider FA Battalions. Also the advance detachments of the 87th Armored FA Battalion, 294th ECB and the 42nd Field Hospital team of 8 Officers and 74 enlisted men whose duty was to set up the first US hospital on the Cotentin Peninsula. Just this one ship was carrying unit's representative of nearly all of Major General Collins VII Corps including the 4th Infantry Division, leaders of the assault on UTAH Beach. Tragedy would strike the ship but not her vital cargo*.

Newport was the only South Wales port to be originally selected in the OVERLORD 'C' plan and which had involved loading far fewer troops and equipment. Together with Avonmouth, the two BCP's would have received units marshalled at Camp Llanmartin for Newport and Muller's Orphanage for the Bristol port, carrying out a rolling programme with only 2,400 troops every 24 hours. How plans had changed; now MTV's had quadrupled as had the number of vehicles. The addition of two troopships had also escalated the out loading and embarkation to over 13,000 men in just one 24 hour period.

The 90th Division troopships were scheduled so that the *Susan B Anthony* with the Advanced HQ and 2/359th Infantry would leave on the first tide to join with others from Swansea, followed on the next tide by the *Excelsior* with the 358th RCT. She would be joined by the *Explorer* with RCT 357 out of Cardiff, less their 3rd Battalions, both of which were loaded on the *Bienville*.

There were worries for some officers however. All troop carriers would have a hundred 5 gallon gasoline drums as deck cargo to enable assault craft to refuel as they embarked troops. A logical step but one that was unfortunately not communicated to the ship masters and one which quite naturally caused great concern. The hazards of volatile fuel stored in the open air on vessels scheduled for a war zone were made plain, but there was no alternative at such short notice.

Footnote. The sinking of the Susan B Anthony and the simultaneous rescue of her troop cargo and crew remains the singularly most successful of all time, incredibly with no loss of life. The verbatim minute by minute report as filed by her master Commander Gray is detailed in Appendix 5.

ALEXANDRA SOUTH DOCK – 2 personnel ships and 18 MTV's

Index No.	Name	Tons/Yr.	Tps.	Vehs.	Beach	Convoy
MT 226	*Frank S. Stockton*	7,176 / 43	503	112	U	EBM 2
MT 227	*George E. Pickett*	7,244 / 43	561	191	"	"
MT 228	*Jedidiah Smith*	7,176 / 43	522	192	"	"
MT 229	*Josiah Nelson Cushing*	7,176 / 43	547	154	"	"
MT 230	*Edward W. Scripps*	7,176 / 43	495	135	"	"
MT 231	*Ephraim Brevard*	7,177 / 43	529	87	"	"
MT 232	*Robert L. Vann*	7,176 / 43	426	63	"	"
MT 233	*Francis C. Harrington*	7,176 / 43	417	89	"	"
MT 234	*Charles M. Hall*	7,181 / 42	475	120	"	"
MT 235	*Walter Page*	7,176 / 43	598	124	"	"
MT 236	*Horace Gray*	7,200 / 43	514	134	"	"
MT 237	*Stephen B. Elkins*	7,180 / 43	623	144	"	"
	Completed loading by 1955 hrs 2 June.					
MT 219	*Abiel Foster*	7,176 / 42	531	197	U	EBM 3
MT 220	*Enoch Train*	7,176 / 43	502	176	"	"
MT 221	*Joshua P. Lippincott*	7,176 / 43	516	206	"	"
MT 222	*Amos G. Throop*	7,176 / 43	521	190	"	"
MT 223	*Charles Morgan*	7,224 / 43	530	162	"	"
MT 224	*Clara Barton*	7,176 / 42	552	205	"	"
	Completed loading by 1300 hrs 3 June.					
PP 17	*S.B. Anthony* (2,288)	8,101 / 30	2,193	-	U	EBP 1/B3
	Completed loading by 1530 hrs 4 June.					
PP 12	*Excelsior* (2,590)	6,685 / 43	1,953	-	U	EBP 2
	Completed loading by 1700 hrs 4 June					

CARDIFF- Marshalling Sub-Area 'V' EMBARKATION PORT

Roath Dock was devoted to NEPTUNE with the east end surrounded by barb wire and MP's. All troops arrived at the dock entrance at the end of Moorland Road via Constellation St., Pearl St. and Splott Rd, rather than the usual main gate at the bottom of Bute Terrace. The late Malcolm Harris related;

When I was 4-5 years old, I remember a lot of noise and everyone running out of their houses to see what was happening. I stood with my parents, sister and lots of local people on the corner of Clifton St. and Pearl St. We watched and cheered the Yanks as they came by. The tanks came first hence the noise. Then truck after truck full of soldiers throwing sweets and chewing gum at us children who were shouting, "Give us some gum chum". The Yanks as generous as always were pleased to do so.'

The 87th Armored FA 'Bushmasters' detrained just after daylight on 2 June.

> *'Here the 87th waited in a huge warehouse for several hours while the Transportation Corps loaded the batteries on their respective boats. The American Red Cross served hot coffee and doughnuts, which was a welcome substitute for breakfast. About mid-morning, the battalion loaded on Liberty ships, by battery. Vehicles and equipment for the men aboard had been loaded previously and securely fastened on the different decks in the ships hold. Most of the afternoon was spent getting the ship organised for a short sea voyage. One deck of the rear hold had been installed with folding bunks, about four inches in height. Upon counting noses, it was discovered that there were two men to each bunk, so emergency measures were employed. Sleeping would be done in twelve hour shifts, with one man up and the other one down.'*

According to their History the 345th Field Artillery marched from Camp Heath.

> *'Dressed in cotton underwear, long johns, 1 pair wool socks, 1 pair of wool impregnated socks, wool ordinary dress uniform, impregnated fatigue uniform, impregnated shoes, field jacket, full field and raincoat'* the men left on a sunny 3rd June afternoon as part of the 1,743 strong marching column bound for Cardiff Docks 5 miles away. *90th Signallers, Quartermasters, Engineers, Medics, Mechanics, MP's and artillerymen swung out onto Allensbank Road, easing left onto Whitchurch Road before swinging down Cathay's Terrace through the City, under the Newport Rd. railway bridge near Queens Street and away via Commercial Road to their Troopships and MT Liberty ships awaiting them in Roath Docks.'*

Not all loading was going to plan though. John Nasea Jr. of the ship-boarded section of 101st Airborne Division 321st Glider FA Battalion noticed that his ship *John S Mosby* was being loaded with the unloading chart. The 'Peashooters' (75mm howitzers) were loaded down in the hold while the 6x6 trucks were loaded up on deck! No one seemed particularly bothered though*. The USN 81st Construction Battalion ('SeaBees') embarked on the *Thomas B. Robertson* and they would stay on board off OMAHA Beach as their job was to man the Rhino Ferries, warping craft and repair barges on site.

There were very strict instructions laid down by Movement Control and Operations Headquarters regarding MTV's and coasters at all embarkation ports,

---

*Footnote: The loading of the John S. Mosby did in fact cause problems. Many of the 321st Glider Field Artillery gunners travelled across on the Susan B. Anthony separate from their guns. It took 3 infuriating days with Battalion officers harassing the Navy before they were traced deep down in the holds of the MTV. Similar problems were experienced by the 907th GFA.

relating to the stowage of all vehicles and the discipline required of personnel both during loading and transit:-

---

Battery leads to be connected, radiators not to be drained.
Safety margin in petrol tanks.
Fuel and Water in Jerri cans.
Lubricating oil in containers.
No tinned Petrol aboard Ammunition carrying coasters.
All securing gear to remain on board and available for re-use.
All lifts to be capable of being handled by ship's gear.
Preloaded MTV's to have 'As Stowed' plans showing vehicle position
Adherence to Pre-loading storage plans essential.
Attention to NO SMOKING rule.

Access to Roath Dock Embarkation Area was easy by train as the rail network took in the dockside wharfs. However vehicles came from 3 directions, A48 east with a straightforward left turn off Newport Road at the RP. Traffic from the west had joined that coming from the north at Gabalfa before coming down North Road, before travelling along Newport Road to the RTRP. Marching troops from Heath Camp were kept away from vehicles by taking a route down Cathay's Terrace before joining with any road transport to pass under Newport Road Railway Bridge serving Queen Street Station, then via Fitzallan Rd., Pearl Street and Splott Road, over the railway to Moreland Road and finally down to Dock Gates East.

Maintaining secrecy was of course paramount all through the build up to the operation and communication was verbal more often than not in the embarkation ports with Movement Control Officers issuing instructions and with the full knowledge of additional Military Police back-up being available. Morale however, among the troops was to be kept at as high a level as possible, and any worries regarding loading and embarkation were to be kept to a minimum with as little hassle as possible.

What did concern some Movement Control and Operation Headquarters officers though, was the lack of information that had been given to the troop ship masters who bore such tremendous responsibility in respect of their passengers.
Lt. Col. Deisher, as Supply Officer, was surprised to find that overall there was a degree of ignorance regarding the preparations required for the loading of personnel and equipment by the masters and they didn't appear to have been briefed at all. In many ways this was not surprising as instructions and orders were only given on a 'need to know' basis. Most had only been ordered to the Bristol Channel Ports following their arrival in convoy TCU24 a week before – BIGOT was adhered to and it was simply that old maxim of unless you are instructed differently, obey the last order!

ROATH DOCK –2 troop ships, 10 MTV's, 2 accomod'n ships, 2 coasters.

Index No.	Name (Owner)	Tons / Yr.	Tps.	Vehs.	Beach	Convoy
PP 689	*Obsidian* (Robertson)	811 / 22	65	-	WTF	EBC 2Y
PP 802	*Royal* (Norwegian)	759 / 18	44	-	"	"
	Completed loading by 1930 hrs 2 June					
MT 214	*Oliver Woolcott*	7,181 / 42	613	213	'O'	EBM 2
MT 215	*Ezra Weston*	7,176 / 43	481	119	'U'	"
MT 216	*Robert E. Peary*	7,181 / 42	579	166	"	"
MT 217	*John S Mosby*	7,225 / 43	679	154	"	"
MT 218	*Benjamin Hawkins*	7,191 / 42	543	177	"	"
	Completed loading by 1955 hrs 2 June.					
USN	*George W. Woodward*	7,176 / 43	(900)	-	'G'	EBM 3
USN	*Thomas B. Robertson*	7,176 / 42	(900)	-	'U'	"
MT 209	*Charles C. Jones*	7,198 / 43	564	163	"	"
MT 210	*Charles D. Postem*	7,176 / 43	533	160	"	"
MT 211	*Collis P. Huntington*	7,177 / 42	516	173	"	"
MT 212	*Eugene B. O'Donnell*	7,176 / 43	480	137	"	"
MT 213	*Webb Miller*	7,176 / 43	531	98	"	"
	Completed loading by 1300 hrs 3 June.					
PP 14	*Explorer* (2,198)	6,736 / 39	1,928	-	'U'	EBP 2
PP 9	*Bienville* (1,850)	6,165 / 43	1,925	-	"	"
	Completed loading by 1700 hrs 4 June					

BARRY – Marshalling Sub-Area 'W' EMBARKATION PORT

The smallest of the four principal South Wales Embarkation Ports was devoid of the larger troopships and small pre-loaded coasters, concentrating on MTV's and coasters with hatch gangs aboard. Pvt. J.K Sunshine, 42nd Field Hospital remembers having travelled down from Camp Pontllanfraith;

> *'We are taken in trucks to the port of Barry on the Bristol Channel. The harbour is jammed with shipping. Long lines of men, troops, trucks and guns waiting on the wharves to board freighters and transports lying bow to stern at the piers. We load, but the boats do not move for reasons not given to us'.*

42nd Field Hospital Memoirs

From St. Donats Castle camp, the 12th FA Battalion together with various 2nd Division elements arrived by train for embarkation, their guns and tow trucks already stowed. The 'Seabees' were joining ship here as well. Two converted Liberty ships assigned to the US Navy took men aboard at Barry with the 111th

Construction Battalion embarking on the *Bernard Carter* which would be home for the time they would spend operating the Rhino Ferries, warping tugs and naval repair craft off Utah Beach. These large motorised rafts and smaller far shore craft such as the LCA's and LCVP's would need refuelling once their first assault landing trips were complete. It had been overlooked and was a small but serious omission in the planning but it was resolved by SOS as soon as it was realized.

MAIN DOCK – 9 MTV's, 2 Accommodation ships and 4 coasters

Index No.	Name	Tons/Yr	Tps	Vehs.	Beach	Convoy
PP 505	*MoWT Josiah P Cressey*	1,791 / 43	144	-	WTF	EBC 2Y
PP 494	*MoWT Jessie G Cotting*	1,791 / 43	84	-	"	"
PP 906	*Stuart Queen* (Br. Ch.Is).	1,224 / 41	100	-	'U'	"
	Completed loading by 1930 hrs 2 June.					
USN	*Bernard Carter*	7,191 / 42	(900)	-	WTF	EBM 2
USN	*Eleazor Wheelock*	7,192 / 42	(900)	-	'O'	"
MT 205	*Charles Wilson Peale*	7,176 / 42	506	148	"	"
MT 206	*Charles Sumner*	7,176 / 43	558	156	"	"
MT 207	*John Steele*	7,176 / 42	527	164	"	"
MT 208	*Henry W. Grady*	7,201 / 43	413	84	"	"
MT 225	*Edwin Abbey*	7,126 / 43	487	96	'U'	EBM 2
	Completed loading by 1955 hrs 2 June.					
MT 201	*Clinton Kelly*	7,176 / 43	477	137	'O'	EBM 3
MT 202	*Hellas* (Greek)	7,176 / 43	462	181	"	"
MT 203	*John Hay*	7,176 / 43	557	166	"	"
MT 204	*Louis Kossuth*	7,176 / 43	537	137	"	"
	Completed loading by 1300 hrs 3 June.					
PP 72	*MoWT Bailey Foster*	1,791 / 43	161	-	WTF	EBC 3
	Completed loading by 1500 hrs 3 June					

SWANSEA – Marshalling Sub-Area 'X' EMBARKATION PORT

On 4 June reserve troops at Singleton of the 115th and 175th Infantry Regiments 29th ID marched to their ships with the 517th Port Battalion going 2 days before. No road march to ship for the 2nd Division's battalion Headquarters Sections and reserves at Mynydd Lliw. Those of the 9th and 38th RCT' plus the entire 1/23rd Infantry were either trucked to Swansea Docks or entrained at Gorseinon rail station between 2nd and 4th June. Whilst troops in Swansea camps marched to ship, the 2nd & 3rd Battalions 23rd RCT with their 37th FA Battalion, and 'B' Companies of the 2nd ECB & 2nd Medical Battalion were trucked to the docks from Camp Corner House at Scurlage. Nearly 300 vehicles were taken down to

Swansea a day or so earlier for loading into the specially prepared coastal MTVs, with the 'deuce and a half's' of the augmented 3345th Quartermaster Truck Company based at Mumbles Car Park then transporting 2,629 troops between the 2nd and 4th June. The Overlord 'D' (revised) plan detailed precise routes with MP's and local constabulary ensuring clear unobstructed roads, the convoys travelling via Parkmill, Upper Killay and Uplands before crossing town and the Tawe into the heavily cordoned off east end of King's Dock. From the east, the 3/9th RCT and the 38th RCT Battalions arrived by train at Kings Dock, stepping down to those same platforms that had tramped by thousands of men over the past months, their first steps in Britain being here in Swansea. Now troops were going the other way, wondering yet another exercise?

Additional coasters were loaded in the Prince of Wales Dock and various small craft were moored in South Dock but generally it was the docks to the east of the Tawe that provided for Invasion shipping. Queens Dock was exclusively for the import of crude oil for Llandarcy and export of product, aviation gasoline, kerosene, paraffin, petrol, diesel and bunker fuels. There were 120 'Snowdrops' were on guard and no person, civilian or service was allowed into or out of the area unless authorised once troopships had commenced loading. Special arm bands for BCP staff (600) in all were issued for ID purposes. Life preservers were issued on arrival and it was only once aboard that briefings were carried out regarding destination. All in all, Swansea out loaded over 13,000 troops and 755 vehicles, not to mention the number of additional preloaded stores ships that had gone before. Also Port Talbot sent out another 7 ships with 755 troops including the 2nd Division Quartermaster Company plus V Corps troops from Margam Park and Castle Camps with over 100 vehicles.

PRINCE OF WALES DOCK. - 4 Personnel Coasters for Convoy EBC2Y

Index No.	Name (Owner)	Tons/Yr	Tps.	Vehs.	Beach
PP 938	*Thore Hafte* (Norwegian)	626 / 96	28	-	WTF
PP 383	*MoWT Fylla* (ex-Danish)	792 / 06	65	-	"
PP 507	*Julia* (Belgian)	597 / 07	65	-	"
PP 1013	*Wild Rose* (Hughes)	873 / 2	39	-	"

Completed loading by 1930 hrs 2 June.

Kings Dock was the primary embarkation point with the entire east end cordoned off just like Cardiff with barbed wire and heavy Military Police guard. A number of installations had to be shut down in the interests of security - the Power House, Trinity House, GWR Workshop, Stores and No's 13 & 14 coal hoists. Within the security area, straw paliasses and life preservers were issued and the essential coffee and doughnuts! Part of 303rd Port Company from 519th Battalion provided hatch gangs here with the rest of the company travelling on to Southampton. Also sailing in advance on 2 June from the Bristol Channel was the *ASIS Donaghmore,* a naval stores pre-loaded coaster which would join EWC1A convoy in the Solent.

KINGS' DOCK. 21 MT Coasters for Convoy EBC 2Z
Number of Berths: Tennant 6, No1 Quay 5, No2 Q. 1, No3 Q. 6, Rose 4.

Index No.	Name (Owner)	Tons/Yr	Tps.	Vehs.	Beach
MT 334	*MoWT Empire Sedge*	2,852 / 41	130	40	'O'
MT 338	*MoWT Empire Strait*	2,824 / 40	140	47	"
MT 345	*Erica* (Norwegian)	1,592 / 19	119	34	"
MT 355	*MoWT Fano* (ex-Danish)	1,889 / 19	133	40	"
MT 397	*Glanton* (Sharp)	2,822 / 29	139	50	"
MT 415	*MoWT Graslin* (ex-French)	2,323 / 24	38	26	"
MT 504	*Josewyn* (Dillwyn)	1,926 / 19	139	20	"
MT 511	*MoWT Juta* (ex-Estonian)	1,559 / 08	118	32	"
MT 517	*Katowice* (Polish)	1,995 / 25	161	47	"
MT 536	*Krakow* (Polish)	2,017 / 26	170	37	"
MT 672	*Newlands* (Tully)	1,556 / 21	86	25	"
MT 601	*Lysland* (Norwegian)	1,335 / 07	149	23	"
MT1001	*Westburn* (Westwick)	2,842 / 29	175	75	"
MT1043	*Zealand* (Dutch)	2,726 / 30	138	63	"
	MoWT Aaro (ex-Danish)	1,426 / 25	146	45	"
MT 67	*MoWT Avance* (ex-Danish)	1,582 / 20	121	36	"
MT 171	*MoWT Circe II* (ex-French)	2,031 / 26	60	27	'U'
MT 178	*MoWT Claudius Magin* (ex-Fr)	2,310 / 21	173	29	"
MT 238	*Dalewood* (Fenwick ex-Fr.)	2,774 / 31	51	17	"
MT 535	*Kordecki* (Polish)	1,975 / 30	54	20	"
MT 948	*MoWT Tomsk* (ex-Danish)	1,229 / 11	41	22	"
Y40	Water Tanker				"
Y41	"				"

Completed loading 2400 hrs 3 June.

KINGS' DOCK. 5 Troopships. N & S Mole, No.4 Quay E & W & F Shed.

Index No.	Name (Owner)	Tons/Yr	Tps.	Vehs.	Convoy
PP 15 (P2)	*George W. Goethals* (1,936)	12,093 tons	2,143	-	EBP 1
PP 93 (P3)	*Gen. Geo. S. Simonds* (1,936)	8,357 tons	2,003	-	"
PP 10 (P4)	*Borinquen* ((1,450)	7, 114 tons	1,602	-	"
PP 16 (P5)	*Marine Raven* (2,546)	11,757 tons	2,169	-	EBP 2
PP 13 (P6)	*Exchequer* (2,216)	6,683 tons	2,582	-	"

Completed loading between 15.30 and 1700 hrs 4 June

PORT TALBOT QUAY. 4 Personnel Coasters and 3 MT coasters.

Index No.	Name (Owner)	Tons / Yr	Tps.	Vehs.	Beach	Convoy
PP 759 *Quentin* (Gibson)		500 / 40	65	-	WTF	EBC 2Y
PP 895 *Staley Bridge* (Summers)		297 / 40	44	-	"	"
PP 130 *Brockley Coombe* (Ald)		662 / 38	87	-	"	"
PP 494 *Coral Queen* (Br.Ch.Traders)		303 / 41	44	-	"	"

Completed loading by 1930 hrs 2 June.

MT 281 *Eastwood* (Fenwick)		1,551 / 24	138	37	'O'	EBC 2Z
MT 475 *MoWT Isac* (ex-French)		2,385 / 26	206	37	"	"
MT 525 *Kmicic* (Polish)		1,894 / 23	171	32	"	"

Completed loading by 2400hrs 3 June

GARSTON – Preloaded Coasters

PP 584 *Loanda* (Evans)		534 / 36	65	-	WTF	EBC 2Y
PP 1027 *Wooler* (Tyne Tees)		507 / 36	65	-	"	"

Completed loading before 2 June

AVONMOUTH – Preloaded Coasters

PP 172 *Citrine* (Robertson)		783 / 39	104	-	WTF	EBC 2Y
Y23	Water Tanker			-	'O'	EBC 2Z
Y25	"			-	'U'	"
Y26	"				"	"

Completed loading by 1930 hrs 2 June.

Early on Sunday morning cables were slipped from their moorings and the vessels began moving, leaving the ports through the lock gates and assisted by tugs, just as any vessel would have done in peacetime. The tug *Cardiff* and *Lord Glanely* undertook their respective tows in their home port and at 4.14am the *Broadbent* and *Herculean* guided the first to leave Swansea, the *Goethals* in a freshening breeze, followed an hour later by the *General Simonds* in the care of the *Wallasey* and *Harrington*. Then at 6.10 the *Herculean* provided her second tow of the morning with the *Waterloo* moving out the *Borinquen*. Coasters had no need of such assistance, but certainly the troopships needed care and attention. The various convoys were assembling just outside the individual ports, awaiting their consorts just as they would have done in practise. The escorts, Hunt class destroyers *HMS Mendip* and *HMS Blencartha* with *HMS Wanderer*, *HMS Walker* and *HMS Watchman* took station and all was now ready for departure. The biggest troop force in the entire OPERATION NEPTUNE was about to set sail.

Force 'O' and Force 'U', some of whose landing craft from Devon and Cornwall, were already at sea and heading up east in rather threatening weather.

Force 'B', fully loaded, was either leaving the Fal Estuary or assembling at Fowey; amongst the 50 'large slow targets' were 4 LST's carrying the 366th Engineer Beach Group complete with 15 priority ammunition loaded DUKW's of the 458th and 459th Amphibian Truck Companies. A further 6 LST's had elements of the PESBG spread throughout as part loads all for landing on the third tide which would turn out to be early on 7June. The Bombardment Fleets had left Belfast Lough (US Navy) and the Clyde (Royal Navy), the battleship *HMS Nelson* having been at Milford on the 2nd was down at Plymouth with her escorts. Even the very slow fleet of 59 block ships, the 'Corn Cob Fleet', including the *Artemus Ward*, was making its way up the Channel having crept down from Scotland.

But in Portsmouth the Supreme Commander General Eisenhower made the decision at 0400hrs to postpone the landings by twenty four-hours. The weather was simply too bad to contemplate attempting to land troops in such conditions either by sea or air. Convoys were re-routed; some back into the ports they had just left, others like the Bombardment fleet did an about turn for twelve hours up the Irish Sea before turning back to their original heading. The Corncob fleet anchored in Poole Bay. Swansea Bay turned into one massive anchorage almost resembling the Solent as vessels hove to, joining those that had left Swansea and were now awaiting orders. The planners fears were becoming evident - thousands of men on ships in poor weather. Those steak sandwiches, so appreciated early on, were now causing some discomfort! Gradually, the seas became calmer as the gale moved away to the south-east. Local schoolboy, now author Paul Ferris relates;-

> *'Sunday 4 June sixty or so ships were there, facing east into the tide as it ebbed. When it turned, in the middle of the morning, the ships turned with it, slowly, on their anchor chains, as though taking part in a marine display, to face the flood-tide coming up from the west.'* That afternoon, or perhaps the day before, two of us went to the end of Mumbles pier, within earshot of a coasting vessel where black American soldiers were lying on deck in the sun, playing Glen Miller music on a gramophone. 'American Patrol' and 'Chattanooga Choo-choo' came over the water. We hoped they had something to do with invading Europe.'
>
> 'Gower in History'- Paul Ferris

Joining them now were the ships scheduled for the next tide with the *Exchequer* guided by the hardworking *Heraculeum* and the *Broadbent* coming out of Swansea followed by the tugs *Waterloo* and *Canada* battling an increasingly strong wind catching their tow, the big C4 *Marine Raven*.

Monday morning June 5th and the approximate ship-count off Mumbles had reached thirty-five troopships and freighters, thirty coasters and half a dozen tankers. Such an armada of shipping anchored ruined the Hais (PLUTO) line on the sea-bed which was so badly damaged that it had to be taken out of service permanently. But it had served its purpose as a guinea pig. At this very moment six huge 'conuns' (floating cable drums) each with 70 miles of flexible undersea

Hais pipe were at Southampton with their tugs *Bustler*, *Danube V* and *Marauder* and attendant cable laying ships ready to begin laying PLUTO due to take over from the short turn TOMBOLA supply from tankers anchored off the beach.

Meanwhile, nearby in Portsmouth Eisenhower agonised over the decision that he, and only he could make. All the advice and forecasts had been discussed. A potential weather window had been identified – not perfect - but if the invasion was delayed any more, it would have to be called off for the best part of a month until the tides and moon would be right again. Moreover there were newly arrived troops in the UK already going into camps only just vacated a few days earlier and several thousand were even now crossing the North Atlantic in the 39 ships of convoy CU26. In just a few words, 'OK, Let's go' 'Ike' launched the biggest amphibious invasion in history. Early Tuesday morning half the moored ships left Swansea Bay with the remainder following on the next tide that evening. Robertson's 2nd ID was finally heading to OMAHA to reinforce the 1st and 29th Divisions. The 5th and 6th ESB troops aboard would bring the Beach Groups up to full strength and the 90th ID were ready for UTAH following their two detached battalions in the assault together with remaining elements of the 1st ESB. Finally, the troops in the seaborne parts of the 82nd and 101st Airborne would be re-united with their comrades. Skirting minefields, the convoys hugged the north coast of Devon and Cornwall, with their escort's ever watchful and anti-submarine screens active in the Western Approaches. Here were the additional covering force of the ECG comprising the carriers *HMS Tracker, Emperor* and *Pursuer* with 6 other anti-submarine Escort Groups. Above Group 19 Coastal Command from St Davids and Carew Cheriton and the Devon and Cornwall airfields of St. Eval, Chivenor, Dunkeswell and Davidstow were on watch. Pembroke Dock 'Sunderlands' made 57 attacks on U-boats on D-Day alone. The BCPLBU Force was on its way.

Photo: AP72 Susan B Anthony, Force Command Ship. (Courtesy of Nav. Source).

*****

Chapter XII

6 JUNE '44 - D-DAY

"Supreme Headquarters Allied Expeditionary Force has today issued a Communiqué. 'Under the Command of General Eisenhower, Allied Navies supported by strong Air Forces began landing Allied Armies on the northern coast of France.' This ends Communique No.1"   BBC 06.06.'44.

Photo: Troops of 'B' Company 1/359th Infantry aboard LCI (L) 326 following up the 4th Infantry Division assault on Utah Beach at 6.10 hrs on D-Day 6th June 1944. The distinct outlines of three other LCI's following are visible each towing a Balloon providing anti-aircraft protection under the care of a 320th VLA Battalion 3 man squad.   Courtesy of the National Archives.

WESTERN TASK FORCE

FORCE 'O'   823 ships - 29,714 troops and 3,241 vehicles.
Assault Group 01
APA 26 Samuel Chase, APA 45 Henrico, LSI Empire Anvil.
US *LST* No's. *309, 314, 357, 373, 374, 376.*
LCH87. LCC No's. *10 & 20, LCI (L) 5, LCT*'s *44, LCM (3)* 18
Assault Group 02
APA 28 Charles Carroll, APA 30 Thomas Jefferson, LSI Empire Javelin.
US *LST No's 310, 315,316, 317, 332, 372*
LCH 86. LCC No's *30, 40, 50. LCI (L) 17, LCT*'s *45, LCM(3)* 18
Assault Group 03
XAP 76 Anne Arundel, XAP 67 Dorothy Dix, XAP 77 Thurston
US *LST* No's. *6, 51, 75, 133, 134, 157, 285, 286, 347, 350, 375, 502.*
LCH 492. LCI (L) 11, LCT's *39.*   LSD *HMS Oceanway* (sailed with Force B).
Assault Group 04
LSI(S) Prince Baudoin, Prince Charles, Prince Leopold.
LSI (H) Ben My Cree, Amsterdam, Princess Maud. LCT (5) 1

FORCE 'U'   800 ships - 30,452 troops and 3,569 vehicles.
Green Assault Group
APA 13 Joseph T Dickman, LSI Empire Gauntlet. US LST 48, 47, 281.
(Follow-up *US LST 49, 50, 491, 283, 492, 57, 290, 501, 351, 500, 508, 539*).
LCC No's *60, 70. LCI (L) 23, LCT (5) 14, LCT (6) 26. RN LCT (4) 14, LCT (5) 15.*
Red Assault Group
APA 5 Barnett, APA 33 Bayfield (HQ) *US LST 282, 230.*
(Follow-up *US LST 284, 311, 346, 371, 380, 382, 400, 499, 46, 294, 509, 515, 58*).
LCC No's *80, 90. LCI (L) 22. LCT (5) 16. LCT (6) 26 RN LCT (4) 16, LCT (5) 22.*

FORCE 'B'   110 ships - 26,492 troops and 4,431 vehicles.
LST No's *5, 7, 16, 27, 28, 53, 54, 55, 56, 59, 61, 212, 262, 266, 288, 289, 291, 292,*
306, 307, 325, 331, 335, 336, 337, 338, 355, 356, 369, 388, 389, 391, 392, 393,
494, 495, 496, 497, 498, 504, 505, 506, 510, 511, 512, 516, 523, 532, 533, 538.
US *LCI (L)* 13. RN *LCT (4) 46. AKA 53 Achernar* (1st Army HQ.)

BCPLBU FORCE   83 ships - 42,410 troops and 6,435 vehicles.
AP 72 Susan B Anthony, George W Goethals, Gen. George S Simonds, Borinquen.
Excelsior, Explorer, Bienville, Exchequer, Marine Raven.
MTV's 37, MTC's 24, PP Coasters 22, USN Accomodation Ships 4.
Water Tankers 5.

Such a simple statement of fact made no attempt to reveal anything more. In fact, it was several hours before anyone in the UK, or anyone else for that matter knew anything, either military or civilian regarding events unfolding in Normandy. The much vaunted Assault Plan for the Infantry, Special Engineer Task Force and DD tanks on both UTAH and OMAHA were to be supported by a simple but extensive bombardment lasting 45 minutes by sea and air, right up to the moment the Infantry and SETF NCDU boat teams and swimming tanks landed.

The UTAH assault on a single Brigade or RCT front of two battalions with a third in support was made by the 8th Regiment backed by the 70th Tank Battalion and SETF troops, none of whom had been based or trained in South Wales, although the 'wading' Shermans and the light 'D' Company with their Stuart tanks had spent a couple of weeks on live fire training at Castlemartin. A limited number of 1st ESB with its 531st Engineer Shore Regiment had taken part in exercises on Gower, primarily as observers. The arrival of the BCPLBU Force the following day would change that with the 90th ID coming in support of the 'Ivy Leaves'.

Bombardment of both Normandy beach areas began simultaneously and followed similar timings, UTAH differing in as much as it was the 267 'Marauder' Medium bombers of the 9th USAF who dropped 4,404 bombs of 250 lbs each onto 7 targets. Also all measures were smaller in scale and number than OMAHA. What was similar was that although much of the bombardment fell on the planned area (where targets could be spotted,) but it was of little effect, especially as the assault went in a mile to the south due to strong tidal drift. The landings were 'a picnic' in comparison to the rest of the Invasion, with 20,000 men ashore in the first 15 hours. Clearing the beach early on and with topography of just sand dunes above the high water line meant relative ease of movement despite the hinterland being flooded and causeways few in number. The worst individual event was the loss of 60 men of the 29th FA Battalion whose LCT was sunk at sea. Overall there were 197 casualties in the entire 4th Division assault and amazingly only 12 fatalities in the 8th and 22nd Infantry Regiments leading the charge ashore.

Things were very different at OMAHA, 3 miles of beach backed by a shingle bank and low sea-wall for the most part, with bluffs rising between 100 and 150 ft behind a narrow stretch of marsh and mostly too steep for even tracked vehicles. Five 'draws' provided possible exits, but all were blocked either by tank trap ditches or massive concrete roadblocks. Concealed blockhouses and gun pits were well positioned and slit trenches on the bluff tops had dozens of heavy machine-gun positions. Line upon line of mined obstacles stretched across the beach between low and high water lines ready to trap and destroy landing craft. To make matters worse and unknown to the planners, the experienced 352nd Wehrmacht Infantry Division had just arrived in the area from the Eastern Front for recuperation and further training.

Beginning at 05.50 hours, the battleships *USS Arkansas* in the east supporting the 01 Assault Group and *USS Texas* in the west supporting the 02 Group plus the accompanying Allied cruisers opened fire on OMAHA. However the various bombardments proved relatively unsuccessful although some open field gun pits surrounding the draws were later found destroyed.

a) H- 45 to H-5 mins.	Navy - bombardment of 13 pre-identified targets.
b) H-30 to H-5 mins.	8th USAAF - 13,000 bombs (1,286 tons) on the bluffs.
c) H-30 to H-5 mins.	Army - 36 SP FA 105mm salvoes from LCT's on run-in.
d) H-20 to H-Hour.	Navy - 5 LCG (L) 4"guns shelling of 11 beach targets.
e) H-15 to H-Hour.	Army - 32 M4 Tanks on LCT (A)'s shelling 10 targets.
f) H-3.	Navy - 9 LCT(R)'s 9,000 rockets on 11 beach targets.
g) H-3	Army - 64 'DD' M4 Tanks firing at will.

The naval bombardment certainly woke everyone one up and kept the defending German troops in their bunkers; the overcautious 8th Air Force bombers, 446 B24 'Liberators'of the 2nd Bomb Division, instructed to delay release by 30 seconds if ground unclear (which it was) missed the beach defences and bluffs completely but certainly disrupted communications, not to mention livestock, inland. Rough water causing pitching on the LCT's and LCG's ruined accuracy and the rockets either fell short or landed beyond the bluffs thanks to the state of the sea. Whilst the 32 DD tanks of the 743rd Tank Battalion did not launch 6 miles out from the beach as planned, 8 were still lost in support of 116th Infantry on the western Dog Green. Further east, no fewer than 29 were launched at sea by the 741st Battalion and all foundered, the only ones making it to the beach having been brought right in as the lead tank had got stuck on the LCT ramp. The two battalions of the 16th Infantry had little or no support early on.

The moment 1,450 infantrymen landed over the 6,000 yards of OMAHA, mostly sea-sick and already tired, 'all hell broke loose' as the LCA or LCVP ramps dropped. Enemy machine-guns, mortars and artillery 'zeroed-in' at previously set distances from the surf line generally decimated infantry and engineers. The west to east drift in the rising tide caused further problems for many commanders as they were landing without recognising where they were. On the 16th RCT front Easy Red, the longest of all the beach sub sections had little in the way of defences, but sadly due to the west to east drift, few craft landed there. Yet on the narrower Fox section a little further to the east 16th Infantry were intermingled with 116th Infantry 30 man assault sections way off course adding to the congestion and providing even easier targets. The specially formed 397th AAA Provisional Machine-gun Battalion formed at Llanmartin only a month or so before and spread across the whole of the assault front was unable to offer much in the way of support losing 28 of its 36 machine guns in disembarking.

'What the hell has happened? It wasn't supposed to be like this. Defences are supposed to have been flattened!' was many a thought as men landing in the next waves attempted to seek shelter. Many of those in the first wave were either dead, wounded or totally shell shocked and leaderless. Any plans had now 'gone out of the window' as Combat Engineers became Infantrymen, replacing comrades mown down together with Medic's who attempted to treat them. Even MP's who were supposed to in the early stages direct traffic off the beaches had no where to send what was left of them, so became rescuers to the countless numbers of both fit and wounded men in the surf. By 0930 hrs the 6th Naval Beach Battalion which would suffer proportionately the highest number of casualties in the 5th ESB, ordered no more craft to land except Infantry and Engineers. Exactly the same was happening to the west in the 6th ESB beach area where the 7th NBB did likewise.

Photo: ESB men (white helmet arc visible) sheltering behind tetrahedron obstacles. Omaha Beachhead – Historical Division, U.S.War Department.

It was into this chaos that the first of the Combat Engineers of the 5th ESB who had trained on Gower had arrived, led by the reconnaissance team of the 37th Engineer Beach Group. They were battered by the waves and neighbouring assault craft seeking ways past obstacles and when their LCVP appeared to beach, the ramp dropped and they were out – into five foot of cold swirling sea-water. Not that that mattered too much, they were soaked to the skin anyway; what did matter was the fight for survival, having to shed equipment, get ashore and find shelter from the murderous machine-gun fire. All around craft were attempting to land their troops.

Frustration was adding to fear offshore with troop and equipment laden craft trying to land. By 10.30 hours the young commanders of two craft had enough and decided to crash through obstacles, come what may.

> '*LCT-30 (Lieutenant [jg] Sidney W Brinker USNR) crashed through the obstacles opposite the Fox Green exit leading to Colleville and beached, her automatic weapons blazing at a German strongpoint in an isolated villa that was holding up the troops. She managed to silence the enemy guns, but they riddled her with 88mm and machine-gun bullets and she had to be abandoned. At the same time, LCI-544 (Lieutenant E.B. Koehler USNR) was ramming her way through obstacles with all guns firing that would bear, and one of the infighting destroyers closed to cover her. She landed her troops and retracted with no loss, after accelerating the movement of troops off the beach.*'

The Invasion of France and Germany 1944-1945. Samuel Eliot Morison.

The 37th ECB Command Section aboard another LCVP from the assault group HQ ship *APA26 Samuel Chase* fared equally badly getting caught up on a mined beach stake later in the morning and before anything else could go wrong the newly-promoted C/O Lt. Colonel Lionel Smith ordered the ramp down. Immediately they were hit with a wall of water as the sea surged in and the 30 or so men were out into neck-deep water. Eventually gaining the low shelter of the pebble bank, the officers began working out how best to command and issue orders in the surrounding chaos, only to receive a direct mortar round hit, killing the S-2 Captain Paul F. Harkelroad and S-3 Captain Allen H Cox. For the Battalion worse was to happen as the highly popular and respected C/O was also hit by artillery shell fragments, falling and making the supreme sacrifice on the section of the beach that retains his name in memory. Two LCVP's and six out of twelve LCT's carrying 37th Engineers received direct hits from artillery fire on the shoreline, and this was just part of one supportive engineer battalion – the infantry with their own Engineers had fared even worse.

Junior Officers began to take command. First Lieutenant Robert Ross ordered a leaderless company of 16th Infantry to join his 37th Engineer 1st Platoon Company 'A' and set about clearing paths through wire and up the bluffs, all the while taking casualties from further above. On the beach, Private Vinton Dove and his co-driver Private William Shoemaker led charmed lives with his D-8 bulldozer, cutting a vehicle path through the shingle at E-1 draw and smashing the roadblock, shoving aside obstacles and filling in the deep anti-tank trap at the neighbouring E-3. Not content with that they actually started cutting a new road up the draw until they were told to stop until the enemy had been cleared from further up ahead. E-3 then became the first access opened on the entire beach.

Captain Louis J. Drnovich and the rest of Company 'A' were undertaking mine, wire and obstacle clearance at this time together with the attached 348th Engineers trying to clear the lateral beach road. He became incensed by one 88mm gun that was taking out tanks and vehicles attempting to climb the draw so he undertook a mission with a squad to destroy it. The mission was successful but at the cost of the Captains' life as he was found 3 hours later with a single shot through the head. Snipers, if found, would get no mercy from vengeful GI's.

Gradually things started to improve, thanks in no small measure to the Navy captains who with little or no radio transmissions from the beach, brought their destroyers so close in to the beach that many a keel scrapped the sand, but with point blank accuracy took out gun enfilading emplacements that had caused so many early casualties. By 1200 hrs the remaining Sherman tanks of the 741st Battalion were coming ashore and they were joined during the afternoon by those of Company 'B' 745th Tank Battalion from LSD *HMS Oceanway* which we had last seen in Swansea. The 18th RCT was ashore with the 26th RCT imminent from 'Force 'B'.

By 1330 hours the command group 5th ESB's LCVP had beached and the supportive 348th and 336th Engineers were following their Infantry Regiments. Even now very little co-ordinated or planned engineer work was taking place, except for mine and obstacle clearance and desperate humanitarian support. Two officers of the 348th ESB were to receive medals for saving 30 drowning infantrymen from their sinking LCVP. The boat team including non-swimmers were rescued by Lieutenants Morris W Selfe and Walter Sidlowski by one swimming out to the craft with a line whilst the other anchored himself in the surf – all made it safely ashore. Elsewhere units were being landed often in completely different locations from those planned. One of the LST's of the 336th Engineers ended up at Dog Green at the D-1 Exit over 1½ miles away from where they were supposed to be at E-3 draw. Much of the 336th reinforced the 348th during the landings with 330 men attached, but none the less many of their vehicles and road construction equipment still occupied 3 LST's of Force 'B' with other 5th ESB and PESBG vehicles spread around another seven. *LST 53* with the on-board troop commander being Captain Thomson F Hutchinson of Company 'B' 336th, embarked 59 vehicles with priority given to the 15 ammunition bearing DUKWs of the 458th Amphibian Truck Company, last to load having driven into the tank deck at the River Fal 'hard' ready to be first off (in reverse) out at sea. Sharing the tank deck were Hutchinson's Jeep, a truck mounted crane, two crawler cranes, two D-7 bulldozers towing Athey trailers, another truck mounted crane of the 348th ECB and squeezed in yet another Jeep this time from 5th ESB HQ. Company. Above on the main deck and first to load via the onboard elevator were mainly 2 ½ ton fully loaded trucks, water and weapon carriers with trailers, two more R-4 tractors and ¼ ton jeeps mainly of the 336th but also from the 61st Medical Battalion, 210th MP Company, 296th JASCO and 5th ESB HQ. Similarly Captain Lawrence Lothspeich of 'A' company had an almost identical load aboard *LST 533*. Both officers would also be responsible for all vehicle and marching troops onboard. An example of the troop muster on *LST 53* is indicative of how units were broken down into separate parties so that in the event of tragedy striking one vessel units would still be able to operate although obviously with a reduced capability until the 20% over-strength sections caught up to fill gaps.

336th ECB Company 'B'- 77
458th Amphibious Truck Co. (Part) - 42
HQ and HQ Company 533rd QM Battalion Detachment - 15
Medical Detachment - 8
4141st QM Service Company - 83
294 Joint Army Signal Company - 25
210 Military Police Company - 61
HQ 5th ESB group - 59
348th ECB HQ and Service Company - 4
320th AA Battalion (VLA) - 3

Neither battalion would suffer the losses experienced by the vanguard 37th ECB.

Four Officers and 17 men killed with 3 missing in action. Two Officers and 70 men wounded. DUKW drivers and mates of the 131st QM Mobile Battalion 459th and 453rd Amphibian Companies also suffered badly with 12 men killed and significantly 30 missing in action plus 19 wounded. The 6th NNB lost four Officers and 18 seamen killed with 12 Officers and 55 sailors wounded. All told the 5th Engineer Special Brigade suffered 131 killed and MIA, 267 wounded and evacuated and a further 127 injured. But they were ashore and with continual reinforcements arriving, 'SNAFU'* was being resolved and with the PSEBG Command Post established in a seized pill - box by the end of the day, problems were being sorted.

However there remained then one area that Brigadier General Hoge had foreseen and which never really got resolved as a result of inter-service rivalry. Communication hold-ups in getting craft to come in and onto the secured beach areas to discharge inevitably meant further delay for the movement of supplies to newly created dumps. The Navy had control of shipping right up to the shoreline, Hoge had argued unsuccessfully that the Army should have control of ship-to-shore movement and frequently resources were wasted with PESBG troops waiting for landing craft to beach. The all important manifests of cargo aboard vessels off-shore were often mislaid as well, so individual officers had to get out on the water aboard DUKWs to seek out who was carrying what.

The weather had played havoc with the planning and whilst a few assaulting troops landed almost unopposed, the majority struggled ashore braving everything in their path, rough surf, obstacles, barbed wire, mines, rifle fire, machine-guns, mortars and artillery. The two American beaches witnessed the extremes on offer, UTAH thankfully saw the lowest casualty numbers of all five Allied assaults but OMAHA turned out to be the worst by far. 'Bloody Omaha', according to the V Corps History, would see almost 2,400 casualties all told. Totals are always contentious as unit 'after action' reports didn't always correspond in the way the statistics (killed, wounded, injured or missing in action) were taken and then collated. What is certain is too many frightened but brave young and some more mature men, all 'citizen soldiers', fell that day.

*****

Footnote. This abbreviation 'Situation Normal All Fouled Up' was a commonly used term in its shortened form although one obvious word was often changed to a profanity!

EISENHOWER'S BROADCAST. Spoken by Col. Ernest Dupuy. BBC 09.32.

People of Western Europe: A landing was made this morning on the coast of France by troops of the Allied Expeditionary Force. This landing is part of the concerted United Nations plan for the liberation of Europe, made in conjunction with our great Russian allies.

I have this message for all of you. Although the initial assault may not have been made in your own country, the hour of your liberation is approaching.

All patriots, men and women, young and old, have a part to play in the achievement of final victory. To members of resistance movements, I say, follow the instructions you have received. To patriots who are not members of organised resistance groups, I say, continue your passive resistance, but do not needlessly endanger your lives until I give you the signal to rise and strike the enemy. The day will come when I shall need your united strength. Until that day, I call on you for the hard task of discipline and restraint.

Citizens of France! I am proud to have again under my command the gallant Forces of France. Fighting beside their Allies, they will play a worthy part in the liberation of their Homeland.

Because the initial landing has been made on the soil of your country, I repeat to you with even greater emphasis my message to the peoples of other occupied countries in Western Europe. Follow the instructions of your leaders. A premature uprising of all Frenchman may prevent you from being of maximum help to your country in the critical hour. Be patient. Prepare!

As Supreme Commander of the Allied Expeditionary Force, there is imposed on me the duty and responsibility of taking all measures necessary to the prosecution of war. Prompt and willing obedience to the orders that I shall issue is essential.

Effective civil administration of France must be provided by Frenchmen. All persons must continue in their present duties unless otherwise instructed. Those who have made common cause with the enemy and so betrayed their country will be removed. As France is liberated from her oppressors, you yourselves will choose your representatives and government under which you wish to live.

In the course of this campaign for the final defeat of the enemy you may sustain further loss and damage. Tragic though they may be, they are part of the price of victory. I assure you that I shall do all in my power to mitigate your hardships. I know that I can count on your steadfastness now, no less than in the past. The heroic deeds of Frenchmen who have continued the struggle against the Nazis and their Vichy satellites, in France and throughout the French Empire, have been an example and an inspiration to all of us.

This landing is but the opening phase of the campaign in Western Europe. Great battles lie ahead. I call upon all who love freedom to stand with us. Keep your faith staunch – our arms are resolute – together we shall achieve victory.

Chapter XIII

AFTERMATH

The South Wales invasion follow-up troops had also gone and the convoys departed, Swansea Bay was empty and the Operational Headquarters could pause and review events, fairly certain that they would not have to face a turnaround of the embarked forces. 'TURCO' had been set up just in case, but was not required. After over a year of planning and preparation followed by the ever increasing 'hubbub' of troop movements for training, concentration, marshalling and finally embarkation, the days immediately after 6 June 1944 seemed strangely quiet, although plenty was still going on with Operation BOLERO continuing and arrivals rising all the while. The month would see the highest total of Army cargo landed in the UK at 635,860 tons with 181, 975 offloaded at the BCP ports.

Photo: A familiar sight in the Marshalling areas, not even a goodbye kiss! (IWM)

OVERLORD hadn't finished, in fact it had really only just begun and similarly NEPTUNE would be ongoing with the shuttle service of men, weapons, vehicles, equipment and stores across the English Channel, ships returning with the wounded and POW's.

The Normandy Landings were looking successful. Off OMAHA Beach, Force 'B' was landing the 26th RCT and the 175th RCT from the 1st and 29th

212

Divisions and the first half of the BCPLBU Force had arrived unscathed at 'Piccadilly Circus' south of the Isle of Wight where they would turn to starboard for the run-in down the mine-swept channels nicknamed 'the Spout' to the transportation areas off the beaches.

In the Eastern Task Force area the same was true, although the MTV 'Sambut' had been bracketed by long range German artillery on the French coast and sunk on the 7th with a loss of life whilst passing through the Dover Straits. Operational Headquarters staff in Newport could breathe a sigh of relief and was stood down with assigned units returning to their former stations. 'Housekeeping' duties at the Marshalling Camps were applauded by the authorities with the 360th and 372nd Engineer detachments returned to advanced training assignments ready for their own inevitable POM – 'Preparation for Overseas Movement'. They, together with all the other units involved, received high praise for the preparation and marshalling duties that had completed the months of work. On the night before D-Day as the Bristol Channel convoys were making their way to Normandy, Colonel James A. Crothers, Commanding Officer of the 17th Major Port stated in a' thank you' message to all under command;

> '...there were a few kinks, but I suppose that was to be expected....I had the opportunity of talking to General McKelvie and General Robertson and their staffs just before they left. They were highly pleased....General McKelvie expressed himself to me as follows: "We are leaving here the best equipped division in ETOUSA".
>
> 'Supply Operations in the Bristol Channel'. - Lt. Col. F. Deisher

The *AP72 Susan B. Anthony* and the BCPLBU force would steam around between the Scillies and Lands End safely; no scares from E-boats or U- boats although once off the beaches mines would take their toll. The '*Susie B*' would suffer and come to the end of the line after attracting one that led to her sinking. Amazingly there were no fatalities and the incident holds the record for the singularly most successful evacuation of a stricken vessel of all time. Most of her troops landed on UTAH Beach although minus much of their equipment. Apart from that, the 90th Division landed without major incident and were able to support Barton's 4th ID according to plan.

Major-General Robertson's 2nd 'Indianhead' Division did likewise with the 9th RCT ashore early on the 7 June, followed by the 38th Regiment. The third regimental unit, the 23rd, was scheduled to be the last ashore and landed under clearing skies. However all three of the Regiments suffered their first fatalities the day before on D-Day itself with 14 soldiers making the ultimate sacrifice as part of the Special Engineer Task Force tasked with clearing beach obstacles. 9th Infantry Regiment lost Privates J.C. Blanton, John C. Freeman, Lester J. Horn and Joe C. Rivas. The 23rd Infantry Regiment lost Pvt. Stanley B. Brumback, and from the 38th Infantry Sgt. George E. Weil, PFC's Clarence Anders, Paul J. Baker, Joe M. Flores, Francis D. Powell, James W. Rew, Floyd Spiker, Murry A. St. John, and

Private Ralph A Tilwell all made the final sacrifice. The regiments had provided security details (i.e. riflemen to be part of boat teams as protection). Amazingly the 90 or so 2nd ECB men who were also included as part of the multi-service individual boat teams emerged unscathed despite one third of the casualties on OMAHA beach on D-Day being Engineers.

Photo: 2nd Division troops appropriately in 'Indian' file trudging up the Omaha bluff at D3 exit, the beach below showing signs of order. (IWM)

The two Divisions that sailed from South Wales went slightly different ways after Normandy. The 2nd Division would cover 1,750 miles in combat from Omaha via Brittany, Belgium and Germany, ending the war in Pilzen, Czechoslovakia, suffering a loss of 3,108 men killed and missing in 337 days of combat, plus 10,924 wounded. The 90th after initial inept leadership and subsequent heavy casualties in July fought its way across France with a succession of highly praised commanders, crossing the Rhine upstream of Frankfurt and ending the war at Susice, amazingly just down the road from the 'Indianhead's'.

The 'Tough 'Ombres' of the 90th Division lost 3,871 Officers and men in combat with 15,076 wounded. Both divisions ended up as part of Patton's' Third Army and it was ironic that having landed in Normandy as part of the same First Army pre-loaded build up force, they should end up sharing adjoining locations – troops from both divisions even being present at the surrender of the 11th Panzer Division at Vseruby on the 4 May 1945.

Back on the beach the build-up started in earnest. Coasters were beaching as planned to be relieved of their cargoes direct to trucks, while DUKW's received netted cargo from coasters still off shore. Early concerns that LST's could be in danger of breaking their backs proved unfounded and beaching greatly speeded up the urgent off loading.

Brigadier General Hoge and his Provisional Engineer Special Brigade Group continued work up until the 26 June when assets were used to form Headquarters Omaha Beach Command. The ESB's carried on with the 5th ESB continuing to operate Omaha until it was closed out on 19 November, moving to the Seine Sector in Paris to supervise construction there. Similarly the 6th ESB left Omaha by the New Year for construction work at Verdun. Both sailed home from Le Havre 3 days apart in July 1945.

Photo: Beached LST's from Force 'B' unload direct to land. LST 310 at right with her VLA Balloon was from Force 'O, beached after partial unloading to rhino ferry earlier. *(IWM)*

The reunited men of the 'All American' 82nd Airborne Division fought in the Cotentin Peninsula until returning to the UK on 13 July for rehabilitation. Fully fitted out they air assaulted the Nijmegen-Grave region of Holland as part of Operation MARKET GARDEN finishing the war on the River Elbe having suffered 1,951 killed and missing and 6,560 wounded in combat. Similarly the

101st 'Screaming Eagles' left UTAH beach with the 82nd on the same day for the UK, before flying out again on 17 September to seize the bridges at Veghel and Zen north of Eindhoven. They were undergoing rehabilitation when the Ardennes counter-offensive began and they were rushed to the front, getting surrounded but not defeated, earning the nick-name of the 'Battling Bastards of Bastogne'. Further R & R was required and by 7 May they had reached Berchtesgaden, Hitler's Eagles Nest, when hostilities ended. They had lost 2,090 in action with 6,388 wounded.

Shoulder patches: 1st ID., 29th ID., 2nd ID., 4th ID., 90th ID., 82nd & 101st AD. Provisional Engineer Special Brigade Group (Amphibious Troops) central.

Those men in the units that had taken part in looking after the Field Forces for the Invasion now prepared for their future roles, most 'shipping out' eventually to France. Similarly, others who had spent time in South Wales did likewise.

12th Evacuation Hospital moved to Sale billets near Manchester for a rest period before travelling back south in mid May to set up a transit hospital at Moreton, Dorset ready to receive casualties from Normandy.

89th Quartermaster Truck Battalion continued trucking duties right through the next two months before going to France at the beginning of August. They became part of the 'Red Ball Express' the famous Transportation Corps organization that kept the US Armies supplied in the East during the Battle of the Bulge and the subsequent Rhine Crossings.

93rd Medical (Gas Treatment) Battalion spent 11 weeks all told in Pontypridd before landing in France as part of Patton's Third Army.

95th Engineer General Service Regiment completed their training in Llanelwydd on 21 June and moved to a bivouac camp at Painswick, Gloucestershire for concentration, then to the Marshalling area at Southampton, sailing for France on the 4th July.

111th Ordnance (Medium Maintenance) Company had noticed a drop off in requested work as the 28th Infantry Division had left for pastures new and the 2nd Division had been re-equipping during the month they were South Wales. But in the first week of June they were instructed to finish and clear away any jobs in the workshops, so they realized something was up. On 5 June, the C/O received a long distance phone call to prepare for movement by road at midnight to a new location. If the unit needed any further confirmation of imminent activity, then they didn't have long to wait, for at 10.30pm the men gazed in awe at the sound and sight of twin engine DC-3's towing gliders streaming overhead as the 101st Airborne assembled and circled prior to turning south-east to their UK departure point over Portland Bill bound for Normandy. Then as darkness fell - British double summertime meant it was light until 23.00 hours - they loaded up and were away. Following a 9 hour drive for the faster first serial of two, the mechanics arrived at a marshalling camp near Plymouth, bleary eyed but grateful for breakfast, a shower and six hours sleep. Waterproofing and preparations for a SSV took a couple of days and then the trucks all loaded with vehicle spares such as complete axle units and towing trailers of 105mm ammunition set off for the embarkation hards to be loaded on LCT's. On 11 June morning they landed on Omaha, evidence of the horror of the assault 5 days earlier still around.

360th Engineer (GS) Regiment received orders on D-Day to prepare for movement to a new destination and all detachments closed in at Camp Dan-Y-Parc on 16 June. A Regimental Field Day was held appropriately on the Fourth of July, concluding with a Regimental Review. The troops were inspected by Major-General Halstead, the British Commander of the South Wales District and by their C/O Colonel Barkesdale. July 12 they moved to a bivouac camp north of Bournemouth, then for an odd unknown reason back to Island Farm Camp, South Wales on 23 July for just seven days. Finally they were marshalled near

Southampton and landed in France on 4 August.

366th Engineer (GS) Regiment remained at Monmouth Camp until 30 June when the Regiment less the 2nd Battalion left for a concentration area near Bournemouth. The 2nd Battalion rejoined them having been recalled from depot duties. Following various 'clearing up' operations at the now partially redundant invasion marshalling camps in the south of England they sailed from Southampton to UTAH Beach on 19 August.

623rd Quartermaster Laundry Company departed Caerphilly on 25 August leaving half a dozen GI brides behind them just from the 623rd and landed on Utah Beach 1 September. The platoons were split up for most of the time being assigned to various Evacuation and Field hospitals to provide laundry cover. The brides didn't depart for the States until late 1945! The exact figure regarding South Wales G.I. war brides is thought to be about 700, with almost 40,000 in the whole of the United Kingdom.

372nd Engineer (GS) Regiment left their Ewenny Park camp on 21 June for Rendcombe Park Camp near Cirencester for a very wet two weeks before moving on to dry billets at Fairford Park. Various improvements to hospital sites were carried out by them, but then in July there was an urgent order from the Office of the Chief Engineer to report to Purfleet S3 Camp for a major construction job. Replacement and additional Phoenix caissons were desperately needed for the Mulberry Harbours following the storm in mid to late June and the Regiment built three in Tilbury Dry Docks, so it wasn't until 9 October that they landed on Utah Beach.

373rd Engineer (GS) Regiment closed in at St. Donats Castle between the 11 and 15 June for training and final preparations before leaving for the staging area down south on 13 July prior to sailing.

863rd Ordnance (Heavy Automotive Maintenance) Company moved to Camp Heath on 14 June continuing with operations before being transferred to Ordnance Depot O-616 at Wallasey with the men being billeted in New Brighton. Other formations not actually involved in the Invasion as field or static forces continued with their own training and preparation work. G-40 at Barry got even busier handling huge amounts of engineering equipment on the completed extension and sending consignments as required to France from the BC Ports. The US Army hospitals at Govilon, Rhyd Lafar and Carmarthen needless to say got even busier with the incoming flow of wounded brought from the South Coast aboard the hospital trains. The US Navy hospital at Milford received casualties for a while, the *USAH Refuge* taking 600 seriously wounded back home in early July.

99th Infantry Bn. (US/Norwegians) following their move from Glanusk Park to Hereford, would weather the storm of 19-22 June aboard LCI's off OMAHA beach. Fighting across France, seizing the Elbeuf Bridge over the Seine, they were the unit that repelled Col. Otto Skorzeny and his infamous Panzer Brigade 150 (Nazi's in US Army uniforms) in the Ardennes. They guarded seized gold worth 2 billion dollars, finishing the war in Norway as part of the 474th Infantry Regiment charged with receiving the surrender of 300,000 German troops.

526th Armoured Infantry Battalion (Separate) continued to train in the Preseli's, spending D-Day sweeping roads whilst gazing and marvelling at the constant stream of airborne troop and equipment C47's overhead even so far west. Most of the skies over England and Wales were used to assemble fleets of aircraft prior to heading south to France. Together with their associated Tank battalions and Ordnance support they would embark for France in July, sailing from Swansea.

756th Railway Shop Battalion Company B had prepared something like 750 locomotives during their time at Ebbw Junction of which 355 of the 2-8-0's and 104 of the 0-6-0 'shunters' and 56 diesels went to the nearby storage sites of Tonteg, Penrhos, Cadoxton and Dyffryn Isaf, not to mention work on the 147 that the GWR had on loan during the period. Work on return of these would be carried out by the 757th RSB prior to shipping out to France in September. The 756th had rejoined their Battalion in Hainault where they continued assembling rail wagons until late October when they transferred to Marseilles to continue producing rolling stock as cases of parts arrived from the States.

757th Railway Shop Battalion spent a happy 2 months in Caerphilly servicing locomotives being returned from the GWR and despatching the stored loco's to Cardiff and other ports ready for shipping. They landed in France in July and carried on locomotive repairs and maintenance plus rolling stock refurbishment at Cherbourg before moving through France and finishing the war in Germany.

771st Tank Destroyer Battalion were trucked out of South Wales on 1 May to the now defunct Assault Training Center in North Devon, the 'Gypsies' pitching camp on Saunton Golf Course. Now they were to get ready for action with more training on Exmoor and firing practice on the Minehead Range. Further 'repple-depple' training for new July arrivals and consequent vehicle repair work took time, but by September POM's were in place and they left for OMAHA on the 15th.

Figures for the end of June saw a remarkable but not entirely surprising drop in the numbers of troops landed in the Bristol Channel ports with just 506 debarking. There were still 121,502 servicemen and women who had all arrived on the Clyde or the Mersey during the month. Despite the congestion in ports caused by Operation OVERLORD /NEPTUNE and the Invasion of Normandy, there was now a recorded total of 1,792,512 arrivals.

The Second World War had another 11 months to run in Europe, at the end of which the Supreme Commander General Eisenhower made and published his report. In it he was keen to point out that the success of the Invasion of Normandy rested not just on the valour of the men who took part or in the combined arms of the services, but also on the importance of the steady supply of the forces. He highlighted the fact that the German strategy was to "Deny the Allies the use of ports and they will be unable to support their armies ashore." The artificial Mulberry harbours undoubtedly played their role, but it was the fact that troops were basically supported as they landed, not being beleaguered in the feint hope that help and supplies would be on the way.

The Provisional Engineer Special Brigade Group could take pride in the knowledge that at least on OMAHA beach, despite the early carnage of the initial assault, they were able to facilitate the distribution of large amounts of stores and ammunition from the massive seaborne operation to the troops quickly. Eisenhower quoted from a captured enemy document, written by a German division commander, which paid as great a tribute to all the forces responsible for supply of the front-line troops as could be found:

> *"I cannot understand these Americans. Each night we know that we have cut them to pieces, inflicted heavy casualties, mowed down their transport. We know, in some cases, we have almost decimated entire battalions. But in the morning, we are suddenly faced with fresh battalions, with complete replacements of men, machines, food, tools, and weapons. This happens day after day. If I did not see it with my own eyes, I would say it is impossible to give this kind of support to frontline troops so far from their bases."*

Report by the Supreme Commander to the Chiefs of Staff on
The Operations in Europe of the Allied Expeditionary Force.
6 June 1944 to 8 May 1945.
HM Stationary Office.

High on the bluff overlooking OMAHA beach stands the Normandy American Cemetery and Memorial. Here lie 9,386 service men and women, far from home.

Behind the Memorial at the top of the picture lies the Garden of the Missing, its semi-circular wall inscribed with 1,557 names of those who paid the ultimate sacrifice in the service of their country that have no known grave.

THINK NOT ONLY UPON THEIR PASSING
REMEMBER THE GLORY OF THEIR SPIRIT

More than a few of those interred here came from the 28th Infantry Division that had become synonymous with South Wales. Many National Guardsmen mustered in the coal-mining towns of Pennsylvania such as Scranton, home for so many families of Welsh origin. Spared the devastating losses of their sister 29th Division on the sands of Omaha, none the less lives would be lost in the Battle for Normandy following their arrival in July. They would suffer their own Armageddon further east just before Christmas. So many US Army and US Navy units spent time in South Wales during the twelve months leading up to D-Day but for over half of that period it was the 14,500 men of the Pennsylvanian NG that epitomised the 'friendly invasion'. The 28th Infantry 'Keystone' Division and the men of the units that had been in South Wales since October 1943 had made many, many friends during their stay.

Back in April when they were suddenly transferred away, Lt. Col. Cummings, Commanding Officer of 3rd Battalion 110th Infantry Regiment had taken the trouble, as many Commanders did, to write letters of thanks. One to the Mayor of Haverfordwest Councillor John White was published in The West Wales Guardian 12 April 1944.

> 'My dear Mr White.
>
> *I am taking this opportunity of apologising for our unceremonious departure from your midst and for not having bid you farewell in person. However, at this "stage of the game", our moves, destination etc, cannot be made known ahead of time. I want you to be fully aware of my own personal thanks, and through me of those men who were with me, for all that you have done for us during our stay with you and the fine people of Haverfordwest. No unit would have been more fortunate in its neighbours, and we are fully aware of our blessings in that way. Many excellent friendships were made during our stay with you and I know they will be lasting. The spirit of cooperation and desire to be of so much assistance during our stay with you was always apparent and greatly appreciated by us. With again many thanks for all you have done for us, and with hope that we shall be able to again meet under less trying conditions.*
>
> *I remain, sincerely,*
>
> *E.A. Cummings*
> *Lt. Col. Infantry.*

Many such proposed meetings would never take place. The Division landed in France in July, and the 110th Infantry Regiment had the honour of leading the Liberation Parade down the Champs Elysee's in Paris on August 29th 1944.

The 'citizen soldiers' fought with distinction and honour, like so many in this story, but were decimated in the Hurtgen Forest and the Ardennes 'Battle of

221

the Bulge'. The 28th Division earned another nick-name especially among its veterans and opponents, being known as the 'Bloody Bucket' Division, so named after its red keystone badge and as a result of suffering over 17,000 casualties in World War II of which 3,000 men were killed or missing in action. RIP.

Photo: 110th Infantry Regiment, 28th 'Keystone' Division marches in Paris.

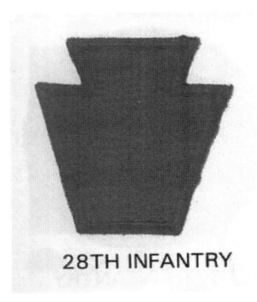

Shoulder patch of the Division.

Inducted into Federal Service 17th Feb. 1941 Philadelphia PA. as the 28th Division. Redesignated 28th Infantry Division 17 Feb. 1942. ('Keystone Division')

*****

APPENDICES

Appendix 1.

US TROOP CONVOYS TO THE UNITED KINGDOM
7 June 1943 – 6 June 1944

Chronological departure order. Differing speeds coupled with unsettled weather meant some voyages took longer.
Troop numbers in brackets indicate estimate or capacity often well exceeded.
Note: Additional troops were also aboard some slower vessels in HX series.

Prefix	Ship/Convoy	Troops	Departure	Arrival	Date

Period covered in Part 1. (Chapters I - V

JUNE '43

Prefix	Ship/Convoy	Troops	Departure	Arrival	Date
AT 48	Queen Mary	(12,000)	NY 01/06/43	> Gourock	07/06/43
AT 49	Emp'of Scot'	(4,000)	HX 11/06/43	> Liverpool	18/06/43
AT 50	Andes	(4,500)	HX 17/06/43	> Liverpool	24/06/43
AT 51	Pasteur	4,498	HX 24/06/43	> Liverpool	30/06/43
AT 52	Queen Mary	15,281	NY 24/06/43	> Gourock	29/06/43

JULY

Prefix	Ship/Convoy	Troops	Departure	Arrival	Date
AT 53	Aquitania	(7,000)	NY 08/07/43	> Clyde	15/07/43
AT 54	Q. Elizabeth	(14,000)	NY 01/07/43	> Clyde	06/07/43
CU 3	23 tankers		Cur 11/07/43	> Clyde	24/07/43
AT 55	Pasteur	4,495	HX 17/07/43	> Clyde	22/07/43
AT 55A	4P 1T 1Sp	(15,968)	NY 17/07/43	> Clyde	27/07/43
AT 56	Q. Elizabeth	14,994	HX 23/07/43	> Clyde	27/07/43
AT 57	------------------------------ No record ---				
AT 57A	Mariposa	(4,700)	BO 07/08/43	> Reyk/Clyde	17/08 /43
AT 58	Queen Mary	15,740	NY 23/07/43	> Gourock	30/07/43

AUGUST

Prefix	Ship/Convoy	Troops	Departure	Arrival	Date
AT 58A	Athlone Castle	3,520	NY 09/08/43	> Liverpool	17/08/43
AT 59	Mauretania	5,089	NY 06/08/43	> Liverpool	11/08/43
AT 60	Pasteur	4,485	NY 14/08/43	> Liverpool	21/08/43
AT 62	Q. Elizabeth	15,116	NY 20/08/43	> Clyde	25/08/43
UT 1	5 ships	(12,786)	Nor 21/08/43	> Clyde/Liv	04/09/43
CU 4	22 tankers		Cur 26/08/43	> Liverpool	09/09/43
AT 61	Queen Mary	15,116	NY 27/08/43	> Gourock	31/08/43

SEPTEMBER

UT 2	19 ships	(42,570)	NY 05/09/43	>	Liv/BCP's	15/09/43
AT 62A	*Gen. J. Pope*	(4,500)	HR 05/09/43	>	Clyde	12/09/43
AT 63	*Mauretania*	7,620	NY 12/09/43	>	Liverpool	19/10/43
AT 65	*Aquitania*	7,984	NY 01/10/43	>	Clyde	09/10/43
AT 66	*Queen Mary*	14,800	NY 20/09/43	>	Gourock	25/09/43
AT 64	*Q.Elizabeth*	14,998	HX 23/09/43	>	Clyde	19/09/43

OCTOBER

UT 3	24 P's 87,897	(66,933)	NY 08/10/43	>	Liv/BCP's	17/10/43
AT 67	*Queen Mary*	12,007	NY 09/10/43	>	Gourock	15/10/43
AT 68	*Mauretania*	7,599	BO 09/10/43	>	Liverpool	17/10/43
AT 69	*Q. Elizabeth*	13,000	NY 13/10/43	>	Clyde	18/10/43
CU 5	19 – 18T 1 RG		NY 13/10/43	>	Liv/BCP's	24/10/43
UT 4	23 + escorts	(46,416)	NY 21/10/43	>	Liv/BCP's	31/10/43
AT 70	*Aquitania*	(7,000)	HX 23/10/43	>	Clyde	29/10/43

NOVEMBER

AT 73	*Queen Mary*	11,800	NY 24/10/43	>	Gourock	02/11/43
CU 6	18 T, 1RG.		NY 26/10/43	>	Liverpool	12/11/43
AT 71	*Q. Elizabeth*	12,000	NY 03/11/43	>	Clyde	09/11/43
AT 72	*Mauretania*	7,079	HX 02/11/43	>	Liverpool	08/11/43
UT 4A	8 + escorts	(12,443)	NY 05/11/43	>	Clyde/Liv	15/11/43
AT 74	*Aquitania*	(7,000)	NY 17/11/43	>	Clyde	24/11/43
AT 74A	*Andes*	5,004	NY 12/11/43	>	Liverpool	20/11/43
AT 77	*Queen Mary*	2,146	NY 15/11/43	>	Gourock	20/11/43
CU 7	14T 1RG 2GP	793	NY 20/11/43	>	Liv/BCP's	01/12/43
AT 75	*Q. Elizabeth*	12,981	NY 03/11/43	>	Clyde	28/11/43

DECEMBER

AT 76	*Mauretania*	7,567	HX 25/11/43	>	Liverpool	01/12/43
AT 76A	*Pasteur*	4,477	NY 26/11/43	>	Liverpool	03/12/43
CU 8	12T 2P 3Ots		NY 02/12/43	>	Liv/BCP's	13/12/43
AT 78	*Queen Mary*	11,907	NY 03/12/43	>	Gourock	09/12/43
AT 79	*Aquitania*	8,000	NY 12/12/43	>	Clyde	19/12/43
UT 5	28 + escorts	(58,798)	NY 05/12/43	>	Liv/BCP's	15/12/43
AT 80	*Q. Elizabeth*	13,000	NY 04/12/43	>	Clyde	19/12/43
AT 81	*Mauretania*	7,494	HX 15/12/43	>	Liverpool	21/12/43
AT 81A	*Pasteur*	4,478	HX 15/12/43	>	Liverpool	21/12/43
CU 9	14T 1GP 2C		NY 15/12/43	>	Liverpool	26/12/43
AT 82	*Queen Mary*	12,100	NY 23/12/43	>	Gourock	29/12/43

Period covered in Part 2 *(Chapters VI – VIII)*

JANUARY '44

CU 10	12T 1P 1GP 2RG		NY 26/12/43	>	Liv/BCP's	06/01/44
UT 6	19P3AC1T1C	(56,485)	NY 29/12/43	>	Liv/BCP's	08/01/44
AT 83	---------------------------------- No record ----------------------------------					
AT 84	*Q. Elizabeth*	12,922	NY 02/01/44	>	Clyde	08/01/44
AT 85	*Aquitania*	(7,000)	NY 02/01/44	>	Clyde	10/01/44
AT 86	*Mauretania*	7,586	NY 09/01/44	>	Liverpool	17/01/44
CU 11	13T 3P 3GP 1C		NY 09/01/44	>	Liv/BCP's	20/01/44
AT 87	*Ile De France*	9,787	NY 17/01/44	>	Clyde	25/01/44
UT 7	23P 3AC 4Ots	(55,960)	NY 18/01/44	>	Liv/BCP's	29/01/44
CU 12	16T 3P 4R/C		NY 19/01/44	>	Liv/BCP's	30/01/44
AT 87A	*Pasteur*	4,488	HX 21/01/44	>	Liverpool	27/01/44
AT 88	*Queen Mary*	12,018	NY 22/01/44	>	Clyde	28/01/44

FEBRUARY

AT 89	*Aquitania*	7,634	NY 29/01/44	>	Clyde	05/02/44
AT 90	*Mauretania*	7,583	NY 31/01/44	>	Liverpool	08/02/44
CU 13	19T 1GP 3RG		NY 01/02/44	>	Liv/BCP's	13/02/44
AT 91	*Q. Elizabeth*	13,065	NY 02/01/44	>	Clyde	08/02/44
UT 8	25P1AC3Ots	(73,692)	NY 11/02/44	>	Liv/BCP's	23/02/44
AT 93	*Queen Mary*	12,081	NY 12/02/44	>	Gourock	18/02/44
AT93A	*Andes*	4,052	NY 09/02/44	>	Liverpool	17/02/44
CU 14	15T 6Ots.		NY 12/02/44	>	Liv/BCP's	24/02/44
AT 92	*Ile De France*	9,819	HX 16/02/44	>	Clyde	22/02/44
AT 93B	*Pasteur*	4,500	NY 21/02/44	>	Liverpool	28/02/44
CU 15	16T 1P 2Ots.		NY 22/02/44	>	Liv/BCP's	06/03/44
AT 94	*Aquitania*	7,664	NY 21/02/44	>	Clyde	28/02/44
AT 95	---------------------------------- No record ----------------------------------					
AT 96	*Mauretania*	7,625	NY 27/02/44	>	Liverpool	08/02/44

MARCH

UT 9	21P 5AK 4Ots	(60,555)	NY 27/02/44	>	Liv/BCP's	09/03/44
AT 97	*Queen Mary*	11,950	NY 01/03/44	>	Gourock	07/03/44
CU 16	19T 3RG 5Ots .		NY 01/03/44	>	Liv/BCP's	12/03/44
CU 17	17T 2P 4Ots.		NY 10/03/44	>	Liv/BCP's	20/03/44
AT 98	*Ile De France*	7,709	NY 13/03/44	>	Clyde	21/03/44
AT 99	---------------------------------- No record ----------------------------------					
AT100	*Aquitania*	7,660	NY 17/03/44	>	Clyde	21/03/44
AT100A	*Pasteur*	4,524	NY 25/03/44	>	Liverpool	21/03/44
CU 18	17T 1AKA 6Ots.		NY 19/03/44	>	Liv/BCP's	08/04/44
AT101	*Queen Mary*	12,072	NY 21/03/44	>	Gourock	27/03/44

Prefix	Ship/Convoy	Troops	Departure		Arrival	Date
			APRIL			
UT 10	19P 1AC 5Ots.(60,123)		NY 26/03/44	>	Liv/BCP's	03/04/44
CU 19	16T 3P 6Ots.	8,062	NY 28/03/44	>	Liv/BCP's	08/04/44
AT102	*Mauretania*	(7,000)	NY 31/03/44	>	Liverpool	08/04/44
AT103	*N'w Amsterdam*	7,564	NY 26/03/44	>	Clyde	01/04/44
AT103A	*Empress / Scot.*	4,936	HX 11/04/44	>	Liverpool	18/04/44
AT104	*Q.Elizabeth*	13,042	NY 31/03/44	>	Clyde	06/04/44
CU 20	19T 3GP 5Ots.	2,983	NY 06/04/44	>	Liv/BCP's	18/04/44
AT104A	*Andes*	4,082	HX 31/03/44	>	Liverpool	07/04/44
AT104B	*Pasteur*	4,491	HX 05/04/44	>	Liverpool	11/04/44
AT105	*Ile De France*	9,759	NY 07/04/44	>	Clyde	15/04/44
AT105A	*Wakefield*	7,033	BO 13/04/44	>	Liverpool	21/04/44
UT 11	24P 2Ots.	(61,540)	NY 16/04/44	>	Liv/BCP's	06/04/44
AT106	*Aquitania*	(7,000)	NY 06/04/44	>	Clyde	14/04/44
AT107	*Queen Mary*	11,979	NY 10/04/44	>	Gourock	16/04/44
CU 21	15T 1AC 9Ots.		NY 16/04/44	>	Liv/BCP's	26/04/44
AT108	*Q. Elizabeth*	13,021	NY 20/04/44	>	Clyde	26/04/44
AT109	*N'w Amsterdam*	7,500	NY 18/04/44	>	Clyde	26/04/44
AT110	*Mauretania*	7,598	NY 22/04/44	>	Liverpool	30/04/44
			MAY			
CU 22	16T 3GP 10Ots	1,689	NY 24/04/44	>	Liv/BCP's	06/05/44
AT111	*Andes*	4,740	NY 10/05/44	>	Liverpool	17/05/44
AT112	*Ile De France*	9,227	HX 30/04/44	>	Clyde	06/05/44
AT113	*Empress / Scot.*	4,912	HX 04/05/44	>	Liverpool	10/05/44
TCU23	16T 10P17Ots.(39,288)		NY 03/05/44	>	Liv/BCP's	14/05/44
AT114	*Pasteur*	4,536	NY 07/05/44	>	Liverpool	14/05/44
AT114A	*Wakefield*	6,918	BO 12/05/44	>	Liverpool	19/05/44
TCU24	21T 8P 5Ots. (11,806)		NY 12/05/44	>	Liv/BCP's	23/05/44
"	9P.	16,429	BO 13/05/44	>	"	"
TCU24B	3T 10C	-	NY 14/04/44	>	Liv/BCP's	25/05/44
AT115	*Mauretania*	1,090	NY 15/05/44	>	Liverpool	22/05/44
AT116	*Andes*	5,001	HX 03/06/44	>	Liverpool	09/06/44
CU 25	22T 6P 10Ots.	6,838	NY 21/05/44	>	Liverpool	31/05/44
AT117	-------------------------------- No record --------------------------------					

Period covered in Part 3 (*Chapters XI – XII*)

JUNE

AT118	*Empress / Scot.*	4,883	HX 26/05/44	> Clyde	01/06/44
AT119	*Pasteur*	4,486	NY 29/05/44	> Liverpool	05/06/44
AT119A	*Mariposa*	(5,000)	BO 03/06/44	> Clyde	11/06/44
AT119B	*M't Vernon*	6,057	BO 03/06/44	> Liverpool	10/06/44
AT120	*Q. Elizabeth*	13,125	NY 30/05/44	> Clyde	05/06/44

Abbreviations for ships in convoys:

P	- Personnel (Troopships)	G	- General cargo (P with troops)
AKA -	Attack Transport (USN)	ST - Seatrain specialist carrier	
T	- Tanker	AC - Aircraft Carrier	
R	- Refrigerated Cargo	RG - Refrigerated and General Cargo	
Ots.	– Others		

Convoys listed include fast Independents (AT), multiple ship (UT) convoys, plus CU convoys that ultimately combined with UT convoys. The 11 UT convoys conveyed 592,041 troops, an average of 53,822 each, with no loss.

*****

Appendix 2

WBS – XXIX DISTRICT INSTALLATIONS

Numbers 1 – 44

Index	Location	Town	Officers	Men	Map Ref.
1	Eastnor Park	Ledbury	-	2500	VP 1908
2	Billets	Ledbury	-	250	VP 1558
3	Highwell House	Bromyard	20	228	VP 1176
4	Billets	Bromyard	-	250	VP 1076
5	Frenchay Park	Bristol	162	500	VU 0898
6	Nass Camp	Lydney	33	704	VP 0922
7	Billets, S.Fishponds	Bristol	-	800	VU 070960
8	Billets, Fishponds	Bristol	-	800	VU 070960
9	Henbury Hill	Bristol	5	100	VU 015987
10	Billets, Brislington	Bristol	-	1000	VU 060910
11	Drill Hall Camp	Ross-0n-Wye	50	1000	VP 050450
12	Billets	Ross-on-Wye	-	250	VP 040550
13	Patchway Camp	Bristol	35	715	VU 058016
14	Billets, Knowle	Bristol	-	1000	VU 040910
15	Knowle	Bristol	15	271	VU 048917
16	Filton Camp	Bristol	54	1000	VU 038019
17	Billets, Horsefield	Bristol	-	1000	U 140980
18	Lines, Whitchurch	Bristol	3	70	V 040980
19	Billets, Southmead	Bristol	-	400	U 030990
20	Overcourt Manor	Bristol	9	177	T 031031
21	Mullers Orphanage	Bristol	40	2808	U138966
22	Billets, Bishopston	Bristol	-	300	U 030960
23	Cabot Café.	Bristol	50	-	V 026937
24	White City, Bedminster	Bristol	50	1190	V 009928
25	Whiteladies Garage	Bristol	-	30	U 019948
26	Southmead	Bristol	5	110	U 028986
27	Henleaze	Bristol	37	741	U 015971
28	Billets, Westbury	Bristol	-	500	U 010980
29	Billets, Bedminster	Bristol	-	1000	O 010920
30	24 Henfre Road	Bristol	-	24	V 018927
31	Billets, Stoke Bishop	Bristol	-	1000	U 000960
32	Billets, Henlaye	Bristol	-	1000	V 020970
33	Clifton College	Bristol	75	3500	U 010948
34	7 & 9 The Glen, Clifton	Bristol	5	92	U 017963
35	Stoke Bishop	Bristol	-	50	U 005969

Numbers 36 – 74

Index	Location	Town	Officers	Men	Map Ref.
36	Seamills Camp.	Avonmouth	34	1710	T 985980
37	Billets, Seamills	Avonmouth	-	500	T 990960
38	Ashton Court	Bristol	38	752	T 995928
39	Southside Wood	Bristol	28	570	T 995986
40	RACE COURSE CAMP	Chepstow	129	2751	O 970160
41	SEDBURY CAMP	Sedbury	34	749	O 995159
42	BULWARK CAMP	Chepstow	56	1246	O 978135
43	Billets, Shirehampton	Bristol	-	250	T 970980
44	Berrington Park	Leominster	120	2380	O 963884
45	Failand Camp	Bristol	68	1946	T 965927
46	Transit Camp	Avonmouth	12	498	T 960995
47	Bullingham Convent	Hereford	20	250	O 960610
48	G-20 Depot	Morton-on-Lugg	-	1250	O 954672
49	Brickworks Camp	Hereford	30	870	O 960610
50	Old Barracks Block	Hereford	10	240	O 960610
51	Race Course Camp	Hereford	-	120	O 960610
52	Billets	Hereford	-	500	O 960610
53	Lansford House	Hereford	5	70	O 960610
54	Tyntesfield Hospital	Nr Bristol	79	350	T 940930
55	Town Block	Monmouth	30	870	O 950340
56	Wonastow Court	Monmouth	18	396	O 920330
57	Billets	Leominster	-	500	O 950800
58	Town Block	Leominster	75	1425	O 946802
59	Baron's Cross Hospital	Leominster	149	390	O 927787
60	Wraxall	Bristol	-	30	T 932930
61	*Unknown*	Portishead	3	80	T 908971
62	Tyntesfield Camp	Nr Bristol	68	1406	T 943933
63	Foxley Hospital Camp	Nr Hereford	-	2500	O 869675
64	Foxley Canadian Camp	Nr Hereford	30	700	O 869677
65	*Unknown*	Weobley	5	130	O 852757
66	LLANMARTIN	Newport	112	3008	O 828098
67	Jarris Charity School	Staunton-on-W	10	132	O 815663
68	Clytha Park	Raglan	6	132	O 808290
69	Stannage Park	Kington	60	1190	O 778938
70	Q-303 POL Depot	Eardisley	10	140	O 765717
71	LLANOVER PARK	Abergavenny	112	3008	O 763300
72	Village Block	Kington	10	190	O 710790
73	Stowe Hill Block	Newport	79	10	O 752097
74	LLANTARNUM PARK	Newport	56	1240	O 750140

Numbers 75 – 114

Index	Location	Town	Officers	Men	Map Ref.
75	Shaftesbury St. Block	Newport	6	200	O 752108
76	Malpas Camp	Newport	56	1504	O 745126
77	Polo Fields, New Inn	Pontypool	56	1246	O 745208
78	Tredegar Park	Newport	28	600	O 730068
79	Tredegar CRS O-605	Newport	6	78	O 731060
80	Tredegar Hill	Newport	6	150	O 732062
81	QM Distribution Point	Abergavenny	3	40	O 735630
82	Kington Hospital	Kington	204	3548	O 729760
83	Aberbaiden House	Gilwern	20	320	O 720350
84	Whitney Court	Whitney'Wye	18	276	O 715694
85	Govilon Hospital	Gilwern	158	544	O 710300
86	Moor Camp	Hay-on-Wye	18	396	O 690640
87	CWRT Y GOLLEN	Crickhowell	112	3008	O 680382
88	ST. MELLONS	St. Mellons	56	1550	T 685093
89	DAN Y PARC	Gilwern	56	1504	O 670365
90	Village Block	Crickhowell	12	228	O 670400
91	LLANGATTOCK PARK	Crickhowell	34	749	O 660390
92	Institute, Llangattock	Crickhowell	12	228	O 060390
93	GLANUSK PARK	Crickhowell	44	1001	O 640420
94	PONTLLANFRAITH	Pontllanfraith	112	2480	O 620170
95	Drill Hall, Park Street	Cardiff	24	504	T 623974
96	Billets, Whitchurch	Cardiff	-	1750	T 620980
97	MAINDY BARRACKS	Cardiff	28	600	O 619998
98	HEATH CAMP	Cardiff	85	1750	T 614005
99	129 Cathedral Road	Cardiff	25	2	T 608980
100	Marcross Lodge	Cardiff	15	2	T 597993
101	Block I, Llandaff	Cardiff	24	504	T 596995
102	Billets.	Bargoed	-	500	O 590220
103	Pontygwindy Hostel	Caerphilly	8	520	O 590100
104	Billets	Caerphilly	-	250	O 590050
105	Silverton L. Fairwater Rd.	Cardiff	9	143	T 594995
106	Hayes Lane Camp	Barry	72	1512	T 584895
107	Ridge Camp, Sully	Barry	68	1432	T 578883
109	G-40 Depot Expansion	Barry	12	266	T 578883
110	G-40 Officers Quarters	Barry	78	-	T 584895
111	WENVOE CAMP	Nr Barry	56	1546	T 567932
112	GOLF COURSE	Barry	56	1546	T 552918
113	Rhyd Lafar Hospital	Nr Cardiff	155	390	T 555013
114	Town Block	Pontypridd	34	719	O 515115

Numbers 115 – 153

Index	Location	Town	Officers	Men	Map Ref.
115	Billets	Pontypridd	-	500	O 510120
116	Llanelwydd Camp	Builth Wells	60	1190	O 498757
117	Billets, Dowlais	Merthyr Tydfil	-	850	O 490280
118	Billets	Mountain Ash	-	500	O 490200
119	Billets	Llantwit	-	250	O 490050
120	Billets	Porth(amer)	-	250	O 470120
121	Billets	Porth	-	250	O 470130
122	Miners Welfare Club	St Athens	14	316	T 469888
123	St. Athens Housing	Llantwit Major	14	220	T 458894
124	Billets	Aberdare	-	100	O 450250
125	Billets	Tonyrefail	-	250	T 440090
126	Billets, Ferndale	Rhondda	-	250	O 440190
127	Billets, Pen y Graig	Rhondda	-	250	O 440130
128	Billets, Tonypandy	Rhondda	-	250	O 440140
129	Billets, Pentre	Rhondda	-	250	O 440130
130	Billets, Treorchy	Rhondda	-	250	O 400180
131	ST.MARY'S HILL	Nr. Bridgend	56	1504	T 418012
132	Village Block	Llantwit Major	14	276	T 408905
133	ST. DONATS CASTLE	Llantwit Major	28	692	T 458894
134	Billets, Treherbert	Rhondda	-	250	O 380280
135	Billets, Blaengarw	Nr Bridgend	-	250	U 350150
136	Blaengarw Hotel	Nr Bridgend	5	-	O 346147
137	HERONSTON	Bridgend	34	749	T 350998
138	Billets	Bridgend	100	2100	T 346016
139	ISLAND FARM	Bridgend	56	1504	T 345998
140	Nottage Block	Porthcawl	12	228	T 262999
141	North Block	Porthcawl	12	250	T 260990
142	Seabank Hotel	Porthcawl	18	396	T 258984
143	Hutchyns Close	Porthcawl	28	692	T 253990
144	Miners Rest	Porthcawl	18	396	O 247022
145	KENFIG BURROWS	Kenfig Hill	56	1550	O 243028
146	MARGAM CASTLE	Port Talbot	31	206	O 250080
147	MARGAM PARK	Port Talbot	12	280	O 256080
148	Billets	Port Talbot	-	500	O 210120
149	Vivian Hotel	Port Talbot	-	60	O 193112
150	Jersey Beach Hotel	Port Talbot	-	140	O 193112
151	Alexandria Restaurant	Port Talbot	8	-	O 193112
152	Vivian Park Camp	Port Talbot	-	80	O 193116
153	Billets, Ystrad Farm	Nr. Neath	-	250	O 200300

Numbers 154 – 192

Index	Location	Town	Officers	Men	Map Ref.
154	Taibach Gibeon Chap.	Port Talbot	5	250	O 220100
155	Forward Movement M.	Neath	5	250	O 199198
156	Billets	Neath	-	500	O 190190
157	Calan Searchlight Site	Baglan	5	300	O 195144
158	Public Hall	Briton Ferry	5	250	O 188162
159	Cross Inn Hotel	Pontardawe	5	250	O 167260
160	Billets	Pontardawe	-	250	O 160260
161	Abermarlais Park	Llangadock	33	772	O 143515
162	Elba Works, Pt.Tenant	Swansea	12	414	O 073168
163	Billets	Swansea	-	250	O 100150
164	Winsor Works	Swansea	8	240	O 115214
165	Transit site	Swansea	16	126	O 112147
166	Clase Farm Hostel	Swansea	56	1504	O 103208
167	Billets, Mumbles	Swansea	-	500	O 090080
168	Taliaris Park	Llandeilo	6	50	O 090500
169	Guide and Church Hall	Llandeilo	3	110	O 078455
170	MANSELTON	Swansea	68	1582	O 086177
171	Rhyddings Hall	Swansea	5	250	O 085145
172	Glanmor School	Swansea	18	396	O 080154
173	Billets, Cockett	Swansea	-	500	O 080160
174	SINGLETON PARK	Swansea	68	1582	O 076140
175	Cockett	Swansea	5	250	O 073168
176	Penllegaer House	Nr. Swansea	39	177	O 068212
177	Trelog Camp	Llansawel	18	396	O 048574
178	Underhill P'k, Mumbles	Swansea	5	250	O 053099
179	Newton Hall Camp	Swansea	4	222	O 047100
180	MYNYDD LLIW 1	Nr Swansea	56	1246	O 045236
181	MYNYDD LLIW 2	Nr Swansea	56	1846	O 045236
182	Caswell Bay Hotel, M.	Swansea	4	190	O 044096
183	Summerland Camp, M.	Swansea	4	226	O 043104
184	Old Church School	Pontardulais	5	250	O 042253
185	Billets	Pontardulais	-	250	O 040280
186	QM. Sub-Depot	Pontardulais	3	97	O 136258
187	Billets, Gowerton	Swansea	50	950	O 130180
188	Aberglasney House,	Drwyslyn	3	220	O 028443
189	Penclawdd Camp	Penclawdd	48	1128	N 983177
190	Furnace Camp	Llanelly	37	952	N 961224
191	Highmead House Cp.	Llanblathen	72	1260	N 950655
192	CORNER HOUSE Cp.	Scurlage	88	2002	N 906097

Numbers 193 – 222

Index	Location	Town	Officers	Men	Map Ref.
193	Bronhewlog House	Burry Port	-	80	N 888235
194	Old Harbour	Burry Port	5	113	N 884232
195	Pembrey Beaches	Burry Port	18	396	N 866234
196	Broomhill House	Kidwelly	12	150	N 854291
197	Cwmgwili House	Carmarthen	2	90	N 874455
198	Rhyd-y-Gors House	Carmarthen	11	91	N 852412
199	Ystrad Cp, Johnstown	Carmarthen	45	1100	N 845412
200	Expeditionary Hospital	Carmarthen	196	392	N 857424
201	Velindre Camp	Velindre	34	504	N 803607
202	Cilgwyn House	N'castle Emlyn	10	75	N 762634
203	Pen-y-Coed House	St. Clears	6	132	N 717407
204	QM Distribution Pt.	Whitland	2	68	N 646391
205	Town Block	Cardigan	12	228	N 628687
206	Albro Castle,	St. Dogmaels	12	228	N 611694
207	Hean Castle	Saundersfoot	12	268	N 282270
208	Town	Tenby	100	200	N 576230
209	Penally Camp	Tenby	43	790	N 555216
210	Clynderwen House	Clynderwen	9	6	N 575426
211	Sodston Manor	Narberth	12	228	N 547392
212	Cresseley House	Cresseley	14	340	N 510290
213	Picton Castle I Camp	Haverfordwest	36	590	N 459336
214	Picton Castle II Camp	Haverfordwest	12	350	N 459366
215	Slebech Park	Haverfordwest	12	228	N 478364
216	Lamphey Camp	Nr Pembroke	14	400	N 459215
217	Town Block	Pembroke	30	630	N 420241
218	Llanion Barracks	Pemb. Dock	113	2000	N 415268
219	Cwm Brandy Camp	Fishguard	24	459	N 400596
220	Town Block	Haverfordwest	31	605	N 398384
221	Merrion Camp, Linney	Castlemartin	76	900	N 359212
222	East Blockhouse Camp	Angle	30	700	N 288256

Locations in CAPITAL letters denotes D-Day Marshalling Camp
Map reference as per Ordnance Survey of the time. 'V' prefix applicable to all.

*****

Appendix 3

MARSHALLING CAMP INDEX and MAPS

CAMP		VEHS.	PERSONNEL BY				
			Rail	Truck	Walk	Ord V.	TOTAL
Sub AREA 'U'							
40	Chepstow Race Course	244	2572	-	-	56	2628
41	Chepstow Bulwark	320	1212	61	-	24	1297
42	Chepstow Sedbury	119	485	-	-	-	485
66	Llanmartin	356	739	2274	-	-	3013
71	Llanover Park	388	1278	1130	-	-	3008
74	Llantarnum	206	165	265	-	324	1354
87	Court-y-Gollen	628	2841	36	-	-	2877
89	Dan-y-Parc	266	1337	183	-	364	1884
91	Llangattock (R)	148	301	-	-	108	409
93	Glanusk Park	147	416	229	-	6	651
Sub AREA 'V'							
88	St. Mellons	213	1331	262	-	-	1693
94	Pontllanfraith	426	1674	503	-	215	2392
97	Maindy Barracks (R)	-	-	-	-	-	-
98	Heath Camp	314	-	1733	-	-	1733
131	St. Mary's Hill	297	919	596	-	-	1515
137	Heronston	77	302	67	-	-	369
Sub AREA 'W'							
111	Wenvoe	354	1282	69	939	32	2322
112	Barry Golf Course	285	1888	-	733	-	2621
133	St. Donat's Castle	268	1057	-	-	-	1057
145	Kenfig Burrows	326	2079	21	-	-	2100
139	Island Farms (R)	-	437	918	-	-	1355
Sub AREA 'X'							
146-7	Margam Park	96	114	14	395	-	523
170	Swans. Manselton (R)	228	411	467	252	-	1130
174	Swans. Singleton	-	-	104	868	-	972
180-1	Mynydd Lliw	465	1937	495	-	-	2432
192	Corner H'se, Scurlage	293	-	2629	-	-	2629

US Army in World War II, European Theatre of Operations. Logistical Support of the Armies Vol. 1 states there were 24 Marshalling Camps and 4 Residue camps, indexed as above by Western Base Section District XXIX..

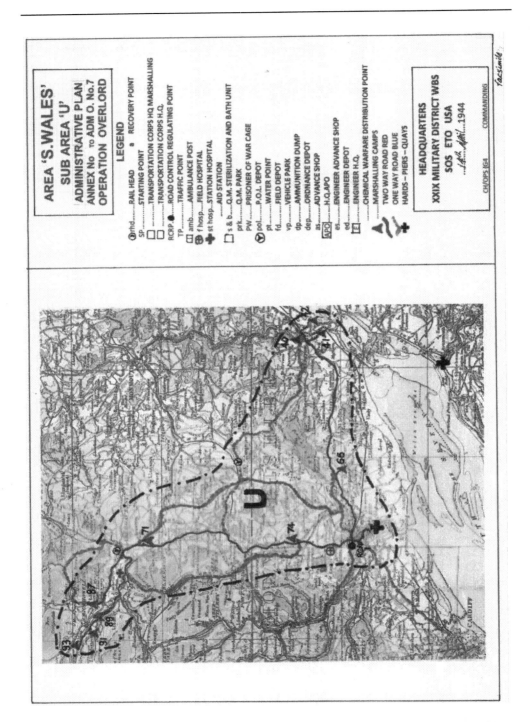

Facsimile of Marshalling Plan 'D' – South Wales Area 'U'. Created from NARA RG-407 Entry 427 Box 24301 at 270/65/10/6 Pre-Invasion File #135

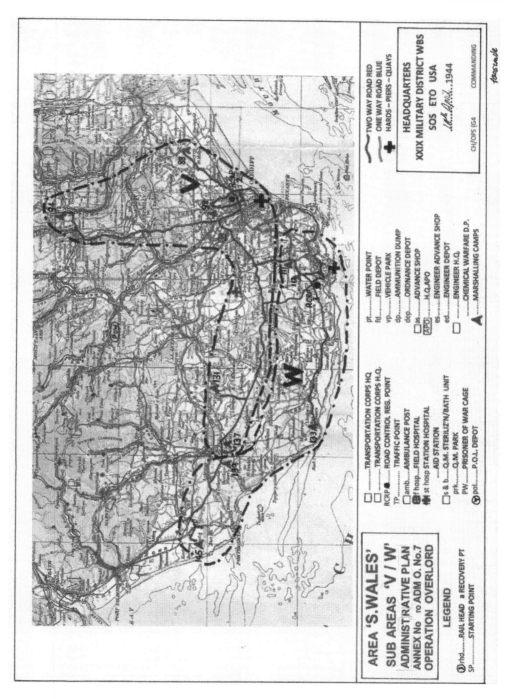

Facsimile of Marshalling Plan 'D' - South Wales Areas 'V' and 'W'. Created from NARA RG-407 Entry 427 Box 24301 at 270/65/10/6 Pre-Invasion File #135

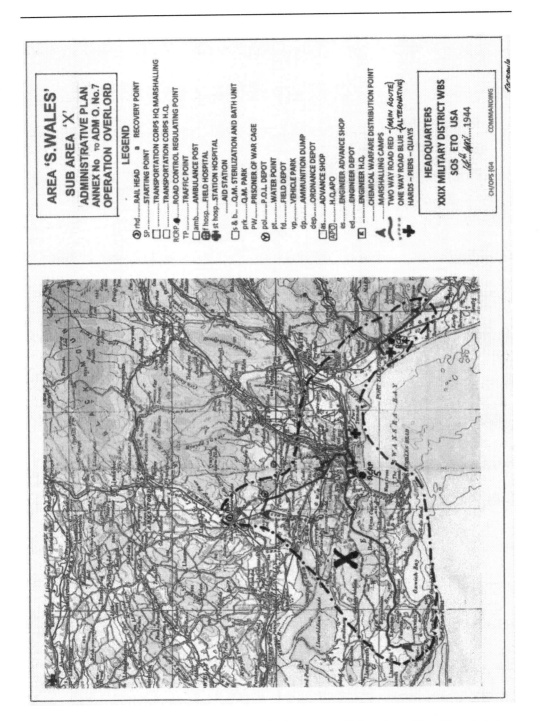

Facsimile of Marshalling Plan 'D' – South Wales Area 'X'. Created from
NARA RG-407 Entry 427 Box 24301 at 270/65/10/6 Pre-Invasion File #135

Appendix 4

LOADING MASTER PLAN

The principal invasion force assaulted the five beaches by sea with airborne divisions to the flanks. 3 glider troop battalions (2US & 1BR) were also seaborne.

Seaborne Elements

The true scale of the South Wales part in Operation OVERLORD and its naval offshoot NEPTUNE can only be really appreciated when seen in the context of the overall plan. OVERLORD included Operation DRAGOON, the amphibious landings in the South of France 5 weeks later. Many of the ships that had taken part in the Normandy Landings including bombardment and escort warships would continue with duties in the Mediterranean. Similarly some troopships and MTV's would be off on transatlantic convoys again whilst many like the *USAT Borinquen* would be part of the cross channel shuttle aided by LST's, LCT's and smaller craft. Troop and vehicle loading differed enormously across all the Embarkation Areas. Marching troops, ie those that did not man vehicles, were embarked in two distinct ways, the most straight forward being from dock or pier side up the 'gangplank' directly on to ship or Landing Craft Infantry. Alternatively men were shipped from shore in tenders; sometimes the very same LCA's or LCVP's that they would board again off the assault beach for the run in through the surf. Examples of both were prevalent in Southampton where the excellent loading facilities resulted in many of the British 'SWORD' assault troops being embarked direct from shore to ship whilst some were transferred by paddle steamer out to their moored LSI's on Southampton Water. Canadians for 'JUNO' all boarded their troopships at the berths (37-40) and 'GOLD' assault troops loaded at the Old Docks direct. LCI's were all loaded direct, often from prefabricated scaffold walkways such as that on Southsea Common, Portsmouth. US troops destined for the advance waves at OMAHA and UTAH were all embarked at anchorage from landing craft; LCI's were loaded as previously described.

Vehicle loading of LST's and LCT's was carried out from 'hards', all vehicles having to reverse aboard LST's and most LCT's, there being only a few of the newer LCT 5's that were ramped at bow and stern. Troop embarkation onto the 'Large Slow Targets' was similar to LCI loading along elevated gangways. Forces 'B'and 'L', being the first of the follow-up groups scheduled to land its forces, was composed almost entirely of LST's, whereas the preloaded elements destined for the next tide were ship born aboard either troopers or Motor Transport Vessels. Review of how the South Wales Marshalling Area and the BCPLBU Force fitted into that plan can be seen from the sketch map of southern UK following the list of Marshalling / Embarkation Areas.

EASTERN TASK FORCES – 'S', 'J' and G'

Area/Camps		Port / Location	EMB	Hards	Berths
A 22	Portsmouth E.	Dockyards	EAA3		LSI tenders
		Southsea Common	"		1 LCI
	Portsmouth	W.Stokes Bay	EA A4.	'G1'	4 LCT
		"	"	'G2'	"
		"	"	'G3'	"
		"	"	'G4'	"
	Gosport	Floating Bridge	"	'GF'	2 LCT
		Hardway	"	'GH'	2 LST
B 10	Beaulieu.	Lepe	"	'Q1'	4 LCT
		Stanswood Bay	EAB2.	'Q2'	3 "
	Lymington	Harbour	"	'A'	2 "
		"	"		LCI's
C 24	Southampton	Berth 101 East.	EAC5.	'S1'	2 LST
		East of Royal Pier	"	'S2'	2 "
		East of Town Quay	"	'S3'	2 "
		Dibbles Wharf	"	'S4'	2 "
F 10	Dover	Admiralty Pier	EF2	'ND1'	2 LST
		Ferry Dock	"	'ND2'	1 "
		Boundary Groyne	"	'ND4'	4 LCT
	Deal	R.M. Baths	EF3	'NW1'	4 LCT
		South Street	"	'NW2'	"
		Granville Road.	"	'NW6'	"
		Cambridge Road.	"	'NW11'	"
G ?	Folkestone	Railway Pier	EG2	'NT1'	1LSI/3LCT
	Hythe	Stade Court	EG2	'NR1'	4 LCT
		Imperial Hotel	"	'NR2'	"
		Lifeboat Station	"	'NR3'	"
H 5	Hastings	Breakwater East.	EAA1	'NB1'	4 LCT
		" West	"	'NB2'	4 LCT
	Seaford	Tidemills	EAA2	'C2'	"
J 10	Shoreham	Inner Harbour	EJ2	'K'	5 LCT
		Outer Harbour	EJ3	'H'	4 LCT
	Newhaven	Sleepers Hole	EJ4	'L'	3 LCT

APPENDIX 4 - LOADING MASTER PLAN

EASTERN FOLLOW UP - FORCE 'L'

Area/Camps	Port / Location		EMB	Hards	Berths
Q 8	Lowestoft / Yarmouth		E1/2/3/4	reserve	
R 8	Felixstowe	Seaward of Pier		'NF1'	4 LST
		Pier to Crane		'NF2'	4 LCT
		North of Crane		'NF3'	2 LST
S 20	Tilbury	Main Dock West.	E5	'NZ1'	4 LCT
		" East	"	'NZ2'	4 "
		West Branch Dock	"	'NZ3'	1 LST
		Centre Dock	"	'NZ4'	"
		East Dock	"	'NZ5'	2LST
		Landing Stage	E6	-	4* PP

WESTERN TASK FORCES - 'O' and 'U'

Area/Camps	Port / Location		EMB	Hards	Berths
D 16	Poole	Hamworthy	EAD6	'P'	4 LCT
	Weymouth	Riverside	EAD7	-	LCI's
		Pierside	"	-	LSI tenders
	Portland	Castletown	EAD8	'R'	4 LCT
		Castletown Pier	"	'R2'	2 LST
		Mere 2	"	'R3'	3 LST
K 11	Torbay	Torquay	EA68	'PY'	LSI tenders
				-	1 LCI
	Dartmouth E.	Upper Ferry	EA69	PC1'	2 LCT
				-	1 LCI
	Dartmouth W.	Lower "	EA70	'PC2'	4 LCT
		New Ground	"	'PC3	2 LST
		Brixham	EA72	'PU'	4 LST
		"	"	-	1 LCI
L 5	Plymouth E.	Turnchapel	EA37	'PK'	2 LST
		St. Budeaux	EA35	'PP2	4 LCT
			EA41	-	1 LCI
M 9	Plymouth W.	Jupiter Point	EA32	'PS'	4 LST
		"	"	'PS2'	2 LCT
		HMS Raleigh	"	-	1 LCI
		Upper Barn Pool	EA33	'PP1'	4 LST
		Lower Barn Pool	"	'PP3'	4 LCT

WESTERN FOLLOW UP - FORCE 'B'

Area/Camps		Port / Location	EMB	Hards	Berths
N 4	Falmouth E.	Polgerran Wood	EA10	'PF1'	2 LST
		Turnaware Point	EA11	'PF2'	4 LST
O 4	Falmouth W.	Harveys Yard	EA7	'PF3'	2 LCT
		Taylors Garage	"	'PF4'	4 LCT
			"	-	1 LCI
	Helford.	Polgwidden Cove	EA8	'PH'	2 LST

BRISTOL CHANNEL PRE-LOADED BUILD UP FORCE

U 10	Newport	Alexandra Dock	N/R	Berth	2 AP/PP
"					MTV
V 6	Cardiff	Roath Dock	"	"	2 TP
W 5	Barry	Main Dock	"	"	MTV
X 5	Swansea	Prince of Wales Dock	"	"	5 TP
"		Kings Dock	"	"	MTV
	Port. Talbot	Wharf	"	"	MTC
	Avonmouth	Docks	"	"	water tankers
	Garstang	Docks	"	"	MTC

THAMES BUILD UP FORCE (not preloaded)

T 8	London	King George V, West India, V&A Dock	3+ TP

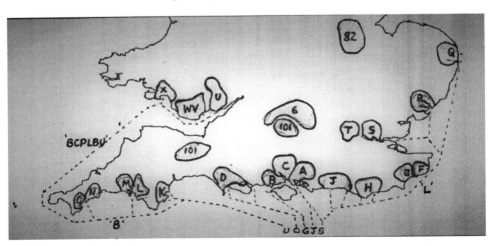

Sketch Plan: Normandy Invasion marshalling areas

Airborne Elements

Organisation of the British and US Divisions was very similar, paratrooper force with heavy weapons in gliders followed up by further glider reinforcement.

EASTERN FORCE - 6th AIRBORNE DIVISION – 'Tonga'
3rd and 5th Parachute Brigades

Group	Squadron	Role	Airfield	No / No	Combination
38	295 / 570	*Pathfinders*	Harwell	3 / 3	Albermarles
	298 / 644	*'Deadstick'*	Tarrant Rushton	3 / 3	Halifax+Horsas
	"	*Main Force*	"	15 / 15	Halifax+ Horsas
	"	"	"	2 / 2	Halifax+Hamilcars
	295 / 57	*Advance*	Harwell	7 / 7	Albermarle+Horsas
	"	*Merville H/W*	"		4 Albermarle+Horsas
	"	*Main Force*	"		21 Albermarle+Horsas
	296 / 297	*Merville CDM*	Brize Norton		3 Albermarle+Horsas
	"	*Main Force*	"		17 Albermarle+Horsas
	"	"	"		17 Albemarles
	190 / 620	*5th Para Bde.*	Fairford		45 Stirlings
	196 / 299	"	Keevil		46 Stirlings
46	233 Sqdn	*3rd Para Bde.*	Blakehill Farm		6 Dakota+Horsas
	"	"	"		37 Dakotas
	512 /575	*3&5th Para Bde.*	Broadwell		54 Dakotas
	48 / 271	*3rd Para Bde*	Down Ampney		7 Dakota+Horsas
	"	"	"		39 Dakotas

GLIDER MISSION - D-Day pm. – 'Mallard'
6th Air Landing Brigade (inc.Armoured Recon.Regt.and 211th Light Battery RA)

38	296 / 297	*Reinforcements*	Brize Norton	19 / 20	Albermarle+Horsas
	190 / 620	*Devons 'A' Co.*	Fairford	18 / 18	Stirling+Horsas
	295 / 570	*Ox/Bucks*	Harwell	20 / 21	Albermarle+Horsas
	196 / 299	"	Keevil	17 / 18	Stirling+Horsas
	298 / 644	*Arm.R.Regt .*	Tarrant Rushton	15 / 15	Halifax+ H'cars
	"	"	"	1 / 1	Halifax+Horsa
46	512 & 575	*RUR*	Broadwell	8 / 19	Dakota+Horsas
	48 & 271	"	Down Ampney	22 / 15	Dakota+Horsas

PARACHUTE RESUPPLY MISSION – D+1 – 'Rob Roy'

46	All 5 Sqdns	Blakehill, Broadwell, Down Ampney	50 Dakotas

WESTERN FORCE – 82nd and 101st AIRBORNE DIVISIONS

Group	Squadron	Airfield	Type
IX Troop Carrier Cmd. Pathfinder Gp.		North Witham	C-47/53

82nd AIRBORNE DIV. - 52nd Transport Wing USAAC.

Group	Squadron	Airfield	Type
61st T. Gp	14, 15, 53 & 59th	Barkston Heath	C-47/53
313th "	29, 47, 48 & 49th	Folkingham	C-47/53
314th "	61, 63, 32 & 50th	Saltby	C-47/53
315th "	34th & 43rd	Spanhoe	C-47/53
316th "	36, 37, 44 & 45th	Cottesmore	C-47/53

101ST AIRBORNE DIVISION - 50th and 53rd Troop Carrier Wings

Group	Squadron	Airfield	Type
439th T. Gp.	91, 92, 93, & 94th	Upottery	C-47/53
440th "	95, 96, 97, & 98th	Exeter	C-47/53
441st "	99, 100, 301, & 302nd	Merryfield	C-47/53
435th "	75, 76, 77, & 78th	Welford	C-47/53
436th "	79, 80, 81, & 82nd	Membury	C-47/53
438th "	87, 88, 89, & 90th	Greenham Co.	C-47/53

GLIDER MISSIONS – D-DAY (4), D+1 (2)

Group	Mission (AD)		Airfield	Number / Glider
434th T. Gp.	'Chicago' (101st)		Aldermaston	52 C-47 / Waco
437th "	'Detroit' (82nd)		Ramsbury	52 C-47 / Waco
434th "	'Keokuk' (101st)		Aldermaston	32 C-47 / Horsa
437th "	'Elmira' (82nd)	'A'	Ramsbury	8 C-47 / Waco
			"	16 C-47 / Horsa
		'B'	Greenham Common	14 C-47 / Waco
			"	36 C-47 / Horsa
436th "		'C'	Membury	2 Waco / 48 Horsa
435th "		'D'	Welford	12 Waco / 38 Horsa
437th T Gp.	'Galveston'	'A'	Ramsbury	32 Waco / 18 Horsa
434th T Gp.		'B'	Aldermarston	50 C-47 / Waco
439th T Gp.	'Hackensack'	'A'	Upottery	20 Waco / 30 Horsa
441st T Gp.		'B'	Merryfield	50 C-47 / Waco

Note. All C-47 towing either CG4A Waco or Airspeed Horsa gliders

*****

Appendix 5

REPORT OF LOSS OF AP 72*SUSAN B. ANTHONY*
06/07/44 OF NORTH COAST OF NORMANDY, FRANCE

NARRATIVE

1.	0750	7 June 44. Convoy BBP1 – Anthony, Goethals, Borinquen and Simonds in column 600 yards between ships. ETA Omaha 0830.
2.		HMS PELICAN leading in middle of swept channel No. 34. Speed 12 knots. All water tight doors closed – Degaussing on. Mess crews clearing up after troop & crew breakfasts.
3.		Wind 320° Force 3. Sea 3. (log states 4). Easterly 1-2 knots.
4.	0757	Violent explosion under ship. High column of water to port and starboard of No.4 hatch.
5.		No text
6.		No text.
7.		No text
8.		Engine room and holds 4 and 5 flooding.
9.		No 'general quarters' sounded as undesirable (troops to quarters).
10.		No text
11.		No text
12.		Hoisted international code signal 'come alongside'. Vessels signalled USS PINTO, 2 LCT's, 1 LCI & 2 British Escorts.
13.		Commander Gray requested USS PINTO to tow in tandem to shallow water. PINTO agreed but to tow along portside.
14.		Increased flooding fire & engine room, No 4 & No. 5 holds.
15.		No text.
16.		Brig. Gen. Sam Williams *(Deputy CO. 90 Inf. Div.)* requested permission for troops to return to quarters for arms and equipment. Declined - unsafe and ship stable thanks to excellent troop discipline. However salvage parties could pass equipment onto deck.
17.		No text.
18.		PINTO fouling davits – moved to starboard side.
19.		Senior M.O. Lt. Commander Pendleton to prepare casualties.
20.	0830	PINTO back to port side. Ship settling accelerated.
21.		CO. to devote efforts to landing 2317 combat troops.
22.		Permission granted to Comms Officers to destroy documents.
23.	0850	HMS Mendip alongside outboard of PINTO.
24.		Health records of SBA crew transferred to PINTO

25.	0857	HMS Norborough* alongside starboard.
26.		CO "USS SBA is greatly indebted to the CO. of HMS Norborough not only for the large number of troops who transferred onto and across his decks but also for the example he set the more timid craft by his determined seamanship in bringing his vessel alongside under difficult conditions." Life rafts not required!
27.	0905	Stern main deck awash.
28.	0908	LCI 489 alongside starboard quarter.
29.	0912	HMS Rupert alongside outboard Norborough.
30.		No text.
31.	0920	Secured gun crews.
32.	0925	LCI 496 alongside port forward – 300 troops on.
33.	0935	Troops continuing to abandon ship.
34.	0943	100 troops remain on foredeck port side.
35.	0950	Salvage party ordered to abandon ship.
36.	0955	Ship listing heavily to port. – All craft clear. Remaining 20 crew ordered into water and swim. CO. followed about 10.00hrs.
37.	1010	USS SUSAN B. ANTHONY disappeared completely. No troops lost. 1 Officer and 14 crew injured inc. 3 broken legs.

ENDS

Formerly the Grace Line 'Santa Clara' built at Camden, New Jersey, the 'Susie B' had already had an eventful wartime history taking part in the Operation TORCH landings in North Africa and Operation HUSKY, the invasion of Sicily. Frequent troop convoy crossings of the North Atlantic had occupied 1943 and the first half of 1944, ports of call including Belfast in Northern Ireland, Holy Loch, Gourock and Glasgow in Scotland, Hvalfjordur and Reykjavik in Iceland and Milford Haven and her final port of departure Newport in South Wales.

The *Susan B Anthony* still lies in the Bay of the Seine.

*****

Footnote. The spelling 'Norborough' is incorrect as the vessel was HMS Narborough.

Appendix 6

SOUTH WALES MEMORIALS DEDICATED TO US FORCES

There are few located here, perhaps there should be more? The inscriptions read:

**THIS AVENUE OF TREES
WAS PLANTED ON BEHALF OF
THE 2ND EVACUATION UNIT**
OF THE
UNITED STATES ARMY
AS A TOKEN OF GRATITUDE
FOR THE HOSPITALITY EXTENDED TO THEM
BY THE PARISHIONERS OF WHITCHURCH
DURING THE SECOND WORLD WAR
1939 – 1945

Whitchurch Common, Cardiff - unveiled and dedicated circa 1945

**This Memorial is dedicated to the US Forces who lived and trained
at the former Saint Peter's Church Hall on this site,
and in Mumbles, Caswell, and surrounding areas
prior to leaving for Normandy beaches in June 1944.**

**We remember those who made the ultimate
sacrifice for our freedom on the long road to final victory
during the Second World War.**

Newton Village Hall, Gower - unveiled and dedicated 2nd November 2012

**This memorial from the people of Pembrokeshire
is dedicated to honour the memory of all
U.S. troops stationed in this county during
1943 – 1944
in preparation for the Normandy Landings
'They fought for our freedom'**

Carew Cheriton Airfield, Pembrokeshire - unveiled & dedicated 22nd October 2019

*****

Abbreviations

AAA AW	Anti-Aircraft Artillery Automatic Weapons.
AB/D	Airborne Division.
ABP	Associated British Ports.
AFV	Armoured fighting vehicle.
AD	Armored Division (US spelling)
ADC	Aide-De-Camp.
AFA	Armored Field Artillery
AT	Convoy prefix
ATC	Assault Training Center. (US spelling)
AP	Assault Personnel (US Navy terminology)
APA	Assault Personnel - Attack (USN)
AKA	Assault Cargo - Attack. (USN)
B&M	Brecon and Merthyr Railway (old line adopted by GWR)
BAB	Base Automotive Battalion (US Ordnance type)
BBG	Battalion Beach Group (Engineer)
BO	Boston and Port of Embarkation.
BCP's	Bristol Channel Ports
BCPLBUF	Bristol Channel Pre-Loaded Build-Up Force
BMA	Beach Maintenance Area
Brecs	Brecknock (modern day Powys)
C1	Ship Class – Built 1940-'41. 6,500 GT. 4,400 HP
C2	Ship Class – Built 1941-'43. 6,500 GT. 6,600 HP.
C3	Ship Class – Built 1941-'44. 7,000 -9,000GT. 8,800 - 9,350. HP
C4	Maritime Commission -'44, 'Marine' prefix. 12,000 GT. 9,900 HP
C47/53	Dakota or Skytrain troop carrying aircraft.
Card	Cardiganshire (modern day Ceridigion)
Carms	Carmarthenshire
CE	Corps of Engineers
CO	Commanding Officer
CU	Convoy designation. Curacao – United (Kingdom)
DD	Destroyer prefix.
DE	Destroyer Escort prefix. (USN terminology)
DP	Distribution Point (QM)
DUKW	D = year '42. U = utility. K= all wheel drive. W= twin axle drive.
EA	Embarkation Area.
E (GS)R	Engineer General Service Regiment.
ESB	Engineer Special Brigade.
ETOUSA	European Theatre of Operations United States Army.
FA	Field Artillery
FDT	Fighter Direction Tender
FOYNES	US / British divisions transferred to UK for D-Day.

G-	General Depot (followed by serial number)
Glam	Glamorgan (old county name)
GFA	Glider Field Artillery
GWR	Great Western Railway
HAM	Heavy Automotive Maintenance (Company)
HMT	His Majesties Transport.
HR	Hampton Roads.
HX	Halifax (Nova Scotia) convoy prefix.
HU	Hospital Unit (one of three platoons separated'
ID	Infantry Division.
IR	Infantry Regiment.
IWM	Imperial War Museum
KMF	Convoy designation (United) Kingdom- Mediterranean Fast
LCA	Landing Craft Assault. (British)
LCT	Landing Craft Tank
LCM	Landing Craft Mechanised.
LCS	Landing Craft Support.
LCVP	Landing Craft Vehicle and Personnel (US)
LSD	Landing Ship Dock.
LST	Landing Ship Tank (or Large Slow Target)
Lt. Col.	Lieutenant Colonel
MAM	Medium Automotive Maintenance.(company)
MKF	Convoy designation Mediterranean – (United) Kingdom Fast.
MO	Medical Officer.
Mon.	Monmouthshire (Modern day Gwent)
MOWT	Ministry of War Transport.
MV	Motor Vessel.
MVA	Motor Vehicle Assembly (US Ordnance Company type)
MVD	Motor Vehicle Distribution (US Ordnance Company type)
NARA	National Archives and Records Center (US)
NBB	Naval Beach Battalion.
NCDU	Navy Combat Demolition Unit.
NY(PE)	New York (Port of Embarkation).
O-	Ordnance depot (followed by serial number)
ON(S)	Transatlantic Convoy designation (Slow)
OSS	Office of Strategic Services.
PESBG	Provisional Engineer Special Brigade Group.
PFA	Parachute Field Artillery.
Pfc.	US Army Private 1st Class Soldier
PH	Photographic
P / O	Pacific and Orient shipping line.
POE	Port of Embarkation.
POL	Petrol, oil and lubricants.
POM	Preparation for Overseas Movement.

Pvt.	US Army Private soldier.
PX	Shop
QM	Quartermaster (Corps)
QSMV	Quadruple screw motor vessel.
RASC	Royal Army Service Corps (British)
RCT	Regimental Combat Team.
RE	Royal Corps of Engineers.
RSB	Railway Shop Battalion.
S-	Signal Corps Depot (followed by serial number)
SETF	Special Engineer Task Force.
SRD	Service (Supply) Reserve Depot.
SS	Steam Ship
SSV	Short sea voyage
SOS	Services of Supply.
T	Truck
T2	Type of oil/fuel tanker.
TB	Tank Battalion.
TC	Transportation Corps or convoy prefix.
TD	Tank Destroyer (Battalion type or antitank self-propelled gun).
TE	Table of Equipment.
TO	Table of Organisation.
TRP	Traffic Regulating Point.
USA	United States Army
USAAC (F)	United States Army Air Corps (Force)
USNAAB	United States Navy Advanced Amphibious Base (or sub.)
UT	Convoy designation. United (States) Troop
V	Fifth Corps (Gerow) charged with assault on Omaha Beach.
VII	Seventh Corps (Collins) charged with assault on Utah Beach.
VIII	Eighth Corps (Middleton) follow up to Utah Beach
WAGAPU	Welsh Assembly Government Aerial Photographic Unit.
WBS	Western Base Section
WSA	War Shipping Administration.
XII	Twelfth Corps (Cook – Third Army)
XIX	Nineteenth Corps (Corlett) follow up Omaha Beach D-Day+8.
XX	Twentieth Corps. (Walker – Third Army)

NB.1. The use of a numeric battalion number is used in conjunction with a Regiment number where appropriate. eg. 3/358th.

    2. For simplification all Liberty ships mentioned in text do not have a prefix. All other shipping prefixes applied where appropriate.

    3. C1 vessels with bigger turbines at 8,800 HP. *Exceller, Exira, Extavia.*

*****

Bibliography

1. PRIMARY SOURCES

NATIONAL ARCHIVES AND RECORDS ADMINISTRATION

Arnold, Floyd S.	*372nd Engineer Historical Record.* 1945.
Barkesdale, James A. Col. C.E.	*History of the 360th Engineer GS Regiment. 1945.*
Bell, Frank F. Colonel.	*The 373rd Engineer GS Regiment in World War II.* April '43 – 15 Jan. 1945. Dallas, Tx. 1945
Boardman, William M. 1st Lt.	*95th Engineers Unit History* Adjutant. 95th Engineer General Service Regiment. 1941-44 end.
Hagen, TG. Capt. C.E.Adj.	*History of the 366th Engineer GS Regiment. Part II.* 10th October 1943 – 10th October 1944.
Brown, Lloyd D. Maj. Gen.	*History of the 28th Infantry Division,* 29 June1944
ADM 603-0.	*Western Base Command Engineers. Diagrams, Camp Layouts.* Administrative History Collection, Historical Section, ETOUSA.
ADM 603A.	*Western Base Command Letters, History and Daily Journal.* Administrative History Collection, Historical Section, ETOUSA.
ADM 603FF.	*Western Base Section. Final Report 12 June 1944.* Administrative History Collection, Historical Section, ETOUSA.
RG-407.	Entry 427. Box 24301. At 270/65/10/6 Pre-Invasion File #135-Text & Maps. *Mounting Plan Western Base Section "C" 8 March 1944.* HQ. Services of Supply, ETOUSA.
RG-407.	Entry 427. Box 24302. At 270/65/10/6 Pre-Invasion File #149 - 22 Maps & Overlays. *Mounting Plan Western Base Section "C" (Revised) 1944.* HQ. SOS. ETOUSA
AG-119.26	*MRU Station List 14th April 1944* HQ. ETOUSA Portsmouth D-Day Museum.
AG- 119.27	*MRU Station List 31st May 1994.* HQ. ETOUSA Adrian & Neil Turley.
COM NAV EU	*Administrative History Parts V-VI,* Department of the Navy, Office of Naval History. Washington 25. D.C
Jones, Clifford L. Lt. USA.	*NEPTUNE: Training, Mounting the Artificial Ports.* The Administrative and Logistical History of the ETO. March 1946. Hyperwar Foundation Transcribed/formatted for HTML Patrick Clancey

RECORDS

GWR Record of Arrivals and Sailings of Vessels. Swansea Docks. 6/09/43 onwards
West Glamorgan County Archives, Swansea.

History of Llandarcy Refinery 1921 – 1971. Victor Barnes.
Neath Antiquarian Society Archives 1971.

Movement Control Diary 1941-1945 of Lt. Col. L. G. Bevan RE. Port of Swansea.
Reproduced within '*Strands of World War II'*. Volumes 2 and 3. T.E. Stradling.
Private 2001 - Bound by Swansea Library 2007.

UNIT HISTORIES AND ACCOUNTS

After Action Report – June 1944. Headquarters 90th Infantry Division. APO 90, US Army. 90th Infantry Division History and Research.

Annual Report of Medical Department Activities 1944. 53rd Medical Battalion. 25 January 1945.

Building the Navy's bases in World War II. History of the Bureau of Yards and Docks and the Civil Engineers Corps 1940 – 1946. Volume II US Government Printing Office. Washington 1947.

Combat History of the Second Infantry Division in World War II. Reprinted by The Battery Press, Nashville, Ky.

Combat History of the Twenty-eighth Infantry Division in World War II. Reprinted by The Battery Press, Nashville, Ky.

History of the 110th Infantry Regiment in World War II. Reprinted by The Battery Press, Nashville, Ky.

Omaha Beachhead. War Department, Historical Division, Washington DC 1945.

Report of Activities of the 25th Naval Construction Regiment. F.P.O. New York. 30 November 1944

DeArman. CE. Capt. Bde. Historian. *The History of the 5th Engineer Special Brigade*. 1st September 1944

Gordon, A. James. Exec. Officer. *The 561st FA Battalion. World War II Diary*.

Hrdlicka, Ed. Colonel. *The 15th Field Artillery in World War Two*.

Mott, John R. Captain, C.A.C. *462nd Anti-Aircraft Artillery Automatic Weapons Battalion Story*.

Smead, Burton A. Jr. Captain. *History of the Twelfth United States Field Artillery Battalion in The ETO 1944 – 1945*. August 1945. The Command & Staff College Library. Accession No. 66763

WEB SITE RECORDS AND UNIT EXTRACTS.

http://www.6thbeachbattalion.org	*US 6th Naval Beach Battalion.*
http://www.jeopard.us	*87th Armored Field Artillery Battalion WW II.* 1-6 June '45. Noriega, John.
http://www.90th divisionassoc.org	*315th Combat Engineers.* 90th division folders/315.
http://www.90th divisionassoc.org	*358th Infantry Regiment. 3rd Battalion.* 90thdivisionfolders/358th.
http://home.comcast.net/	*119th Anti-Aircraft Artillery Gun Bn. (Mobile)*
http://www.skylighters.org	*225th AAA Searchlight Battalion: Unit History.*
https://www.med-dept.com	WW2 Medical Research Centre., Unit Histories. *12th Evacuation Hospital Unit History* *29th Field Hospital Unit History* *232nd Station Hospital.*
http://www.299thcombat	*299th Engineer Combat Battalion History.*
http://www.6juin1944.com	*Men of D-Day*
http://www.antiaircraft.org	*473rd AAA AW Battalion History.* *481st AAA AW Battalion History.*
http://www.5ad.org	*628th Tank Destroyer Battalion.*
http://history:amedd.army.mil	*643rd Medical Clearing Company. Annual Report*
http://654th.com	*History of the 654th Tank Destroyer Battalion.* Fred E Moon. GoDaddy.com 2009
http://www.geocities.com	*History of the 863rd Ordnance Heavy Automotive Maintenance Company* from Jan.' to Sept.17, '44.
http://www.convoyweb.org.uk	*Arnold Hague Convoy Database.*
http://www.lstmemorial.org	*USS LST Ship Memorial.*

MONOLOGUES and PAPERS

Bekke, Major Douglas.	US Army (ret'd). Curator, Minnesota Military Museum. *Norwegian-Americans and the 99th Infantry Battalion (Separate).* The Military Historical Society of Minnesota.
Caruthers, James H. Lt. Col.	*Travelogue of a Division Quartermaster* Part I. The Quartermaster Review, March - April 1945 Quartermaster Museum - Fort Lee, Virginia.
Dunham H.H.	*U.S.Army Transportation in the European Theatre of Operations 1942 - 1945.* Historical Unit, OCT, Army Service Forces. June '46
Deisher, F. Lt. Colonel.	*Supply Operations in the Bristol Channel Area during 'Operation Overlord.'* 15 April - 6 June 44. (Personal Experience of an Operational Supply Officer.) Infantry School, Fort Benning, Georgia.

2. SECONDARY SOURCES

PERSONAL MEMOIRES

Harner, Harlan Lincoln. *987ᵗʰ Field Artillery Battalion in World War II* (From D-Day in Normandy to VE Day in Czechoslovakia) Veterans Stories. Battle of The Bulge Association.

McConahey, Dr.W.M. *'Battalion Surgeon'*. Veterans History Project. The Library of Congress.Washington. 12ᵗʰ February 2004

Pampeyman, Earl. *'My Story'*. 538ᵗʰ Ord. Heavy Maintenance (Tk) Company.

Nasea, John Jr. *Voices of the 321ˢᵗ Glider Field Artillery Battalion.*

Unangst, Roland C *111ᵗʰ Ord. Medium Maintenance Company. . (Hanover)*

PUBLISHED SOURCES

Addington, Scott *Invasion.* D-Day & Operation Overlord in 100 Moments. Uniform 2019

Balkoski, Joseph. *Beyond the Beachhead*: The 29ᵗʰ Division in Normandy. Harrisburg, Pa. Stackpole Books, 1989.

Bass, Richard T., *The Brigades of Neptune.* US Army Engineer Special Brigades in Normandy Lee Publishing, Exeter, Devon. '94

Bass, Richard T., *Spirits of the Sand*. The History of the U.S.Army Assault Training Centre, Woolacombe. Lee Publishing, Exeter, Devon. 1992

Bradley, Omar N. *A Soldier's Story*. New York: Henry Holt. 1951.

Brown, David. *Landings in Normandy June 1944*. HMSO 1994. Pitcairn-Jones, L.J. Commander. Battle Summary No.39 Operation 'Neptune'. Landings in Normandy 6ᵗʰ June, '44.

Brozyna, Andrew J. *Longshore Soldiers*. Homefront, England, Normandy, Antwerp. Life in a World War II Port Battalion. Apidae Press, Longmont, Col. 2010

Bryan, Keith. *Pack Up and Move*. A Pictorial History of the 348ᵗʰ ECB. The Art Printery, Columbus, Nebraska.

Bykofsky, Joseph. & Larson, Harold. *The Transportation Corps: Operations Overseas*. United States Army in World War II. The Technical Services: Office of the Chief of Military History. Department of the Army. Washington, D.C.:1957.

Colby, John. *War from the Ground Up*. The 90ᵗʰ Division in WWII. Nortex Press, Austin Tx. 1991.

Eisenhower, Dwight D. *Report by THE SUPREME COMMANDER TO THE COMBINED CHIEFS OF STAFF ON THE OPERATIONS IN EUROPE of the ALLIED EXPEDITIONARY FORCE 6 June 1944 to 8 May 1945.* HMSO London 1946.

Elphick, Peter. *Liberty.* The Ships that Won the War.
Chatham Publish'. London 2001.

Evans, W Meurig. *The Furrow of My Life.* The Story of a Dyslexic Farmer.
Private Publisher, Llansadwrn. 2012

Ferris, Paul. *Gower in History.* Myth, People Landscape.
Armanaleg Books, Hay-on-Wye, HR

Gardner, Ian. & *Tonight We Die as Men.* The Untold Story of 3/506th
Day, Roger. Parachute Infantry Regiment from Tocca to D-Day.
Osprey Publishing 2009.

Gawne, Jonathan. *Spearheading D-Day.* American Special Units of the
Normandy Invasion. Histoire & Collections.

Grover, David H. *US Army Ships and Watercraft of World War II.*
United States Naval Institute Press, Annapolis Md. 1987

Harrison, Gordon A. *Cross-Channel Attack.* United States Army in World War
II. The European Theater of Operations: Office of the
Chief of Military History Washington, D.C.: 1951.

Hervieux, Linda. *Forgotten.* The Untold Story of D-Day's Black Heroes.
Amberley Publishing. Stroud. 2016.

Hesketh, Roger. *Fortitude*: The D-Day Deception Campaign.
St.Ermin's Press. 1999

Hoyt, Edwin P. *The GI's War.* American Soldiers in Europe during WWII.
Cooper Square Press 2000.

Kemp, Harry M. *The Regiment: Let the Citizens Bear Arms!* A Narrative
History of an American Infantry Regiment in World War
II. (109th Infantry Regt.). Nortex Press, Austin.Tx. 1990.

Lewis, Adrian R. *Omaha Beach*: A Flawed Victory.
Chapel Hill: University of North Carolina Press, 2001

Mansley, Michael J. *Porthcawl at War. 1939 - 45.* Private Porthcawl Glam '94.

McKenzie, John. *On Time, On Target.* Presidio Press.

Morgan, Sir Frederick. *Peace and War.* A soldier's life.
Hodder and Stoughton. London 1961

Morse, Brian. *A Moment in History.* The story of the American Army in
the Rhondda in '44. Y Lolfa. Talybont, Ceredigion. 2007.

Mountford, E.R. *The USA 756th RSB (Railway Shop Battalion) at Newport*
(Ebbw Junction). The Oakwood Press. 1989.

Parry, Gordon. *Trinity: '43 – '45 A Legacy for Life.*
Trinity College Carmarthen 1996.

Rohwer, J & *Chronology of the War at Sea 1939 – 1945.*
Hummelchen, G. The Naval History of World War Two.
Greenhill Books, London. Second edition. 1992.

Ruppenthal, Roland G. *Logistical Support of the Armies.* United States Army in
World War II. The European Theater of Operations:
Volume I May 1941 – September 1944. OCMH
Department of the Army. Washington, D.C.: 1953.

| Sellwood, Dennis G. | *The Friendly Invasion*. Caerphilly Local History Society. Caerphilly 2002. |

Sellwood, Dennis G.   *The Friendly Invasion*. Caerphilly Local History Society. Caerphilly 2002.

Stanton, Shelby L.   *Order of Battle*, US Army, World War II. With a Forward by Russel F. Weigley. Novato, California: Presidio Press. 1984

Turley, Adrian & Neil.   *The U.S.Army in South-East Shropshire 1944*. Private publisher 2004.

Wardlow, Chester.   *The Transportation Corps: Responsibilities, Organization, Operations*. United States Army in World War II. The Technical Services, OCMH. Department of the Army. Washington, D.C. 1951.

Weaver, Michael E.   *Guard Wars*. The 28th Infantry Division in World War II. Indiana University Press. Bloomington, Indiana. 2010

Winser. John de S.   *The D-Day Ships.* Neptune: the Greatest Amphibious Operation in History. World Ship Society, Kendal, Cumberland. 1994.

NEWSPAPERS

Cardiff and Suburban News.
Carmarthen Journal.
Glamorgan Gazette.
Llanelli Star.
Port Talbot Guardian.
The Welshman.
South Wales Echo.
South Wales Evening Post.
West Wales Guardian.
Western Mail.
Western Telegraph.
Weekly News (Tenby Observer)

LOCAL GOVERNMENT MINUTES.

Cardiff City Council
Carmarthen Borough Council
Carmarthen Town Council
County Borough of Swansea
Gower Rural District Council
Rhondda Borough Council
Swansea Town Council

*****

Index

118th IR (Separate) 177;
175th IR. 59, 101, 138, 197, 204;
325th GIR. 171;
357th IR. 131, 150, 153, 192;
358th IR. 131, 154;
359th IR. 131, 158, 191/2, 201, 203:
506th PIR. 17;
99th IB. (Separate) 72, 84, 60, 162:
Artillery Groups / Battalions:-
174th FA Group, 152;
187th FA Grp; 153; 258th FA Grp, 158;
80th /, 319th A/B PFA B'ns. 141;
320th A/B PFA Bn. 141, 191;
321st A/B GFA Bn. 131, 191, 194;
456th A/B PFA Bn. 141;
907th A/B GFA Bn. 131, 191;
12th FA Bn. 139, 195; 29th FA Bn. 205;
37th FA Bn. 197; 38th FA Bn. 139, 173;
107th FA Bn. .46, 66, 81;
108th FA Bn. 46, 62, 81, 100, 178;
109th FA Bn.. 46, 81;
110th FA Bn.138;
115th FA Bn. 58. 63, 67;
174th FA Bn. 158; 204th FA Bn.. 167;
224th FA Bn. 138, 183;
227th FA Bn. 138, 161, 183;
229th FA Bn. 46. 81;
258th FA Bn.158; 270th FA Bn. 167;
343rd / 344th FA Bn. 131;
345th FA Bn. 193; 561st FA Bn. 143;
559th FA Bn. 143;
690th FA Bn. 153; 915th FA Bn. 131;
987th FA Bn. 104, 152;
991st FA Bn. 158:
Anti-Aircraft Artillery G'ps /Battalions:-
113th AA Group, 155;
128th Gun Bn, 155;
225th Searchlight Bn, 89;
320th Barrage Balloon (VLA), 91;
391st AAA (AW) Bn. 154;
397th AAA (AW) Provisional Machine
Gun Bn.154, 205/6;
398th (AW) Bn. 154;
407th Gun Bn, 89;
447th (AW) Bn.139, 173;
461st (AW) Bn., 155;
462nd (AW) Bn. 63, 71, 100, 154;
465th, 776th, 777th (AW) Bn's 154;

535th (AW) Bn., 173, 191;
601st (AW), 863rd (AW) Bn's, 155;
792nd (AW), Bn. 89:
Engineer Corps:-
Provisional ESB Group units 93/4, 109,
159, 208-10, 212, 214-5, 219;
1st ESB 113, 140, 201;
5th ESB 26, 31, 55, 61, 70, 85, 93, 98,
101, 113, 120, 127, 133, 137, 159, 180,
201, 208, 214-5;
6th ESB 59, 85, 93, 133, 137, 141, 157,
159, 180, 201, 207-210, ;
1053rd /6th /7th / 8th, PCRGp. 119;
1119th ECG 55; 1120th ECG 133;
1199th Eng Base Depot Grp. 105, 181;
Regiments:-
95th EGSR 23, 26/7, 49/50, 52, 84, 94/5,
102, 126, 180/1, 185, 217;
342nd EGSR 32, 119;
347th EGSR, 155;
351st EGSR 119;
355th EGSR 32, 119;
360th EGSR 23, 58, 120, 123, 131, 133,
136, 155, 159, 166, 206, 217, 220;
365th EGSR 32;
366th EGSR 32, 89, 100, 150, 152,
161/3, 218;
368th EGSR 32;
372nd EGSR 31, 32, 60, 94, 102, 104,
156, 166/7, 170, 174/6, 179, 206, 218;
373rd EGSR 32, 84, 87/8, 94, 104, 120,
123, 136, 138, 171-6, 180, 183/5, 218;
398th EGSR 119;
333rd ESSR 32:
Battalions:-
2nd ECB 81, 138/40, 175, 197, 206,
37th ECB 85, 92, 97/8, 120, 126, 181,
208 /10;
103rd ECB 46, 59/61, 66, 73, 81;
146th ECB ; 149th ECB 98;
121st ECB 138, 183, 20;
203rd ECB 85, 137, 159;
294th ECB 133, 168, 191;
299th ECB 122;
315th ECB 131, 191;
336th ECB 85/6, 92, 101, 120, 209/10;
348th ECB 85, 97, 181, 208;
348th Battalion Beach Group120:

*****

Printed in Great Britain
by Amazon

42258509R00161